PERSPECTIVES IN CRITICISM

20:

Elisabeth W. Schneider

The Dragon in the Gate:
Studies in the Poetry of
G. M. Hopkins

UNIVERSITY OF CALIFORNIA PRESS
Berkeley and Los Angeles
1968

University of California Press
Berkeley and Los Angeles, California
Cambridge University Press
London, England

LIBRARY OF CONGRESS CATALOG CARD NO. 68-31434
Printed in the United States of America

To my sister Margaret,
whose name, by chance, is celebrated
in one of Gerard Hopkins's best-loved poems

Preface

THIS BOOK, or, to be exact, another on the same subject, was projected and begun many years ago but was set aside in favor of a series of undertakings each of which at the time seemed more urgent. In the intervening years, studies of Hopkins have flourished, and the comprehensive work that might then have been of use would now be superfluous. Thanks to many admirable studies, both comprehensive and specialized, that have appeared during the past two decades, we are in a position to take for granted much that once had to be laboriously sought or painfully argued. Unwilling to inflict upon the reader, or for that matter upon myself, a tiresome retracing of large tracts of familiar ground, I have tried in the present book to concentrate upon a few central aspects of Hopkins's work that remain incompletely explored or, occasionally, that I take to have been somewhat mistakenly explored. The result is a series of chapters that fall somewhere between a closely knit study and separate essays. The chapters are interdependent, but I have not attempted to draw them into the more intensive unity that might have been secured by imposition of a limiting critical doctrine or by the tracing of a single strand within the poet's complex work, choices either of which would have excluded much that I wished to say. For the most part I have dealt with major poems, in particular with poems upon which little agreement has been reached, in the hope of contributing here and there something toward a fuller understanding and deepened appreciation of the best of Hopkins's poetry. And I have risked, on occasion, a good deal of critical evaluation.

For the unwritten as well as the written chapters of this work I am indebted to more persons and books and articles than can be properly enumerated here. Of my predecessors in the study of Hopkins, the foremost to be named must be those whose nearly always exemplary editing has made available both the poetry and the prose with invaluable annotations. For the poems, all readers are indebted to Robert Bridges to begin with, followed by Charles Williams, then through more than one revision W. H. Gardner, and now also Norman H. MacKenzie; for the three volumes of letters, to Claude Colleer Abbott; for *The Journals and Papers,* to the late Humphry House, whose work was completed by Graham Storey; and for *The Sermons and Devotional Writings,* Christopher Devlin, S.J. My obligations to biographers and earlier critics are almost equally great, as will appear constantly throughout the discussion and notes. To estimate the debt all readers owe to their work, we need only glance back, from where we now stand, at the incomprehension with which the poems were once greeted; without the contributions of these writers we might not yet have got far beyond that initial state. Because of their numbers, however, a study that is not bibliographical must omit many; the others I leave to be named later where their particular contributions are most immediately relevant. To two of these, however, I owe something additional: to Professor W. H. Gardner, who was kind in answering certain inquiries, and to Professor Norman H. MacKenzie who has given me the benefit of valuable judgments, as well as new information, concerning texts and dates. I am grateful also to Professor Jerome H. Buckley of Harvard, Professor John Pick of Marquette University, and Professor William K. Wimsatt of Yale for kind as well as useful comments upon earlier versions of two chapters when these were published as separate articles. No writer on a Victorian subject can fail to be grateful for the existence of Professor Buckley's *The Victorian Temper* and for the comprehensive work of Walter E. Houghton and J. Hillis Miller.

My debt is great to numerous friends: to one of long standing, Abbie Huston Evans, who first introduced me to the work of Hopkins with a poet's appreciation of it, at a time when few members of the academic profession had so much as heard his name; and to another poet and more recent friend, Alan Stephens, with whom informal discussions of Hopkins were fruitful almost equally when we agreed and when we disagreed. Through their early interest in the poems of Hopkins and their subsequent interest in the progress of this study, Elizabeth and Karl de Schweinitz have provided most generous encouragement and support. Other friends and colleagues have been kind and helpful in a variety of ways direct and indirect; among them especially Mabel P. Worthington, Irwin Griggs, Marvin Mudrick, Hugh Kenner, and Frank Gardiner. Neither friends nor predecessors, it goes without saying, bear any actual responsibility for anything I have said.

The staffs of the libraries of Temple University, the University of Pennsylvania, the University of California at Santa Barbara, Los Angeles, and Berkeley, and the Library of Congress have facilitated my work; their help has been generous and their courtesy unfailing. The Bodleian Library was good enough to provide me with a photographic copy of MS B of *The Wreck of the Deutschland* and, a year or two later, with microfilm copy of the whole of MSS B and H. Certain stress marks in chapters 3 and 4 are printed from these manuscripts by permission of the curators of the Bodleian.

Chapters 2 and 3, originally published in slightly different versions in *PMLA*, are incorporated here by permission of the Modern Language Association. Temple University and the University of California have afforded me assistance through grants in aid of research. Finally, I owe thanks to Miss Karen Malone for expert typing and patient retyping of my manuscript, to Dennis Kennedy for preparation of the index, to Mrs. Grace H. Stimson and other members of the staff of the University of California Press for expert and generous assistance, and to my sister Margaret for assistance in reading the proof.

E. W. S.

Contents

Texts and Abbreviations

THE BEST TEXT of Hopkins's poems is now that of the fourth edition: *Poems of Gerard Manley Hopkins*, ed. W. H. Gardner and N. H. MacKenzie, (4th ed., rev. and enlg.; London, 1967). Though it appeared too late for me to make full use of it, my quotations from the poems have been made to conform with this latest text, and in matters of chronology I have consulted it. Otherwise, however, except where noted, I have used the 1956 revision of Gardner's third edition. Because of the number of editions now in circulation, I have not, as a rule, given page references to any.

Texts of the prose are as follows:
The Letters of Gerard Manley Hopkins to Robert Bridges, ed. Claude Colleer Abbott (London, 1935); referred to in my notes as *Letters*, I, and in the text further abridged to the volume and page numbers.
The Correspondence of Gerard Manley Hopkins and Richard Watson Dixon, also edited by Abbott (London, 1935); referred to as *Letters*, II, or simply as II with page number.
Further Letters of Gerard Manley Hopkins Including His Correspondence with Coventry Patmore, also edited by Abbott (2d ed., rev. and enlg.; London, 1956); referred to as *Letters*, III, or simply as III.
The first two volumes of letters remained virtually unchanged in the second edition and their pagination is the same. In *Further Letters* much new material was

included in the second edition; my references are therefore applicable to this edition only.

The Journals and Papers of Gerard Manley Hopkins, ed. Humphry House, completed by Graham Storey (London, 1959); referred to here as *Journals.*

The Sermons and Devotional Writings of Gerard Manley Hopkins, ed. Christopher Devlin, S.J. (London, 1959); referred to here as *Devotional Writings.*

1

Beginnings

THE TIME for attacking or defending Gerard Manley
Hopkins is over, and critical thought has begun to strive
more actively than in the past toward a balanced judgment. Readers temperamentally antagonistic to his
ideas or his often extravagant style, or to his personal
intensities of feeling—and no doubt there will always
be such readers—less often now feel called upon to
castigate the poems in wholesale terms; and on the other
hand his ardent admirers, finding the climate of opinion
altered, more seldom are driven to belligerent defense
of every image, every thought, and every word put on
paper by Hopkins. It is widely agreed now that he was
capable of some of the most beautiful as well as original
effects in English poetry; it is also coming to be recognized that, great as his genius was, his exercise of it was
not unflawed.

Hopkins is possibly not one of our great central poets.
He has neither the broad sanity and wisdom nor the
inexhaustible variety; he lacks the great lordly manner,
or the grand mask, or whatever in defining it to oneself
one requires of the great central poet. To read his
poetry is nevertheless to explore a vein as deep as it is
narrow, and there is no longer any question, as certain
impatient critics once thought, of his being merely the
center of a passing cult that will fade from sight once
the novelty has worn off. Initially, he baffled readers
somewhat as Blake had baffled those of a previous gen-

1

eration; and even now, though his thought and belief, unlike Blake's, were those of a known and established religious system, some idiosyncrasy of language, thought, or feeling from time to time draws his work out of the main currents of English poetry. In our day a cult interest in both writers has sprung up, attracted in part by the combination they both present of strangeness and obscurity. If we leave out of account the body of simple, or apparently simple, lyrics left by Blake, to which nothing in Hopkins corresponds, it is probably safe to say that of poets of stature writing in English before the present century, Blake is the most and Hopkins the next most obscure. In both poets the obscurity goes hand in hand with the strangeness. For readers of Hopkins, since he wrote no Songs of Innocence, this has been of paramount concern. It plagued his earliest friendly critics; they plagued him about it; and it is still a major source of contention. His obscurities, however, are closer to hand than those of Blake, since he presents no original symbolic system that bristles with paradox. His complexities lie rather in the texture than in the substance of the writing, except for a very few passages that have their origin in his studies of technical theology.

Despite the air of strangeness, the actual themes of Hopkins's poems are simple. From time to time an event, a scene in daily life, or some inner spiritual experience moved him deeply, and this, often very soon afterward, became the subject of a poem. As we know, the central events of his life were his conversion to Catholicism and his entrance into the Jesuit order. All his subsequent poetry is referable in one way or another to these great decisions. They never faded into the background of his daily living; his priesthood seems never to have become an unselfconscious, habitual way of life but remained a conscious striving, accompanied by perpetual awareness of the choice he had made. Ranged about this center, the other subjects that moved him were visual natural beauty, his love of England, the writings of Duns Scotus, the separation from family and early friends, his general failure and occasional successes in his calling, and, above all, the problem of reconciling these loves, loyalties, and sorrows with his religious dedication. Nearly every poem written after his conversion has for its theme one or another of these subjects or their relation, in his life, to each other. They are not notably strange themes, nor do they inevitably lead to obscure writing.

Blake, as I have said, lived in an intellectual world that was largely self-created, however often its constituent materials may be traced to other minds. Ultimately Hopkins's world was almost as private—though on the one hand less intrinsically odd than Blake's, yet on the other, doubly private in that a personal idiosyncratic world lay within the larger but still, in England, comparatively isolated world of the nineteenth-century Jesuit. Stepping, with scarcely a breath between, from the life of an undergraduate into the discipline of the Jesuit novitiate, Hopkins missed the common experience of everyday life at large in the world of men and women. He had left Oxford after taking his degree in June 1867, already a Catholic convert but not intimately in touch with Catholic lay life. Between that date and September of the following year, when he entered the Jesuit order, his external life was confined to a stay at home with his parents during most of two summers, a month's sight-seeing tour of Switzerland in the company of an Oxford friend, a week's tour of Paris with another Oxford acquaintance, and a winter under Newman's eye at the Oratory at Birmingham, teaching for a few months, somewhat unhappily, half a dozen fifth-form boys. And that is all. I can think of no other considerable English poet who wrote out of so slight an experience as this of secular life. It is tempting, however idle, to speculate upon the course his poetry might have taken had he remained in the world. We know, at any

3

rate, that he himself felt disadvantaged as a poet, particularly in the hope that for some years he cherished of writing dramatic poetry, by the narrowness of his experience. Once, setting forth to Robert Bridges his plan for a tragedy on the martyrdom of St. Winefred, he paused to assess his own powers: "I seem to find myself, after some experiment, equal to the more stirring and critical parts of the action, . . . but about the filling in and minor parts I am not sure how far my powers will go. I have for one thing so little varied experience. In reading Shakespeare one feels with despair the scope and richness of his gifts, equal to everything; he had besides sufficient experience of life" (I, 92–93).

The early poetry of Hopkins was composed within a period, roughly, of six years and was followed by nearly a decade of silence. A school-prize poem had been written at the age of sixteen, in 1860; after the first months of 1866, he practically ceased to write verse, the few exceptions being mainly Latin verses and translations; and after his subsequent commitment to the priesthood, his duties, or his rigid interpretation of them, allowed only the composition, for his local religious community, of two or three occasional pieces. His new life removed him from the society and influence of his literary and secular contemporaries, and thus his mature poetry, when he began to write again, was separated by a long gap from his early work. Yet the early verse, almost all written before Hopkins reached the age of twenty-two, is worth more than a glance, and this for a number of reasons. It had shown remarkable promise and remarkable versatility in conventional modes. Metrically it was extraordinarily accomplished for a young man's work. Already there were passages of achieved, not merely promised, excellence. Already too, though, there were signs of emotion deflected into unusual and, to many readers perhaps, somewhat repellent channels.

The earliest piece, the school-prize poem on a set

topic, *The Escorial,* is remarkable for its comparative mastery of the Spenserian stanza. It is also notable in its revelation of the boy's temperament, for it is crowded with rich images of sensuous luxury and beauty on the one hand, and on the other is marked by an inclination to dwell upon physical torture, cruelty, and martyrdom: a saint with "crack'd flesh . . . hissing on the grate," a "scourge," the "rod / Of forc'd persuasion," the ground "where the martyr's bones were thickest trod"—these represent an emphasis not demanded by the designated subject. Neither this set piece nor the other early attempt at sustained composition, *A Vision of Mermaids,* which in sensuous descriptive extravagance outdoes even the early Keats, is anything more than an accomplished practice piece. But *Winter with the Gulf Stream,* even in the early form in which it was printed [1] before Hopkins went up to Oxford, and in spite of some technical forcing, various archaisms, strained metaphors, and a superfluity of crimsons, violets, beryls, and tawny-golds, has a genuine poetic quality. For one thing, Hopkins had already learned the secret of that almost indefinable thing, poetic movement, a secret not commonly discovered by a schoolboy. Especially in view of the purely descriptive character of the subject, which offered no ready-to-hand movement such as a narrative theme provides, the poem succeeds remarkably well— mainly through technical mastery of enjambment within the *terza rima*—in avoiding the effect of static description:

> The boughs, the boughs are bare enough
> But earth has never felt the snow.
> Frost-furred our ivies are and rough
>
> With bills of rime the brambles shew.
> The hoarse leaves crawl on hissing ground
> Because the sighing wind is low.
>
> . . . .
>
> A gold-water Pactolus frets

5

Its brindled wharves and yellow brim,
The waxen colours weep and run,
And slendering to his burning rim

Into the flat blue mist the sun
Drops out and all our day is done.

Only the nearly laughable fifth line betrays the writer's youth.

A *Soliloquy of One of the Spies left in the Wilderness*, written during the month of his twentieth birthday, distantly after the manner of Browning's monologues but in heightened poetical style, is another early work that is more than merely promising; it is in fact a quite moving poem though its dramatic machinery creaks and its attempt to convey dramatically both the reality and the delusion of the speaker produces some murky lines. The speaker of the poem is one of those sent ahead by Moses to spy out the promised land of Canaan, who in discouragement report false difficulties and are struck down by a plague in punishment: [2]

Who is this Moses? who made him, we say,
To be a judge and ruler over us?
He slew the Egyptian yesterday. To-day
    In hot sands perilous
He hides our corpses dropping by the way
    Wherein he makes us stray.

The spy longingly imagines himself back in captivity in "Egypt, the valley of our pleasance":

Your parchèd nostrils snuff Egyptian air,
    The comfortable gloom
After the sandfield and the unveinèd glare!
    Goshen is green and fair.

.   .   .   .

Give us the tale of bricks as heretofore;
To plash with cool feet the clay juicy soil,

6

Who tread the grapes are splay'd with stripes of gore,
    And they who crush the oil
Are spatter'd. We desire the yoke we bore,
    The easy burden of yore.

        ✿   ✿   ✿   ✿

Go then: I am contented here to lie.
Take Canaan with your sword and with your bow.
Rise: match your strength with monstrous Talmai
    At Kirjath-Arba: go.—
Sure, this is Nile: I sicken, I know not why,
    And faint as though to die.

There is a living movement of somber speech here, and
at times a masterly handling of the musical resources of
the varied six-line stanza with its demanding four-ply
rhyme. Both this and the less successful *The Alchemist
in the City* (1865) show also an imaginative power in
the invention of personae not for such uses as Browning
sometimes put them to but for the dramatized expression of personally felt emotional conflicts. In the *Soliloquy,* the theme is the self-deceiving attempt to justify
one's failed courage and one's denial of faith; in the
Alchemist, it is the solitude of one who has irreparably
chosen a hopeless path. Both poems are haunted by
loneliness; in both the protagonist is set apart from mankind and knows he is set apart. This loneliness is more
acute and more genuinely felt than the fairly common
literary loneliness of most belated nineteenth-century
Romanticism.

Other early pieces appear to be conscious imitations
of the deliberately quaint ingenuities of George Herbert, whom Hopkins always admired. But more striking
is the influence of Shakespeare. The ten, nearly all somber, early sonnets, though their form is Petrarchan and
their cast of thought usually religious, bear a strong
resemblance in tone and style, and indeed in theme, to
the somberest of Shakespeare's sonnets.[3] The resemblance is in fact so striking that one can scarcely believe
one is not hearing the very progressions and curves of

7

syntax and thought of Shakespeare himself in such passages as this opening—though perhaps it is more accurate to say that what one hears is Shakespeare diluted by Mrs. Browning:

> Where art thou friend, whom I shall never see,
> Conceiving whom I must conceive amiss?

or in the next:

> My love is lessened and must soon be past.
> I never promised such persistency
> In its condition. No, the tropic tree
> Has not a charter that its sap shall last
>
> Into all seasons, though no Winter cast
> The happy leafing. It is so with me:
> My love is less, my love is less for thee.
> I cease the mourning and the abject fast,
>
> And rise and go about my works again
> And, save by darting accidents, forget.
> But ah! if you could understand how then
>
> That *less* is heavens higher even yet
> Than treble-fervent *more* of other men,
> Even your unpassion'd eyelids might be wet.[4]

Yet they are more than mere imitations; they go their own way, uneven though they are—as, notably, in the especially weak concluding line here. If these early pieces did not also contain lines of such good poetry, they would rank as masterpieces of mimicry. The best of the early poems, however, is one of the few that are not notably derivative, the well-known *Heaven-Haven*, with its inspired metrical shift in the concluding line, by which the "swing" of the sea in the curve of the bay becomes audible in the verse—a display of onomatopoeia that just skirts, but does skirt, the metrically os-

8

tentatious. It is a pity the poem that was to have been the counterpoise of this one in theme, "I must hunt down the prize," was left unfinished.

A revealing feature of all this early work is the evident bent of the author toward the conquest of technical difficulties. Of the nearly ninety completed pieces and fragments now in print, scarcely a handful are composed in simple quatrains and couplets; instead, a great variety of lines and stanza forms are tried out. Hopkins liked especially to set himself the task of finding three or four rhyming words rather than only two, and his rhymes, as a rule, were strict: no liberties were taken for mere convenience. In composing sonnets, in spite of the obviously deep influence of those of Shakespeare, he chose the strictest of English Petrarchan schemes, confining his sestet to two rhyme sounds in preference to three; apparently the rhyming of the Shakespearean sonnet was too loose or too easy to attract him.

As a whole, the dominant impression left by Hopkins's early verse is of, first, this remarkable technical mastery, at a remarkably early age, of a variety of difficult forms in which he permits himself no liberties; and, next after this, a highly charged emotional intensity, occasionally running in unusual channels. *The Escorial* is not the only poem that exhibits ascetic feeling carried to what must be called masochistic lengths. In the sonnet *Easter Communion,* Hopkins wrote, "You striped in secret with breath-taking whips," and the stripes are described as marking cruciform patterns on the flesh of the devotee. The fragment of *Pilate* is marked by similar feeling as, repenting in Hell, Pilate plans, with a great deal of explicit and grotesque physical detail, to crucify himself. This preoccupation with physical torment was not perfectly unique with Hopkins in his day: there are traces of it in such works as Christina Rossetti's *The Convent Threshold* ("They bore the Cross . . . / Racked, roasted, crushed, wrenched limb from limb") and in the somewhat gruesome image of the same writer's sonnet *Zion Said:* "Thou who hast bled, see how my heart doth bleed: / Open Thy bleeding Side and let me in." This kind of feeling was not unique, but neither was it a mere chance reflection of the nineteenth century's religious mediaevalism. It was an expression primarily of temperament—in the case of Christina Rossetti, a temperament described even by some of her contemporaries as morbid.[5] There is a hint of similar feeling in an odd remark of Hopkins to his mother, "To be persecuted in a tolerant age is a high distinction" (III, 106). To some extent he outgrew or else suppressed the full expression of such feeling in his later poetry, but an occasional hint of it, and the explosive emotional intensity that in him is always associated with it, remained. Now, masochistic feeling not only unites pleasure and pain; it also unites willful indulgence with rigid subjection of the self. I do not think it is fanciful to see, or to feel, a tinge of these contradictory impulses expressing themselves in Hopkins's subsequent experiments with poetic form. But this is to anticipate. And in any event, those experiments stand independently on their merits; it would be gross distortion to look upon them primarily as expressions of a particular temperament. In some degree, nevertheless, Hopkins was a poet set apart from his fellows from the beginning. He was not then, however, during his school and his undergraduate years, set apart so far as to be, in his writing, eccentric; and he was not at this stage a notably difficult poet. His early work is remarkable in the main simply for its high promise in conventional modes. Its actual achievement, indeed, is scarcely matched in the juvenile writing of any other English poet. Yet even so, it only faintly foreshadows the work of his mature years when he resumed his writing after an interval of nearly a decade, and the mature work is posterity's real concern.

2

The Dragon in the Gate

FOR A LONG TIME the luxuriance of baroque imagery so conspicuous in even the earliest poetry of Hopkins has tended to obscure one of its fundamental characteristics. His is a poetry of statement, intellectually formulated even when at emotional white heat, and scarcely at all, in any usual sense, a poetry of suggestion or atmosphere. He could not have permitted himself to write otherwise even if he had wished, and he did not wish. Though obviously the poetry does not lie in the statement—he himself was explicit about this (*Journals,* p. 289)—still, when he found that even Robert Bridges had continual difficulty in making out his literal meaning, he resolved, he said, "to prefix short prose *arguments*" to some of his work. "These too," he added, "will expose me to carping, but I do not mind" (I, 265).

His writing was contemporary with that of the French Symbolists (he was born in the same year as Verlaine), and after his earliest years both he and they were bringing something fresh to the language and rhythms of poetry. But there is no evidence that he was aware of their work, or of French Impressionist painting either, for all his lively interest in the art of his day; and in method he and they were as far apart as can be imagined. His aim was nearly opposite to that implied in Mallarmé's dictum, "nommer un objet c'est supprimer les trois quarts de la jouissance du poème . . . le suggérer voilà le rêve"; his effort was to name, to pin down with the utmost precision, the individual thing of which

11

there could be no duplicate, the distinctive pattern and design that made the living individual or the natural scene unique; and his roots were all native. The precepts of Ruskin's *Modern Painters* had recently opened the eyes of many Englishmen, and Hopkins's drawings, both of architectural subjects and of nature, were avowedly "Ruskinese" (III, 202). The spirit of Ruskin's chapters on "truth of clouds," "truth of water," "truth of foliage" and branch and twig is present everywhere in the detailed observations of nature recorded in his journals and poetry, as well as in the attention to both detail and design in his drawings. In no sense did he write symbolist poetry or the verbal equivalent of "mood music," though in their passionate exactitude his language and imagery are often supralogical, addressing themselves directly to the sensual imagination. His structure, however, is always logically conceived; its rigid severity suggests mediaeval Aristotelian thought more nearly than poetic imagination.

Like the temperament from which it sprang, however, his is a poetry of extremes, distinguished on the one hand, as was already becoming apparent in his youthful writing, by passionate sensuousness reminiscent of Keats—a love of the richest colors, tastes, physical beauty, sensation of all kinds—and on the other by an equally urgent desire for law, rigid control—by asceticism in fact. Willfulness, then, and an impulse toward extreme license are set against the bent towards self-denial and utter subjection of the will. In his life the extremes were perhaps rarely at peace; in his poetry at its best they are reconciled, and much of the individuality of his work derives from the tension so created. Something resembling this kind of opposition naturally underlies any poetic organization and not Hopkins's only, being in fact present wherever form is imposed. In such a writer as Keats, however, the control is felt to be no more than the normal human love of order at work

12

in creating aesthetic form; there is no tinge of asceticism in it. Hopkins, in whom the ascetic was so strong, as a poet transformed this into a positive power over form, but his form carries the marks of its particularly intense origin. Both form and language are therefore paradoxically on the one hand severe and on the other wayward, extravagant, sometimes outlandish. A single descriptive epithet may be both willfully odd and determinedly subjected to literal fact, his grammar and idiom eccentric and yet precisely explicable by rule or precedent, the thought of a poem eccentrically conceived but developed on a rigidly logical plan. In both its successes and its sometimes embarrassing failures, Hopkins's poetry owes much of its peculiarly explosive character to these oppositions inherent in the detail as well as the whole design of nearly every work.

Under this light, in spite of a number of valuable studies that have appeared in recent years in consequence of which it has ceased to be quite the fearsome "dragon folded in the gate to forbid all entrance" that Bridges once thought it, there remain certain things to be said about Hopkins's longest poem, the first significant work of his maturity.[1] *The Wreck of the Deutschland* is beginning to take its place in the company of the great English odes and elegies. It is not a flawless poem, but we are coming to see it as unmistakably a great one. It is also something of a miracle, for its success is won against every probability. Given all that it attempts and given the intractable, unmastered emotion that went into it, it should have been doomed from the start to failure. The whole undertaking presents itself as a piece of reckless daring, and the poem lays a teasing claim upon our interest, therefore, as an almost unheard-of kind of success.

However much its remarkable language may obscure the fact and however complex its final effect may be, the *Wreck*, like every other completed poem of Hopkins, is extremely simple, not to say also rigid, diagrammatic, in its primary structure. The naked skeleton is not particularly beautiful and its character is likely to be uncongenial to many modern readers, but the skeleton alone gives coherence to the parts, and it alone makes intelligible the shape and proportions of the whole. It therefore needs to be set forth as clearly as possible.

Stated baldly, the poem is an ode on conversion, conversion to the Catholic Church. As Hopkins reminded Bridges, it is an ode, not a narrative; the wreck of the German liner which provides the title is the occasion, not the theme. The poem is in two parts, a mode of thought that in Hopkins seems to have deep roots if one recalls its almost constant appearance in his subsequent work. The main theme of Part the First is his own conversion; that of Part the Second, the hoped-for conversion of all England, for which certain events connected with the shipwreck are conceived as the spark and the signal.[2] Within the limits of its bare thematic frame, however, Hopkins explicitly or by implication crowded nearly everything in life about which he felt deeply. Reading the poem, one has the feeling that, his poetic pen licensed after that decade of largely self-imposed silence, he was writing as if he might never again be free to write and must set down in this one work all that remained to him of value and hope on earth. It is not a promising prospect, for the control of so much intensely felt and apparently disparate material would seem to pose insuperable difficulties.

Among Hopkins's most abiding hopes and deepest longings was the wish that England might become Catholic, not in some remote future time, but soon, or now. To a degree this was natural, especially for a convert; and for a young man whose last experience of secular life had been the Oxford of the fifties or sixties with conversions and rumors of conversion still a matter of high excitement, the possibility need not have seemed altogether absurd. Hopkins would not have forgotten what he had written to Newman while still at Oxford, when four friends had taken the step almost simultaneously, "All our minds you see were ready to go at a touch and it cannot but be that the same is the case with many here" (III, 30). The hope did not die easily: as late as 1881, knowing well how hostile Bridges would be to the thought, Hopkins was nevertheless impelled to write to him of the approaching three-hundredth anniversary of the martyrdom of Edmund Campion, "from which I expect of heaven some, I cannot guess what, great conversion or other blessing to the Church in England" (I, 135–136). On this occasion too he was undertaking to write an ode, in a vein "something between the *Deutschland* and *Alexander's Feast.*"

The basis of Hopkins's longing for others' conversion, however, was personal as well as religious, and the intensity of the personal feeling undoubtedly affected his rational judgment. He had been one of a close and congenial family, and the shock of his conversion and dedication to the priesthood brought grief to all, himself not least; though superficial friendliness was preserved by an effort on both sides, the old intimacy was broken for good. A similar barrier had fallen between himself and certain of his dearest friends. Sensitive and dependent on affection, the happiness of sharing his love of natural beauty, poetry, painting, and high thoughts with family and friends suddenly gone, Hopkins was a lonely, sometimes desperately lonely, man. No new human ties took the place of the old ones, for he did not transfer affections easily and the companions of his new life shared few of his intellectual interests or tastes. As he was fully committed to his adopted religion, nothing short of a general movement of conversion in England could reunite him to those he loved; nothing less could heal the breach within himself that remained a source of the pain described in a sonnet of the next decade:

To seem the stranger lies my lot, my life
Among strangers. Father and mother dear,
Brothers and sisters are in Christ not near
And he my peace / my parting, sword and strife.

His letters show an almost pathetic effort to grasp at
whatever common interests could still be shared without stirring bitter depths. The stanzas of the *Wreck* having to do directly with the conversion of England are
marked by a personal intensity over and above the
natural desire of even an ardent Christian for the salva-
tion of his fellowmen; and the forced significance which
he read into one event of the wreck is accountable,
biographically if not historically or aesthetically, on the
same ground.

A lifelong interest in shipwrecks remained one thing
that he could still share with his family. Wrecks, it will
be remembered, were a main part of the business of his
father, who as head of a firm of marine average ad-
justers not only wrote technical works on marine in-
surance but, only a short time before the *Deutschland's*
disaster, had published *The Port of Refuge, or Advice
and Instructions to the Master-Mariner in Situations of
Doubt, Difficulty, and Danger* (1873), a book practical
in purpose but adorned, beyond its alliterative title,
with quotations from *The Ancient Mariner* and the occasional purple phrases of a man who would have liked
to be a poet (and who in fact did produce some verse
that may be described as well meant). The whole family seems to have been a company of horrified amateurs
of maritime disaster, too high-minded to rejoice in others' misfortune but vividly interested. Hopkins's brother
Arthur exhibited at the Royal Academy paintings inspired by shipwrecks; and, for a landsman's, Gerard's
own poetry is surprisingly full of images and symbols—
nearly always highly charged with feeling—derived
from wrecks, often in the most unlikely contexts. It is
not by accident that in his earliest known poem reli-

gious martyrdom and imagery of shipwreck are brought together in one of the passages so strongly tinged by masochistic feeling: the "poor collapsing frame" of the saint—whose "crack'd flesh lay hissing on the grate"—"hung like a wreck that flames not billows beat." Nor is it by chance that in the late "Heraclitean" sonnet the second turn is marked by the words "Across my foundering deck shone / A beacon, an eternal beam"; and in between these are very many other images of shipwreck, some explicit, some half submerged. When the liner *Deutschland* was lost, Gerard's mother sent him newspaper clippings describing the event, which, he told her, had made a deeper impression on him than "any other wreck or accident" he had ever read of (III, 135). It was a disaster that for personal reasons, therefore, touched him more closely than it did most Englishmen.

It stirred the rest of England too, however, with an uncommon shock of guilt, for the liner had run aground near the mouth of the Thames not far from shore, its distress signals had been seen, yet no attempt at rescue had been made for some thirty crucial hours; and subsequently the vessel was looted by the owners of local fishing smacks who, it was said, even tore rings from the fingers of dead bodies aboard. This was an ugly record for the English with their national pride in maritime competence and in certain kinds of human decency. The inquest and a local inquiry were followed by a full-dress admiralty investigation, and the sense of national guilt was voiced in more than one *Times* editorial concerned with the "painful surprise" and "shame" with which the nation learned "that a wreck could be stranded off the English coast, appealing to English sailors for aid, and for thirty hours should be left without that aid." [3] "It is shameful," the same editorial said further, "that where men were found in considerable numbers thus bold enough to defy the law [i.e., the pillaging smacksmen] there were none found daring enough to risk anything for the sake of saving life." The disaster was thus felt by others besides Hopkins as something of a public moral crisis, and it might therefore without overstraining be looked upon as an event of spiritual significance, though few would have read into it all that Hopkins did.

As the cause of the wreck itself, however, lay not in man but in nature, the blinding winter storm that drove the vessel off course, there was implicit in the event the question of cosmic justice, the old crucial problem for the Christian of explaining the suffering of the innocent and particularly such suffering as appears to be caused by nature, not by fallen man himself. This relation of the natural to the moral world was an issue sharpened in Hopkins's day by the impact of the Darwinian doctrine of the struggle for existence, with "nature red in tooth and claw." For Hopkins personally, nature presented another problem of deep concern, that of reconciling his strong emotional attachment to the physical beauty of the world with the claims of the spirit, a problem that reduced itself to the simple question of whether he might not be guilty of loving material nature too passionately and too much for the sake of beauty itself (on several occasions, once for a period of six months, he renounced the sight of nature as a penance, refraining from looking about when out of doors [4]). On a theological plane both these problems had recently been resolved for him by a doctrine he had found in the writings of Duns Scotus. All this, including the doctrine itself, went into *The Wreck of the Deutschland*.

Then there was the matter of miracles. Hopkins was not among the Victorian Christians who found those a stumbling block in the way of belief. On the contrary, not only did biblical and the early saints' miracles move him deeply, but he also eagerly sought reasons to believe any accounts of contemporary miraculous healing or other supernatural signs of grace, and these appear often to have been associated in his mind with the conversion of England. Miracles enter prominently into the *Deutschland,* and the whole poem really turns on the hint of a miraculous presence through which the wreck and the conversion of England are brought within a single focus.

This is a great deal for a man to dare combine in one ode, particularly when it is all felt with somewhat abnormal personal intensity: the central spiritual event of his own life, his hope for "rare-dear" England, the shipwreck with both its public and its personal significance, the suggestion of a new miracle, the Scotist doctrine of the Incarnation, the reconciliation of evil and suffering in the world with the Christian belief in an all-powerful, all-wise, all-good God. And then there was the final daring of the form. In the *Wreck* Hopkins experimented for the first time with his new "sprung rhythm" and, to increase the difficulty immeasurably, invented for it a new stanza, one of the most complicated ever employed in English verse. No one, it would seem, in his right mind would experiment with such form on such material; few would attempt to cope with the material even in a simple or established form. All this is what I meant by saying earlier that the poem succeeds—supposing that it does so—against all probability. Almost phenomenal technical skill was required and extraordinary control over the refractory and too intense emotional material. Both skill and control, particularly the latter, break down occasionally; the absence of distancing and failure of judgment are felt here and there, somewhat as they are in *Adonais* and for not altogether dissimilar reasons.

To return, however, to the skeleton of thought, which has yet to be traced at its literal level. The two divisions of the poems are unequal, the autobiographical first part being appropriately shorter but still parallel, serving as microcosm, prelude, and, in a sense, pattern to Part the Second, with the implication that what has happened in one soul may happen in all.

The poem opens with a solemn stanza addressed to

God Omnipotent, lord of all living and dead, of land and sea, of the speaker himself—God omnipotent to create and destroy:

> Thou mastering me
> God! giver of breath and bread;
> World's strand, sway of the sea;
> Lord of living and dead;
> Thou has bound bones and veins in me, fastened me
>   flesh,
> And after it almost unmade, what with dread,
>   Thy doing: and dost thou touch me afresh?
> Over again I feel thy finger and find thee.

The imagery is universal and would be appropriate to any poetic acknowledgment of the power of God; at the same time it is deliberately bent toward the particular circumstances so as to sum up much of the poem, living and dead, land and sea foreshadowing the shipwreck on a sandbank as well as embracing all the earth and mankind, and the personal "mastering me" in the first line, which I take to be a deliberate alteration of "masterful" or "all-mastering," signaling at the outset the personal direction of Part I.[5] The last line, with its anthropomorphic image and apparent but not real tautology, is a specific theological statement illumined by Hopkins's own commentary on the *Spiritual Exercises* of St. Ignatius, where the "finger" of God is explained as symbolizing God's power exerted on the external world of matter—here, of course, the wreck—as distinguished from "thee," the very self of God, God as love.[6]

As the oracular tone changes to a more personal one in what follows, the rhythm falls into conventional and soon predominantly anapestic meter with only an occasional sprung foot. In this rhythm the account proceeds of the poet's conversion, or at least of a crucial moment connected with it, a decisive night of violent spiritual terror and suffering that ended with the free choice of his heart, responding to God's grace. The moment of choice is summed up in the somewhat mannered "To flash from the flame [of hell] to the flame [of Christ or the Holy Spirit] then, tower from the grace to the grace," a line that illustrates Hopkins's not always happy efforts to render theology in poetic terms. Poetically there is probably no value in our knowing precisely what the two kinds of grace are; it is, however, well to know that they are doctrinal and definite, not vague or mystical; they are explicitly distinguished in his prose meditations (*Devotional Writings*, pp. 154–158). The resolution of this crisis is succeeded by a spiritual serenity which is the subject of the beautiful "hourglass and well" stanza:

> I am soft sift
>   In an hourglass—at the wall
> Fast, but mined with a motion, a drift,
>   And it crowds and it combs to the fall;
> I steady as a water in a well, to a poise, to a pane,
> But roped with, always, all the way down from the tall
>   Fells or flanks of the voel, a vein
> Of the gospel proffer, a pressure, a principle, Christ's gift.

This is the serenity of Dante's "Our peace in His will" or of that prayed for in *Ash Wednesday*, "Teach us to care and not to care," here symbolized in images that reconcile stillness and motion—stillness in the willing renunciation of individual will, and motion, readiness to act in willing response to God's will—with the profound peace of this reconciliation. So the "soft sift" of the quiescent soul is motionless at the wall of the hourglass but at the center "crowds" and "combs" (like an inbound comber on the shore) in willing motion to fulfill its destined function, the telling of time. And the spirit

21

is confidently quiet like the water in a clear well, yet not stagnant but marked by motion from the inflow of mountain springs, "Christ's gift," that perpetually feed it. (The well is not named in the poem, but the image is of a particular sacred well, that of St. Winefred at Holywell, the scene of a series of reputed miraculous cures including a recent one that had particularly interested Hopkins.) Though parallel and similar in drift, the two images of the stanza are not redundant, for though both represent the will as at once active and passive, motion in the hourglass image implies the spending of self, that in the well renewal. The essence of the whole passage, however, is the serenity of a dedication that has followed upon the agonizing choice of the preceding stanzas.[7]

The doctrinal substance of that serenity is the subject of the next several stanzas. First it is given in emotional terms: the poet accepts and indeed welcomes not only the stars of the world but the storms, the beauty and the terror. The first comes naturally, "I kiss my hand to the stars," from which the spirit of Christ is easily felt to be wafted; the other is achieved through acceptance by faith of the Christian mystery (by "mystery," Hopkins once explained to Bridges, a Catholic does not mean "an interesting uncertainty" but "an incomprehensible certainty"). The great mystery significant for the circumstances of the poem is not Christ's relation to stars (beauty)—that the devout man feels without effort—but his relation to storms, to the suffering attributable in naturalistic terms not to man's sin but to the constitution of the external world.

> I kiss my hand
> To the stars, lovely-asunder
> Starlight, wafting him out of it; and
> Glow, glory in thunder;
> Kiss my hand to the dappled-with-damson west:
> Since, tho' he is under the world's splendour and
> wonder,

His mystery must be instressed, stressed;
For I greet him the days I meet him, and bless when
I understand. (stanza 5)

Another extremely mannered line here, the seventh, I
take to mean simply what has been said above: though
Christ is (i.e., is naturally felt to be) under the world's
splendor (the stars), His mystery also (the storms)
must be instressed (scored in upon ourselves, dwelt
upon inwardly) *when stressed* (by storm) in the natural world. *Stressed* in this reading is simply the equivalent of an elliptical clause, a common enough construction, which elsewhere as well as here Hopkins employed
in eccentric ways.[8]

In the stanzas that follow, the intellectual foundation
of the poet's serenity is presented through a cryptic
summary of the Scotist doctrine of the Incarnation,
which provided the reconciliation of "stars and storms,"
"lightning and love," that met Hopkins's personal need.
He seems to suggest that Scotus's heart, like his own,
must have been "at bay," needing this particular truth
so desperately that the very need generated its intuitive
discovery. Briefly and somewhat crudely summed up,
the doctrine held that the Incarnation was not a consequence of the Fall and so not primarily a sacrifice to
redeem man, but that in some sense it preexisted, that
it is in fact coeval with time itself and hence with
material creation. In this sense the Incarnation rides
the whole course of time "like riding a river"; it is not
confined to the historical life of Jesus however central
that may be to Christianity, is not a moment in the
stream of time but rides that current from beginning
to end. As Hopkins rephrased the doctrine in his meditations, the "first intention" of God outside Himself, the
"first outstress" of His power, was Christ, who went
forth from God "not only in the eternal and intrinsic
procession of the Trinity but also by an extrinsic and
less than eternal, let us say aeonian one." He added,
significantly, "It is as if the blissful agony or stress of

23

selving in God had forced out drops of sweat or blood, which drops were the world." The created world, therefore (I oversimplify, omitting discussion of Lucifer's place in all this), by virtue of its origin "is marked everywhere with the confusion, clashing, and wreck which took place in the higher one." [9] What this comes to—a commonplace, but not of orthodox theology—is that storms as well as stars are part of the essential constitution of matter, antecedent not only to the Fall but even to the creation of man, and further, that they are intimately bound up with the sacrificial Incarnation from the beginning. This view of creation is very different from the usual Thomist one, and it is the doctrine expressly but elliptically asserted in the sixth and seventh stanzas of the poem. "Few know this," the poet says parenthetically, for the Scotist doctrine was not generally accepted though it had never been declared heretical and so was not forbidden to a Catholic: concerning it, therefore, "the faithful waver" (i.e., remain undecided, differ among themselves), while the faithless "fable and miss" altogether. The truth comes home to all sometime; and when it does so, it penetrates the whole being like the physical shudder produced by a sudden sour-sweet taste (stanza 8).

This Scotist doctrine, with its potentially masochistic implications, had found immediate response in the temperament of Hopkins. To conceive Christ's sacrificial Incarnation, as well as the concomitant "storms" of nature, not as solely redemptive of man and therefore not as spiritually practical or functional for man's good, but rather as free supernatural sacrifice for its own sake, is to conceive both sacrifice and storms as exquisite, to be rejoiced in for themselves (not simply endured for the good they may be thought to produce), the pleasure-in-pain sour-sweet of the sloe raised to the highest pitch of emotional and spiritual intensity (the extremely sensuous image of the sloe's taste is exact, though it has been criticized, and I think readers must often find it

24

somewhat repellent). This doctrine, then, in conjunction with the related Scotist theory of the constitution of matter, which, in addition to accounting most satisfactorily for "storms," gave to nature an altogether higher place than it holds in Thomist thought and which thus might afford a fuller spiritual sanction to the peculiar intensity of Hopkins's love of nature, underlay the serenity and peace of the sifting sand in the hourglass and of the water in the sacred well, for it answered to several needs and brought them into harmony: sensuous love of nature, ecstatic asceticism, and the need for an orderly logical framework.

The progression of thought, then, if not the thought itself, in these central stanzas of Part I is rational and simple: first there is the spiritual crisis, then the choice, the serenity following the choice, and the main emotional, followed by the doctrinal, basis of that serenity. Part the First then closes the chapter of spiritual autobiography with two stanzas addressed, like the opening of the poem, to God, but with the stars and storms now reconciled; the poet prays that all men may be brought to God, whether by violence as in the conversion of Paul—and of himself as he has been describing it—or gently as with St. Augustine.

Part the Second prefaces the narrative of the wreck with perhaps the most beautiful passage in the poem, a stanza on the worn theme of the inevitability of death:

"Some find me a sword; some
The flange and the rail; flame,
Fang, or flood" goes Death on drum,
And storms bugle his fame.
But wé dream we are rooted in earth—Dust!
Flesh falls within sight of us, we, though our flower the same.
Wave with the meadow, forget that there must
The sour scythe cringe, and the blear share come.

Death speaks in images that blend the traditional—sword, flame, fang, flood—with the (in 1875) still modern railroad train; and it must be the quiet unmannered precision of the words, as well as their absorption into the remarkably elaborate though unostentatious alliterative and assonantal pattern, that permits this surprising yet, as written, scarcely noticeable collocation. The meeting of flange and rail is the cutting edge of death to the victim in its path, and the image of the railroad train, divested of all else, here becomes one with sword and scythe. "The sour scythe cringe" too is one of those incredibly exact flashes of physical, almost visceral imagination that sometimes distinguish Hopkins's lines. Here it imparts life to the ancient rhetorical device of the transferred epithet. It is the victim, not the scythe, that cringes, but the shape of a scythe is the shape of a cringe. Reading Hopkins's words, one feels the tightening ventral curve with almost the physical immediacy of the prodded caterpillar. The language of this whole stanza deserves (but does not need) an essay to itself.

The story of the wreck follows in a finely controlled, flexible but conventional anapestic meter (or in that logaoedic iambic-anapestic which constitutes nearly all successful verse that goes by the name of anapest). The "sprung" effects that in the earlier stanzas mingle with this standard rhythm and that will reappear later are almost wholly absent here. The narrative is straightforward, literally exact, sometimes following word for word the published testimony of survivors, till Hopkins reaches the subject of the chief of five nuns who perished and the cry she was said to have uttered. Here the factual narrative ends and the poet begins to prepare for his climactic half-statement; and here it is necessary to pause for an explanation of what appears to be the only viable reading of the fourteen stanzas that follow. These seem to me clearly to embody the suggestion that a miracle had occurred, that during the night of terror at sea Christ had appeared to the nun, not in a subjective or imagined vision but as a real miraculous presence and that this event, once acknowledged and published to the world, might become the needed signal, the turning point for the conversion of English Christians.

This reading requires defense. To turn, therefore, first to the external facts with which Hopkins was dealing —for he invented no explicit additions to them. Newspaper reports had detailed the events: the vessel, driven off course in the winter storm, struck a sandbar (the Kentish Knock); its propeller broke; distress signals brought no aid. As the tide rose without setting the vessel afloat, many attempted to take refuge in the rigging; hope dwindled as the water rose; women and children wailed; one heroic sailor died trying to save the more helpless. These events all became part of Hopkins's narrative. Five nuns, emigrating from Germany to America in consequence of Bismarck's repressive measures against the Catholic Church, were among the many who perished; the *Times*'s account of the wreck contained two brief reports of them. One of these said that the women had "clasped hands and were drowned together, the chief sister, a gaunt woman 6 ft. high, calling out loudly and often, 'O Christ, come quickly!' till the end came." The report of their funeral two days later contained a slightly different version: "One [nun], noted for her extreme tallness, is the lady who, at midnight on Monday, by standing on a table in the saloon, was able to thrust her body through the skylight, and kept exclaiming, in a voice heard by those in the rigging above the roar of the storm, 'My God, my God, make haste, make haste.'" [10] Nothing at all beyond this was reported of their actions, no strikingly heroic act, and Hopkins added nothing; yet he made of the leading nun's cry and its meaning (not, it should be noted, of their death, which many Catholics regarded as martyrdom) the central event of the poem. To do so, at such

length, would seem to make sense under one contruc-
tion only.

The chief nun appears first at the end of the seventeenth stanza—"a lioness arose . . . a *prophetess* tow-
ered . . . a *virginal tongue told*"—and the thought of
her call moves his heart to speak out, moves him to tears
too, but tears of joy. Before her call is actually quoted,
Hopkins interposes five stanzas in which the history of
the nuns is interrupted by a recurrence to the Scotist
reconciliation of stars and storms through their coupled
origin in time—"from life's dawn" they have been
joined: St. Gertrude, "lily," and her fellow townsman
Luther, "beast of the waste wood," Abel and Cain,
"storm flakes" and flowers. Foreshadowing the final
hoped-for reconciliation of the specific storm that
wrecked the *Deutschland*, these allusions are further
interlaced with a rhapsody on the sacred symbolism, associated with miracles, of the number five: the wounds
of Christ and their miraculous appearance in the stig-
mata of St. Francis. There were five nuns and they be-
longed to a Franciscan order.

At last the chief nun's call is quoted: "O Christ,
Christ, come quickly" (stanza 24). To most readers
such a cry wrung in such circumstances from anyone
reared in Christian faith would seem the most natural
of utterances. The poet, however, exclaiming, "The
majesty! what did she mean?" and asking the Holy
Spirit to answer his question ("Breathe, arch and original Breath," stanza 25), devotes some four stanzas (out
of a total of thirty-five for the whole poem) to an exploration of her possible meaning, eliminating at last
all explanations but one. Was it eagerness to sacrifice
her life in imitation of Christ? Not even his disciples
were of that mind, the poet says, and recalls the biblical
account of Jesus miraculously calming the waters of
the Lake of Genesareth when his disciples were fright-
ened and the other miracle so often associated with it,
his walking through the storm over the waters to his

disciples and again calming wind and wave. Or was the nun longing for heaven because of the acuteness of her present suffering? Both meanings are dismissed at length on naturalistic, rather penetrating psychological grounds. Yet the whole discussion is far-fetched, gratuitous in fact, except as it is seen leading to the supernatural meaning in the crucial stanza (stanza 28), which implies without quite saying what the nun did mean:

> But how shall I . . . make me room there:
> Reach me a . . . Fancy, come faster—
> Strike you the sight of it? look at it loom there,
> Thing that she . . . There then! the Master,
> *Ipse*, the only one, Christ, King, Head:
> He was to cure the extremity where he had cast her;
> Do, deal, lord it with living and dead;
> Let him ride, her pride, in his triumph, despatch and
> have done with his doom there.

Poetically this does not quite work, but the intention is surely evident. What he has to say, what the nun's cry really meant, is beyond the power of speech except for breathless, fragmentary exclamation, "look at it loom there, / . . . There then! the Master, / *Ipse* . . ."— *his very self*. Hopkins did not ordinarily introduce foreign words into his English poems, but our language has no intensive to match for emphasis and condensation the Latin *ipse*, with its utter concentration of selfhood. For Hopkins, moreover, the word would have carried a further, very particular, association because of its prominence in the Mass, at the minor elevation.[11] The drift of this stanza, then, clearly is that the nun saw Christ's very self; and it seems to me equally clear that what is implied is a supernatural event, not an ambiguous "vision" or a hallucination. If it were either of these, the preceding stanzas would be an absurd building up to an anticlimax and much that follows would be pointless and very nearly meaningless. For the nun is now identified with Simon Peter (to whom in particular Jesus was said to have appeared miraculously walking over the waters) and then, fulfilling an earlier foreshadowing (the "virginal tongue told" of stanza 17), becomes an analogue of the Virgin Mary, to whom also, as the poem goes on to say, the Word, Christ, came— through the Annunciation—and from whom the Word issued: Mary "*uttered* thee ["Jesu"] outright" (stanza 30).[12] The connection between the two stanzas embodying these parallels is cemented formally by a repetition of the three words of the major rhyme, in inverted order, the rhymes *right, night, light* of stanza 29 becoming *light, night, outright* in stanza 30.

There is a preliminary hint of the miraculous event earlier: the nun is said to have "one fetch in her," an odd expression, by some critics interpreted to mean that she has one resource available, her faith. I think it means more than this. In Ireland, Scotland, and much of the north and west of England, *fetch* is a name for an apparition, wraith, ghost, or spirit, sometimes of the living, sometimes of the dead. Scott uses it ("His . . . fetch or wraith or double-ganger"), and so does Yeats. More important, so does Hopkins himself, and with reference to a *miraculous event which he was taking pains to distinguish from a subjective vision,* a context, that is, identical with that of the poem: "At any rate I suppose the vision of the pregnant woman to have been *no mere vision but the real fetching, presentment, or 'adduction' of the persons, Christ and Mary, themselves.*" *Adduction,* according to Father Devlin, is "the technical term used by Scotus . . . where he proves that *it is strictly possible for the same body to be in more than one place at the same time.*"[13]

In Hopkins's circumstances, and for more than one reason, it would not have been proper for him to proclaim a miraculous event explicitly, but there was nothing to prevent his suggesting it as he did, clearly though

30

not quite explicitly, in a poem that he would publish, if at all, only with the approval and under the auspices of his order. When the *Wreck* was rejected by *The Month*, Hopkins gave up the thought of publication (III, 138). Probably his quite exceptional statement to Bridges—"granted that it needs study and is obscure, *for indeed I was not over-desirous that the meaning of all should be quite clear, at least unmistakable*" (I, 50; my italics)—had reference to this particular meaning, for invariably on other occasions Hopkins was more than eager to have his literal sense understood, and I can think of nothing else in this poem that he might have wished to leave half veiled.

It seems likely that many readers have been aware of these implications in the central stanza; one or two critics have referred somewhat neutrally to the nun's "vision." Most have avoided the subject, perhaps because the meaning is distasteful or because it opens Hopkins to the charge of credulity (though extreme and eager credulity in such matters is inescapable in his letters and journals), or because it was desired to save the poem from controversy or skeptical contempt. To ignore the literal meaning of the central stanza would be my own preference if it were not for the fact that this is the pivot upon which the main thought of the poem turns. Without it the structure of the whole falls apart: lines and stanzas of an otherwise inexplicably feverish intensity float loose from either rational or poetic moorings. Much of what is said about the nun before and after this stanza can be justified, as to what is said and at what length, only if a miracle is pointed to. The overall proportions of the poem require it, for we have to reckon with the fact, already referred to, that, though the nuns undoubtedly died bravely, no other specific acts of heroism were attributed to them either in the newspapers or by Hopkins and that essentially all of the fourteen stanzas about them (out of a total of thirty-five in the poem) hinge upon the *cry*, not the martyrdom, or the courage or deeds, of the chief nun. This cry may "startle the poor sheep back," the poet says. But more than those sufferers of the particular disaster are meant as the statement is broadened into a question, "Is the shipwrack then a harvest, does tempest carry the grain for thee?" where the themes of conversion and reconciliation of suffering are explicitly brought together.

The climactic *ipse* stanza brings a return to sprung rhythm, which has been largely in abeyance after the opening lines of Part II, but which from this point on is dominant, becoming more and more irregular, the meter now for the first time stretched to its limits as Hopkins later defined them. The effect is of an increasingly broad, orchestral movement as the theme itself broadens toward its conclusion.

The four closing stanzas begin with a recapitulation of the opening acknowledgment to God the wielder of all power, framed in sea and shore imagery now of even greater magnitude than at first and in language that harks back to the appalling declaration of omnipotence in the book of Job, when the Lord speaks out of the whirlwind. But what in the first stanza was a bare acknowledgment of Power, "Lord of living and dead," and afterward in the climactic stanza was intensified to "Do, deal, lord it with living and dead" (the verbs are indicative, not hortatory), now becomes affirmation as well: "I admire thee," the poet says, and the word *admire* carries both its ancient or Miltonic and its modern sense. This celebration of Power is balanced by a succeeding stanza on divine Mercy and Compassion, and the two stanzas are again bound together within a common rhyme and into a single sentence as well:

> I admire thee, master of the tides,
>   Of the Yore-flood, of the year's fall;
> The recurb and the recovery of the gulf's sides,

The girth of it and the wharf of it and the wall;
  Stanching, quenching ocean of a motionable mind;
  Ground of being, and granite of it: past all
    Grasp God, throned behind
Death with a sovereignty that heeds but hides, bodes
      but abides;

    With a mercy that outrides
    The all of water, an ark
  For the listener; for the lingerer with a love glides
    Lower than death and the dark;
  A vein for the visiting of the past-prayer, pent in
      prison,
  The-last-breath penitent spirits—the uttermost
        mark
    Our passion-plungèd giant risen,
The Christ of the Father compassionate, fetched in
      the storm of his strides. (stanzas 32–33)

The recapitulatory character of this passage is under-
scored by the reappearance of a great many key words,
several of them used earlier in strange or striking ways,
and by recapitulatory images as well: "Thou mastering
me / God! . . . sway of the sea," from the opening
stanza, is now "I admire thee, master of the tides";
"world's strand" is now intensified into "the recurb . . .
of the gulf's sides . . . ground of being and granite of
it"; *fall, wall,* and *past all* repeat rhyme words of the
hourglass stanza (*wall, fall, tall*); *the uttermost mark,*
an unusual phrase, echoes the earlier, mannered line,
"Mark [verb], the mark is of man's make" (stanza 22);
and "*fetched* in the storm of his *strides*" repeats both
the allusion to Christ's walking on the waters and the
strange "fetch" of stanza 19, which had prefaced the
appearance of the "Master."
  The cryptic statement of the second of these stanzas
has been variously read but seems to me to be this,
continuing from the preceding, addressed to God: "past

all grasp God, throned behind death with a sovereignty . . . ; with a mercy . . . an ark for the listener [i.e., for him who already listens to God]; [and] for the lingerer [the laggard in faith] with a love [that] glides lower than death and the dark; a vein [parallel with ark] for the visiting. . . ." The sentence breaks in the sixth line with the dash, and *uttermost* is a summarizing and emphatic substantive, the *very uttermost*, of whom he has been speaking. The word is used both in its sense of extremes (i.e., those in extremity) and in the archaic sense so powerful in Milton, whose *utter* is *outer* as well as extreme darkness, or as in the still current phrase, the "uttermost parts of the earth"; those in extremity, those at the outermost fringes, farthest from God, "mark [a verb] our . . . giant risen, Christ, fetched [a participle: brought to the scene, materialized, like the "fetching" of Christ and Mary described in his prose devotional writing] in the storm of his *strides*" as He had once walked upon the stormy waves of Galilee. The passage is thus part of the recapitulation, paralleling an earlier passage toward the end of Part I: "Hither then, last or first, / To hero of Calvary, Christ, 's feet— / Never ask if meaning it, wanting it, warned of it—men go" (stanza 8).[14]

Finally, in the last two stanzas the poet calls upon Christ as he had called upon God at the end of Part I, praying that He may return upon England not with the destruction of doomsday and not humbly unknown as at his birth but, "royally reclaiming his own" strayed sheep, may return as "a released shower, let flash" to the shires of England, not as a "lightning of fire hard-hurled." And the nun is asked to intercede in heaven to this end, that "our King" may return to "English souls," that the sun may rise again upon "rare-dear Britain."

The fact that it is especially English conversion that Hopkins prays for at the close is signified not only by the specific naming of English souls and shires and Britain itself, but also by the metrical stresses,

> Dáme, at oúr dóor
> Drówned, and among oúr shóals,

in which the second *our*, if not the first, wrenches the natural reading of the line badly, for the sake, evidently, of this special emphasis.[15]

The prayer ends with a series of epithets of Christ, evidently meant to bring the whole to a prophetically triumphant, all-inclusive close like the great resolution of a large-scale organ fugue:

> Pride, rose, prince, hero of us, high-priest,
> Our hearts' charity's hearth's fire, our thoughts'
>   chivalry's throng's Lord.

Poetically, these last two lines seem to me to fail; they are simply too mannered to produce the tremendous, all-stops-opened effect at which they evidently aim. The final line is symmetrically constructed and locked together in the hook-and-eye grip of the possessive case that seems meant to create the closest unity of all human values in Christ; but the effect, upon this reader at least, is of eccentricity rather than power: what should be a satisfying resolution I find myself preferring to forget. It is one of those passages in which Hopkins's art is betrayed by his schematic ingenuity. In a sense, the possessive case may be regarded as the closest of grammatical relationships, most nearly making one thing out of two by force of grammatical law. This, at any rate, seems to me the rationale of the line, but the result is more ingenious than beautiful or moving. Schematic logic seems to have clouded Hopkins's poetic judgment here, and not only in the syntactical linkage. The sound pattern is most elaborate, but its stresses can be made out with confidence only through manuscript authority, which places a stress on the monosyllables: "hearts' . . . hearth's fire; thoughts' . . . throng's Lord," leaving the trisyllabic *charity's* and *chivalry's* arbitrarily without any metrical stress. Alliteration, assonance, and stress (and even singulars and plurals) are thus distributed symmetrically with reference to the monosyllabic and the trisyllabic words. The symmetry increases the more one looks at it, but the effect is arbitrary and labored; one has no sense of the inevitable in the succession of epithets.

No poem of Hopkins shows a more carefully wrought structure than the *Wreck*. The "design, pattern or what I am in the habit of calling 'inscape' " meant to him finding, for an experience that was to become a poem, its individual form, with the particular kind of formal balance it required, the organic symmetry of a living form (though, as we have just seen, overingenious logic now and then betrayed him into a mechanical symmetry instead). In these terms the parts and their proportions in the *Wreck of the Deutschland* are conceived, and the clarity of the design is a remarkable achievement in view of the recalcitrant material. As I suggested to begin with, the primary outline is simple but the detail of the design complex. There is, for example, the framing of the poem by the measured, sonorous apostrophes at the opening and the close: the prayer of submission to the God of power in the first stanza reappearing magnified, altered, and enlarged so as to draw all the strands into the recapitulation. Part I, as the individual rehearsal of the more universal theme, has its own smaller but matching conclusion, Part II its not quite matching opening, in which the note struck is again a universal but a different universal (the human one of death), defeating a too exact symmetry while sharpening its relevance as a preface to the narrative of shipwreck.

The inclination of Hopkins toward two-part forms led him to some extravagant pseudo-rational theorizing about the sonnet, of which the two-part Italian form was for him the only one that counted. On the proportions of the parts he was for a while quite doctrinaire, having got it all down into a mathematical formula of which he found close counterparts in St. Augustine's discussion of the placing of certain caesuras in *De Musica* and in the relation between pentachord and tetrachord in the major and minor diatonic scales and the earlier modes of plainsong in music. Equal proportions alone are too symmetrical and too simple, and so also, he said, is a mere 2:1 proportion.[16] As he did not specifically discuss the proportions of the *Deutschland* in this way, one is not obliged to suppose that a special virtue inhered in its mathematical proportions of 2:5 (10:25 stanzas), though he would be capable of arguing even this. The form is distantly comparable in his terms—or he may have thought of it so—to the plagal mode in music, in which he noted the reversal of the more common order by the tetrachord's being placed first, a form not unlike that of an upside-down sonnet. It is tempting to see in Hopkins's preoccupation with two-part poetic structure, at any rate, in preference to the more common and more easily unified single and three-part forms, a symbolic reflection of the unresolved dualism in his own temperament.

A further element complicates the primary design of the *Deutschland*. The narrative and descriptive account of the wreck itself differs in conspicuous ways from the rest of the poem. Its objective physical literalness causes it to stand out prominently, like the foreground in a landscape, in contrast with the subjective and spiritual matter that precedes and follows it; the narrative stanzas, moreover, move more swiftly in thought, and their verse, almost all smoothly anapestic, moves with corresponding speed. As these objective stanzas occupy the middle place in the poem, they tend to create an effect, structurally, of a three-part form superimposed upon the primary two-part one. So strongly marked is this secondary division that some critics have noticed it alone and, interpreting the poem, have ignored the

37

more fundamental, explicitly numbered two-part form and its correspondent meaning altogether. Other complexities arise out of the knotty texture of the thought in certain passages; and, of course, throughout the whole runs the intricate texture of the language, the several related themes, the recurrent imagery, and the changing music and meter, of which the reader becomes more and more aware as his familiarity with the poem increases. The final effect, obviously, is of a complex, not a simple poetic organization, and also of a tightly knit one, though the shipshape tightness becomes apparent only when the thought structure has been more or less fully made out.

There are two criteria—or it may be they are fetishes —that have particularly marked today's criticism and poetry, and it is interesting to see where Hopkins's poem stands with reference to them. Modern readers have become accustomed to the employment of imagery for structural purposes, and modern criticism has made us so aware of this element in poetry of the past as well as the present that we have come to see it almost everywhere. Actually, however, its use by older writers was sporadic, usually unsystematic, and when present often quite slight. In particular, it is not a notable feature of the Romantic and early Victorian poetry from which that of Hopkins emerged. Its prominence in his work is one of the least noticed aspects of his modern appeal, along with this link to the seventeenth century. No doubt Herbert, whose work he knew and loved, influenced him, though his use of imagery for formal design must be mainly owing to his care for "inscape" in painting and nature and to the precepts of *Modern Painters*.

The other modern principle in the light of which it is interesting to consider *The Wreck* is that now commonly referred to as the need for a "persona." By this criterion the poem, like nearly all the mature work of Hopkins, will be found most unmodern and most "Romantic." When he told Bridges, justifying the poem in the face of his friend's dislike, "I may add for your greater interest and edification that what refers to myself in the poem is all strictly and literally true and did all occur; nothing is added for poetical padding," the contemptuous word *padding* makes it evident that he recognized no aesthetic or theoretical need for a separation between himself, Gerard Hopkins, and the speaker of the poem.[17] Where is the irony, where is the mask, where is even the thin screen of the impersonal that can lend aesthetic distance to make this a poem and not simply an unmodulated, moving perhaps but embarrassing, personal cry of longing and faith? As Eliot long ago pointed out, in somewhat different terms, this is a major weakness in all but the greatest Romantic poetry: as a poet you automatically take a stand slightly elsewhere than where you are, but often, if you are a Romantic poet, you fail to stay there. This results in the uncertainty, the unreliability of tone that so often breaks the charm of that poetry. More recently, the argument has been advanced that even the Romantic poet's "I" is not his real self, and such writers as Byron, Whitman, and later Wilde have been particularly instanced [18] (but what of Wordsworth, Keats, and Shelley?). It may be true that wherever there is aesthetic distancing there is in some sense a "persona," yet I think this rather extends the meaning of a cult word beyond the point of usefulness. I am not sure that I can put my finger precisely on the means by which Hopkins transcends the difficulty of the too personal; and in fact, as I have indicated in other terms earlier, in certain passages he obviously fails to do so. But at his best he does transcend it, and his success must be due mainly to his remarkable mastery over a distinguished form—after all, form is a kind of persona or serves the same purpose —and to the elevation of style, which lifts the speaker above the level of the human Gerard Hopkins to that of a universalized poet-prophet speaking as if out of a vision even when he speaks in personal terms.

39

Considering *The Wreck of the Deutschland* purely as a poem, then, what do we have? Some passages, as I have said, seem to me to fail through loss of the established tone or through eccentricity of taste or feeling, sometimes deriving from the frigidity of scholastic logic insufficiently transformed. One finds oneself put off here and there also by words, phrases, and images that seem out of key. After his undergraduate days were over, the aesthetic side of Hopkins's life had to develop almost entirely in isolation with the partial exception of the friendship of Bridges to be noted later on; and as even from youth his temperament bordered on the eccentric, it was probably inevitable that his thought, feeling, and expression should have become sometimes queer. He knew this. Freer contact with the cultivated lay world might have toned it down, or might not. More pervasive in the *Wreck* is another difficulty, the fact that not all the emotional intensities of the poem are felt to be adequately accounted for within the poem. If the theme is fully understood, however—if the implication of a miracle with profound consequences to come is recognized as the central event—and if the reader is capable of suspending his disbelief for the moment (possibly a large *if*), the discrepancy between heightened emotion and its represented cause disappears except in isolated lines such as that describing the "glee" in his heart as he weeps (stanza 18), where the requisite dignity of tone is wrecked by, I think, unacceptably abnormal emotion.

The *Deutschland* is a poem, then, of unequal but indisputable greatness, to be ranked among the great odes of the English language. Structurally it impresses the reader with the sense of magnitude and order; and as to the detail, in passage after passage a thought, emotion, or sensation seems inevitably married to its language and to the sound of that language. A blizzard at sea is epitomized for all time in the two lines, bound together by their *w* and long and short *i* sounds and

moving with the abrupt fall from quintessential concrete sensation in one line to the depths of abstraction
in the next:

> Wiry and white-fiery and whirlwind-swivellèd
> snow
> Spins to the widow-making unchilding unfathering
> deeps.

Even the worn abstraction of sea into *deeps* here re-
gains a century's lost impressiveness, following as it
does after the concrete distinctive epithets of the snow
and after the abysmal negative abstractions. Nor do I
know any passage in English poetry in which alliteration, assonance, and other kinds of sound pattern are
more expressive, and more fully under disciplined control than in the great stanza on death. Perhaps the poem
will continue to be valued most frequently as a mine of
fine poetical phrases and images, but it is far more than
this; and the phrases themselves are finer when they are
known as part of an intelligible whole.

Finally, there is the remarkable rhythmic beauty and
sweep of the poem and of many individual stanzas,
with the changing movement so subtly responsive to
the shifting mood. It is a new music that we hear, and
stanza after stanza haunts the memory because of it—a
new, flexible, and expressive rhythm the beauty of which
is due at least as much to Hopkins's subtle and sensitive
handling of the dangerously facile English anapest as to
his newly invented sprung rhythm but also—and most of
all—to the refinement with which the two rhythms are
combined and to the structural relation which they
bear to the meaning and design of the whole.

41

3

Evolution of the New Rhythm

I

ONE OF THE MOST CELEBRATED and from a historical point of view most important aspects of *The Wreck of the Deutschland,* the new rhythm which is there employed, has been touched upon only briefly thus far, the whole subject being so large and so complex that its proper consideration had to be deferred if the various threads of the discourse were not to become hopelessly tangled. It should be born in mind now that this separation is in some degree artificial; yet it is not altogether so, for we know from Hopkins's own statement that his new rhythm came into existence as a rhythm before it had a body of thought or theme to inhabit. The separation has at any rate an advantage for readers who admit to finding metrical discussions tedious: they may readily "turne over the leef and chese another tale."

Almost everything would seem to have been said that can be said about sprung rhythm—not that authorities agree.[1] On the contrary, there is every sort of disparity in the accounts of its nature and origin. That Hopkins invented its name is certain and that he himself first used it in *The Wreck of the Deutschland,* but agreement ends there. His rhythm has been traced to, and sometimes identified with, the old strong-stress Anglo-Saxon alliterative measure, or, alternatively, to the choruses in *Samson Agonistes.* It has been called rigidly isochronous; it has also been described as free verse, next door to prose, and quite lawless in spite of his insistence that it was written by strict laws. It has been said to be entirely new and entirely old. When pushed to defend it, Hopkins himself found numerous precedents: brief instances or hints in Shakespeare, Milton, and Campbell, in nursery rhymes and weather saws, in Anglo-Saxon verse and its "degraded and doggrel" survival in *Piers Plowman* (though he did not know the last two, except at second hand and in the briefest of extracts, till some years after he had developed his own system). These predecessors, however, he named merely as precedents; he never called them sources. The only specific statement he made concerning the actual origin of the measure reveals nothing: "I had long had haunting my ear the echo of a new rhythm which now I realised on paper." [2] He hastened to add, as he did also in discussing the meter with Bridges, that he did not claim it as "altogether new"; he did profess to be the first who had avowedly "used it and made it the principle throughout" a poem, to the best of his knowledge.

The sources and the nature of sprung rhythm are not altogether separate questions. Not only its associations but, actually, how we read it in Hopkins, its character, stress, and timing depend partly on our conception of its origins—whether we hear it, that is, as a throwback to strong-stress Anglo-Saxon verse or as a development from traditional literary verse with its mingling of English and southern European roots, or as something still different from either. Bound up with this question is another: whether we are to conceive the rhythm as isochronous, or, if a more or less exact relation between time and stress does not create the rhythm, we have to ask what does. These questions are the heart of the problem. But before looking into them, I should like to draw attention to something about the state of poetry during the last century that from its very obviousness has gone largely unnoticed by literary historians.

Bridges called *The Wreck of the Deutschland* "a

great metrical experiment." It was this, whatever its sources, and more; but it was not an isolated experiment, for as an innovator in form, meter, and style, Hopkins was dealing with a problem that all poets writing in English, and to a lesser extent in French and Italian, were coming to face more or less consciously, the problem of staleness on a scale and for reasons that had not existed before. We hear often of a different phenomenon, the momentary exhaustion that may set in when a movement in any art has run its course, as when the vein of literary Romanticism petered out without engendering a reaction that might have brought freshness; this exhaustion is not what I refer to. By the mid-nineteenth century there was greater reason, of much longer growth, for a feeling on the part of poets that the forms of poetry, its meters, and even its language were wearing out. Conventional English meters have remained essentially the same since Chaucer, a period of some four hundred years by the time Hopkins wrote (since verse written in other modes during the century or two after Chaucer soon dropped from the sight of nearly all but scholars and antiquarians), and the language itself has continued without significant change since the sixteenth century. Every rhyme even —aside from a handful of eccentric or comic, mostly trisyllabic, rhymes—by 1800 had been repeated some thousands of times. What with printing, the growth of population, the rise of a literate middle class, and the prolific English poetic genius, in purely numerical terms there can never have been in the history of the world's cultures any such quantity of poetry composed in a single language and metrical system as came to exist in English, though French and Italian poetry fall not much behind. In recent times it must have seemed to an English poet more true than ever before that "that which is to be hath already been." Prose writers largely escape the difficulty because their subject matter by its nature secures greater variety from the changing circumstances of the society it reflects; and certain of its forms, too, were of later development than verse. But for poetry, especially lyric poetry dealing directly with the universal and the permanent in human experience, the problem was and is real, to whatever extent mitigated by the variety of human genius and the conscious search for new themes, new myths, and fresh attitudes. Though the old forms have continued to succeed, now and then supremely, in the hands of certain poets, the choices have grown narrower; and even a century ago many were beginning to feel that the possibilities of the old forms had been fully explored. This purely historical fact must have been at least as influential as the more obvious wish to be "modern" in animating the metrical and stylistic experiments of the past hundred years.

The American George P. Marsh, in lectures that Hopkins cited in his own lectures on rhythm in 1873-74, was already, in 1859, commenting on the effort of modern poets "to invent new forms and combinations . . . and to infuse fresh life and spirit into movements of the muses which perpetual repetition has made wearisome"; and he added, "The English language cannot long supply the necessities of poetry without the introduction of new elements of verse," referring to the exhaustion of rhymes and his suggested substitution of assonance and half-rhyme.[3] Some poets also have been explicit on the matter, none more so than Bridges. Standard English meter "has long been in the stage of artistic exhaustion of form which follows great achievement," he said. Of all European verse, none before in history had ever been subject to such "various elaboration"; and the question seemed to him urgent "whether any further development on the same lines is possible." A few years afterward, in 1914, he told Edward Thompson: "The old forms are worn out. We have got to find new ones. We shall find them."[4] Four years later he published Hopkins's poems, perhaps with this need partly in mind. Not all poets have been as specific as Bridges about

45

their dilemma, and no doubt many have been less distinctly aware of it, but nearly all must have been affected. The reaction, like the cause itself, has been a movement of longer range than most literary movements. Within shorter spans of time, the heroic couplet once grew out of Elizabethan freedoms, and the verse forms of Romantic poetry, mainly revivals and modifications, proceeded naturally from a surfeit of couplets—to telescope prosodic history somewhat drastically. These were important but relatively short-range changes. The subsequent movement has been more radical because it has resulted from the whole sum of this past. No doubt certain modern experiments reflect simply a new spirit seeking new forms for a new age. But the main reasons for change in verse forms over the past century are probably more poetic than social: the old forms really are well worn, and the experiments are therefore of the greatest importance if English poetry is to have a future as well as a past. Even the moderate prosodic ventures of Tennyson and Browning were a sign of the felt need.

One measure not new to English verse but with possibilities that had been little explored was the anapest. Saintsbury, who was perhaps overfond of it even in its rawest forms, comments in his *History of English Prosody* on the neglect of it over several centuries. With rare exceptions anapestic rhythms had remained too crude and trivial in movement to succeed in serious verse and had been left largely in unsubtle hands like those of Isaac Watts, Southey, and Tom Moore. Occasionally it had been made to produce something fine: the rhythmic ambiguities of "As you came from the holy land / Of Walsingham," which sounds like anapestic verse composed by a man with iambics running in his head, give that poem much of its enchantment; Blake sometimes succeeded with it though at other times he seems to have been bred too long on Watts and Charles Wesley; [5] and there is perfect metrical, if not aesthetic, mastery in Shelley's "When the lamp is shattered." The anapests

46

are conspicuous in *Christabel* too; and it may have been the prominence of that poem, accompanied by Coleridge's controversial account of its meter, that stimulated what grew into something like a stampede of anapestic verse after about 1850. Those of Tennyson have been praised, but I do not think he ever tamed the measure. To my ear, at least, it half ruins the once admired "Break, break, break": "O well for the fisherman's boy, / That he shouts with his sister at play! / . . . But O for the touch of a vanish'd hand, / And the sound of a voice that is still!"—which carries off the broken heart at rather an unfeeling clip. It is Swinburne above all whom we associate with the measure, sometimes for better, often for worse. Almost everyone, however, was using it; and its influence has been pervasive ever since, not always in obvious places. It became one fresh resource, possibly the most significant one, within the framework of traditional English prosody.

The various directions taken by bolder innovations are well known: those of Whitman, the French Symbolists, and countless later writers turning toward greater or even complete metrical freedom (though the actual term "free verse" had been used as early as 1821 by Tom Moore), while others sought to create new forms or systems which would be as strict as the conventional ones but fresh and, it was sometimes hoped, endowed with other advantages of their own. There was the flurry of revived mediaeval French forms: by Henley with his ballades and villanelles on one hand and his free verse on the other; by the now nearly forgotten Alfred Austin and Austin Dobson, "the rondeliers," as Hopkins habitually named them with some contempt. There were new efforts to adapt classical meters, particularly the hexameter: Swinburne wrote some accentual Sapphics; even Hardy, who was scarcely by temperament a technician, tried out Sapphics in one of his earliest poems, as well as triolets and a pseudo-Anglo-Saxon accentual measure. Swinburne, Bridges, and Hopkins tower easily over most of their contemporaries in the earlier experimental measures; but the movement continued, as we know, into the present century, where Bridges' modifications of syllabic verse stand beside Pound's old French forms and free verse and beside Eliot's mediations between free and traditional verse, not to speak of the great variety of still freer experiments that have been tried. Under this light and as a part of this movement of poetry in need of new forms, a genuine technical need deeply rooted in historical circumstance, the "great experiment" of Hopkins's sprung rhythm is before us.

II

The early metrical practice of Hopkins was entirely conventional. It proved, as we saw earlier, that from the beginning he had a fine ear, a remarkably developed metrical skill, and an interest in trying out a variety of forms; but there were no experiments in meter. Between 1866 and 1868, he appears to have written almost nothing (almost nothing, at any rate, survives); and before the middle of the latter year his decision to become a priest had brought a resolution to give up the writing of poetry "unless," as he explained later, "it were by the wish of my superiors." After this, with exceptions to be noted shortly, Hopkins wrote no poetry till he began *The Wreck of the Deutschland* in December 1875. By that time the "new rhythm" had come into being in his mind.

The intervening development can be traced for the most part only by inference. During the years of almost complete poetic silence, two circumstances that we know of drew his thought toward the technical problems of verse. One is that in 1873–74 he was lecturing on "Rhetoric" at Roehampton. These lectures included discussions of both classical and English meters, as his surviving notes on "Rhythm and the Other Structural

48

Parts of Rhetoric—Verse" show.[6] The second circumstance is that he had been reading Swinburne. There may have been other influences at work—he read Tennyson, for example, with great admiration and presumably some profit, and he knew some of the work of Christina Rossetti and of course Browning—but the one contemporary writer of whose influence we can be certain, aside from Bridges, whose own metrical experiments came later, is Swinburne. Writing of the *Deutschland* afterward, Hopkins mentioned "two or three little presentation pieces" as the only exceptions to his self-imposed silence (II, 14), and two that must be among these have been recovered. Both, as Bridges said of one of them, are "in direct and competent imitation of Swinburne." They must belong to the spring of 1871, 1872, or 1873. *Ad Mariam* [7] reads almost like a parody, except for its seriousness, of the celebrated chorus in *Atalanta in Calydon:* "When the hounds of spring are on winter's traces, / The mother of months. . . ." Hopkins employed the same stanza, a variant of *ottava rima* in four-stress anapestic lines; but his poem is full also of verbal and rhetorical echoes of Swinburne's chorus. The pedigree of *Ad Mariam* announces itself in the first line, and the imitation continues throughout:

When a sister, born for each strong month-brother,
   Spring's one daughter, the sweet child May,

. . . .

We have suffered the sons of Winter in sorrow
   And been in their ruinous reigns oppressed.

These last lines suggest Swinburne's "For winter's rains and ruins are over"; and the whole poem, playing as it does on *month, mother, spring, winter, maiden,* and the like, deliberately echoes Swinburne's chorus, even to the regular alternation of feminine with masculine rhyme and the triple rhymes "sing to thee," "bring to thee," "spring to thee" echoing Swinburne's "sing to her,"

49

"spring to her," "cling to her." The second of these occasional poems, *Rosa Mystica*—it may be chronologically the first, for neither can now be precisely dated—is also written in light anapestic verse, less obviously Swinburnian in sound and even more trivial in spite of its serious subject. Neither can be taken seriously as poetry, and Hopkins himself probably did not take them so. They are scarcely experimental, but they point a direction.

The connection of these pieces not only with Swinburne and the wave of anapests in the nineteenth century but also with the development of sprung rhythm becomes apparent when we observe that the "Bremen" stanza (stanza 12) of *The Wreck of the Deutschland*, the one Hopkins said was written first, is not in sprung rhythm at all but in perfectly conventional anapestic meter and cannot be read in any other way. The importance of Swinburne, however, does not end here and may best be disposed of before we turn to Hopkins's developing intention as it can be gathered from one other poem and his lecture notes.

Atalanta in Calydon was published in 1865 and was followed in 1866 by the first series of *Poems and Ballads*. Just when Hopkins read these is uncertain, but that he did so with close attention is not. In a letter of mid-September 1867 to his Balliol friend Mowbray Baillie, Hopkins mildly criticized the morality and the poetic archaisms of *Atalanta* in terms that show the work was not new to him then. Ten years later, defending the strictness of his rhymes and his anapests in the *Deutschland*, he told Bridges, who had treated both severely and parodied the latter: "And my quantity is not like 'Fĭftў twō Bĕdfŏrd Squāre,' where *fĭftў* might pass but *Bĕdfŏrd* I should never admit. Not only so but Swinburne's dactyls and anapaests are halting to my ear: I never allow e.g. *I* or *my* (that is diphthongs . . .) in the short or weak syllables of those feet, excepting . . ." He proceeded to detail his exceptions and went on to describe the new rhythm of the *Deutsch-land*.[8] By this time he had clearly studied the verse of Swinburne with a technician's concentration. Swinburne did not confine himself to anapests, however; and what seems to have escaped the notice of writers on prosody as well as on Hopkins is the fact that in his free handling of other measures Swinburne very often approaches remarkably close to sprung rhythm as Hopkins later defined it. If Hopkins's new measure was in any sense, as I believe it was, an evolution from current versification and not either an altogether novel invention or an Anglo-Saxon revival, then this writing of Swinburne's is an important link.

The most striking and characteristic feature of sprung rhythm, and the basis for its name, is its provision for the juxtaposing of stressed syllables anywhere in the line and as often as is wanted, *without loss of force or length in these syllables*. This last provision is not explicit in Hopkins's definition, but it is a vital difference between sprung and standard rhythms (cf. I, 46). Conventional iambic verse recognizes the so-called hovering accent and spondaic substitution, both of which involve consecutive stresses;[9] but neither of these produces the effect of a sprung line. As its name suggests, the hovering accent, and the spondee also in a slighter degree, weaken the stress or shorten the time given to one or more of the consecutive stressed syllables. This is not a theoretical but an audible fact in the reading of such feet within the rhythm dictated by their context, so clearly so as to have led certain theorists to deny the possibility of a spondee in English. A hovering accent is possible in sprung, as well as in standard, rhythms. Hopkins uses it, often with the two syllables so smoothed by alliteration and inflection that they are psychologically almost one: "Flesh falls within sight of us." An illustration from conventional verse may help to distinguish these from sprung effects. The commonest spondees and those least disturbing to the rhythm of a line are ones that occur paired with and following a pyrrhic foot: "Ănd thĕ / préss'd wátch / returned a silver sound." This is like a small rubato, where both time and stress are momentarily withheld and then paid back, so that the swing of the line as a whole continues undisturbed. It is one of the commonest sources of life and movement in standard English verse. But suppose that either the previously established rhythm or the demands of the meaning, or both, induce us to read, "Ănd thĕ préss'd / wátch / rĕtúrned / a sil/ver sound"; then we have an altogether different timing, rhythm, and inflectional tune, and a rhetorical emphasis so different as to amount to a different meaning. And we have the beginning of sprung rhythm. Or if Wordsworth had wished for a different emphasis and a sprung line, "Ĭ hăd [or Ĭ hăd] / nó hú/măn feárs" might have been "I hăd nó / hú/măn feárs"—if he could have got us to read it so. These are of course distortions.[10] However, it is precisely this transition that we find Swinburne making in *Atalanta*, in a few poems toward the end of the 1866 *Poems and Ballads*, and in *Songs before Sunrise* (in later work too, but these are the volumes Hopkins knew before he developed his new rhythm).

The blank verse of *Atalanta* is probably freer than any that English poetry had seen before, and this is one of its chief innovations.

> Give place unto me; I am as any of you,
> To give life and to take life. Thou, old earth,
> That hast made man and unmade; thou whose
>   mouth . . .[11]

The last of these lines may be read either conventionally "Thăt hăst / máde mán / ănd ún/măde; // thóu / whŏse móuth," or "Thăt hăst máde / mán / ănd ún/măde; thóu / whŏse móuth";[12] and several circumstances make the second perhaps as natural as the first:

the meaning; the frequency of anapests elsewhere in the blank verse, preparing the ear for a trisyllabic foot; and the exceptional weight of the three preceding words, "Thou, old earth," which incline the reader to quicken the next words in compensation. In the speech of Althea beginning, "Girls, one thing will I say and hold my peace," these lines occur:

As with the shadow of shed blood; behold,
I am kindled with the flames that fade in him,
I am swollen with subsiding of his veins,
I am flooded with his ebbing; my lit eyes . . .
(pp. 335–336)

The first line may be read either as "thĕ shád/ŏw ŏf / shéd bloód; / bĕhóld" or "the shá/dŏw ŏf shéd / bloód; / bĕhóld." These again are different rhythms, not just different methods of scansion: the first a conventional variant in which we stretch the weak syllables *-ow of* slightly beyond their ordinary prose length and minimize somewhat the stress on *shed,* in order to retain the semblance of the iambic movement; the second a reading that produces quite a different effect, with a much stronger stress on both *shed* and *blood.* In this line the second reading is encouraged by the extreme lightness of the two light syllables, and by the strong rhetorical pause after *blood,* which together strain the common ‿ ‿ / ′ ′ pattern rather beyond what the ear will accept as normal. The last line quoted provides another instance: "hĭs éb/bĭng; mў / lít eýes" or "hĭs éb/bĭng; mў lít /eýes." Or there is this single-line speech of the chorus among other pentameter lines, "And thy moúth shúddering lĭke a shót bírd" (p. 334), for which it is impossible to think of any reading that is not sprung.

In standard verse, two stresses can be banked against each other without weakening either syllable only by means of a strong, clear-cut inversion. As most commonly employed at the beginning of a line or after a pause, the emphatic back-to-back effect is lost and abruptness disguised or avoided by the pause separating the stresses; but occasionally the inversion occurs without a preceding pause. This is a highly sensitive variant, capable of great expressiveness: Keats's inversion of the second foot, for example, establishing a slow, heavy movement, "Mў héart / áches, ănd a drowsy numbness . . ."; or Housman's heightening of the word *cling* (at the fresh graveside), "The rain, it streams on stone and hillock, / Thĕ bóot / clíngs tŏ / thĕ cláy"; or Yeats's closing line in the early *Ballad of the Foxhunter*, "The hounds wail for the dead." [13] Usually this kind of inversion is so clearly dictated by a special intention in the meaning that we do not think of it as sprung; moreover, in cases like these where there is no pause, the inversion still tends to weaken, if only slightly, the preceding stress and so to soften the abruptness. Swinburne, however, in both his lyric measures and his blank verse, inverted stresses so freely that one sometimes has difficulty in making out the rhythm of a line; at other times, the effect is unmistakably "sprung," as in this line from a chorus in three-stress anapestic verse, "Ăs thĕ móuth / ŏf ă flúte-/pláyĕr" (p. 337), a liberty no doubt traceable to lines ending with "a far countree" in popular ballads, but in Swinburne's line the word accent wins, even though it belongs to the weaker element in a compound word.

After the juxtaposition of accents, the other main feature of sprung rhythm is its logaoedic or mixed character. There is only one stress, but the number of light syllables in a foot varies from none to three (and "for particular effects," Hopkins said, any number). In this direction also Swinburne had gone far. The emergence of anapestic verse in the nineteenth century had already broken the back of the syllable-counted line, for anapests can scarcely be tamed or tolerated without a generous admixture of dissyllabic feet. From the nature of the language, the trisyllabic foot is so conspicuous that if anything approaching half the units of a poem are anapestic this becomes the rhythmic signature of the whole. English anapestic verse in serious poems, therefore, is normally logaoedic.[14] This circumstance constitutes quite as important a contribution to new prosodic resources in the nineteenth century as the emergence of the anapest itself. Occasionally Swinburne introduced still a third light syllable into his trisyllabic verse, but this alone would not likely have suggested to Hopkins a new rhythm, for Swinburne's fourth syllable is usually inconspicuous and often subject to elision: "emp/tying of qui/vers" in the "Hounds of spring" chorus, and in a later one of three-stress lines, "That is wo/ven of the day / on the night" (pp. 271, 294). In his blank verse, however, the number of light syllables between stresses much more often ranges from none to three, which is the regular range of sprung rhythm; and though these variations can perhaps more often than not, with ingenuity, be described in terms of conventional prosodic rules, they are frequent and extreme enough to change the nature of the verse. In an iambic poem, a trochaic inversion followed by an anapest will yield three successive light syllables, but when these occur in a context full of other variations, the conventional terms lose their meaning, for the whole effect becomes different.

The following opening of a long speech of Althea in *Atalanta* offers a fair range of these variations. Several of the lines are open to more than one prosodic interpretation, but all are to be read as pentameter.

O king, thou art wise, but wisdom halts; and just,
But the gods love not justice more than fate,
      [five lines omitted]
O child, for thine head's sake; mine eyes wax thick,
Turning toward thee, so goodly a weaponed man,
So glorious; and for love of thine own eyes
They are darkened, and tears burn them, fierce as fire,
And my lips pause and my soul sinks with love.
But by thine hand, by thy sweet life and eyes,

By thy great heart and these clasped knees, O son,
      [five lines omitted]
Small things and transitory as a wind o' the sea,
I forget never; I have seen thee all thine years
A man in arms, strong and a joy to men,
Seeing thine head glitter and thine hand burn its
    way . . .   (pp. 291–292)

The sixth and seventh of these lines alone illustrate the fundamentally mixed character of the rhythm. A description based on rhetorical units gives us for the first of these a third paeonic, "They are darkened"; an iamb, "and tears"; a trochee, "burn them"; a monosyllabic foot, "fierce"; and an iamb, "as fire"; in the next line, an anapest, "And my lips"; a monosyllabic foot, "pause"; another anapest and another monosyllable, "and my soul / sinks"; and an iamb, "with love." Scanned according to the conventions of its blank verse, the lines may be read:

Thĕy ăre dárk/ĕned, ănd / téars búrn / thĕm, fiérce /
  ăs fíre,
Ănd mў / líps paúse / ănd mў / soúl sínks / wĭth lóve.

We are unlikely to read them in this way, however, for having opened unmistakably with "Thĕy ăre dárk-," in the first line we are led automatically to "Ănd mў líps" as the opening unit of the second, which forces the line into a sprung rhythm. And at the close of a later line no system of scansion can get around the presence of a fourth paeonic foot followed by an anapest: "Small things and tráns/ĭtŏr/ў ăs ă wínd / ŏ' thĕ séa" (or else an amphibrach, "-ĭtŏrў," followed by two anapests). In short, though Swinburne's blank verse is still in touch with the iambic pentameter norm, he has altered it so radically that many passages have the characteristics of sprung rhythm. The same variations from standard meter appear in his shorter rhymed iambic verse, and among the *Poems and Ballads* several pieces are written in a different strong-stress, nonsyllabic meter, which Swinburne evidently arrived at by way of the popular ballad, Morris, and the Pre-Raphaelites. In some of these he is particularly free with the archaisms to which Hopkins objected so strongly—the "I wis," "I rede," "perfay" style—but they offer notable departures from syllabic verse, with juxtaposed stresses and as many as three successive light syllables.[15] These verses must have interested Hopkins, but his own sprung rhythm does not really resemble them in rhythmical effect; it is far closer to the graver measures in which Swinburne played variations upon a conventional syllabic base.

Swinburne's influence, coming from the contemporary world of metrical experiment, is I think one of the mainsprings of Hopkins's new rhythm and may well have provided the first incitement to experiment.[16] For his earliest departure, however—the only one known to have preceded the *Deutschland*—Hopkins cited the precedent of Shakespeare. This was a revision, in 1868, of an early poem in which he altered certain lines to reproduce one particular strong-stress pattern of which he had noticed isolated instances in Shakespeare. He sent the new version to Bridges with the comment: "I hope you will master the peculiar beat I have introduced into St. Dorothea. The development is mine but the beat is in Shakspere—e.g. / Whý should thís désert bé? [17]—and / Thóu for whóm Jóve would sweár—where the rest of the lines are eight-syllabled or seven-syllabled" (I, 24–25; three of the obvious stresses, omitted in the letter, are here supplied from the *Journals*). The original version of this poem, *For a Picture of St. Dorothea,* which also has a mystifying but perhaps chance connection with Swinburne, is in conventional tetrameter verse.[18] There are two later versions, the one sent to Bridges in 1868 and another of unknown date, *Lines for a Picture of St. Dorothea.* Both of these have undergone metrical revision directly imitating the two lines of Shakespeare. The experiment was limited. Hopkins was making no effort to create a whole new metrical texture but was merely attempting to introduce into standard verse an occasional line of exceptional pattern. The poem is not improved by the revision—rather the contrary, for many of the stresses marked by Hopkins are unnaturally forced.

> I bear a basket lined with grass.
> Î am só líght and fáir . . .
> Sérvèd bý méssengér? [etc.]

It was almost entirely an abortive venture and demonstrates little except his interest in the effect of juxtaposed accents, even if he had to hammer down by force and without rhetorical excuse a strong stress on the preposition *by*. Yet this, as far as we know, is the only metrical experiment that preceded that extraordinarily complex poem *The Wreck of the Deutschland*.

If he wrote little, Hopkins at least had opportunity to think systematically about prosody once during the intervening years. His lectures on the rhythms of verse, delivered while he was teaching "Rhetoric" in 1873–74, had to do officially with Greek and Latin, but he made occasion to discuss certain aspects of English verse as well, and several points upon which he dwelt indicate the direction of his thought (*Journals*, pp. 267–290 *passim*). He discussed what he described as the "counterpoint" in the verse of Horace and Ovid, where the word accent and the quantity produce different patterns that run concurrently, a feature of Latin verse that interested him a great deal then and later (II, 25); and he cited an instance of "counterpoint" in the closing line of *Paradise Regained*. He contrasted classical quantitative rhythms with nonsyllabic accentual ones, illustrating the latter first by quotations from Latin Saturnian verse in which, according to the scansion he followed, there are four or five instances in which accents come together; and, similarly, among the classical quantitative feet that he singled out for particular notice is the antispast, which he illustrated by English accentual equivalents, marking their juxtaposed stresses, "Dulness / perháps őften, / at tímes sădness, / regrét nĕver." From the Latin he went on to "Rough English accentual verse," quoting "Márch dúst, Ápril shówers / Bríng fórth Máy flówers" and a few lines of *Piers Plowman*, which, however, like Anglo-Saxon verse, he did not know except in brief extract till many years later. And finally he proceeded to treat of the same developed, that is, English accentual verse, no longer "rough." Accentual rhythm, he thought, "allows of development as much as time-rhythm wherever the ear or mind is true enough to take in the essential principle of it, that beat is measured by stress or strength, not number, so that one strong may be equal not only to two weak but to less or more. In English great masters of rhythm have acted on this." Four isolated lines from Shakespeare are quoted, all in four-beat strong-stress rhythm: "Tóad that únder cóld stóne," "Sléep thou fírst i'th [*sic*] chármed pót," and the two he had cited to Bridges some years earlier, along with several others from Campbell and William Hamilton of Bangour.

Throughout this discussion, Hopkins shows a particular interest in matters, chiefly but not exclusively from classical poetry, that furnished precedents for logaoedic and contrapuntal rhythms (I use the term "counterpoint" in Hopkins's sense; though the analogy has been objected to as inexact, it seems to me clear enough and I know no better term).[19] Some of his observations read more like those of a poet seeking a new rhythm, or possibly seeking a rationale for one already in mind, than notes for the instruction of a class of boys. However, his practice, not his theory, is our main concern here, and the known stages in its development can be summed up very briefly: first the few unsuccessful

59

strong-stress lines injected into "St. Dorothea" (1868); next the Swinburnian anapests of the two Marian poems (1871–1873); then *The Wreck of the Deutschland* (1875–1876). Composition of the long work seems to have extended over a period of some five or six months. First news of the disaster appeared in the *Times* on December 8; by the twenty-fourth, Hopkins was at work on the poem; by the latter part of June 1876, it had been completed and sent to *The Month* (III, 135–138). More than a year then elapsed before he wrote another poem in rhythm that he described as sprung throughout (*Hurrahing in Harvest*, dated 1 Sept. 1877).

III

The Wreck of the Deutschland thus stands somewhat alone in time as a poem avowedly composed in sprung rhythm. In writing it, Hopkins evidently began with the narrative of the wreck, and this part of the poem is written mainly in conventional anapestic meter, more carefully "timed," he asserted in defending it to Bridges, than the dactyls and anapests of Swinburne; and he was right, I think. Swinburne was a great metrist and was capable of most beautiful and subtle effects, but not usually when his metrical base was trisyllabic, the popularity of the "Hounds of spring" and *A Forsaken Garden* notwithstanding. Hopkins defeated the almost inveterate tendency of the anapest to lope in a mechanical rhythm or at too fast a pace for serious verse, through several devices of skillful timing. For one thing, he managed more or less to even his trisyllabic and dissyllabic feet and to do so not by quickening the former but by retarding most of the light syllables of the latter with obstructive consonants or other means. His narrative opens:

> On Sát/urday sáiled / from Brém/en
> Amér/ican-oút/ward-boúnd,

Take sét/tler and séa/men, tell mén / with
    wóm/en,
    Twŏ hún/dred soúls / in the roúnd—
O Father, not under thy feathers nor ever as guessing
The goal was a shoal, of a fourth the doom to be
    drowned;
    Yet did the dark side of the bay of thy blessing
Not vault them, the millions of rounds of thy mercy
    not reeve even them in?

In nearly all the dissyllabic feet here except the first,
the light syllables are retarded either by a long, semi-
diphthongized, almost accented vowel, or by adjacent
consonants ("with wom[en]" is the only clear exception). To pass, for example, from the *ai* of *sailed* to the
accented vowel of *Bremen,* the reader has to proceed
through the sound *l—d—from—Br-;* and similarly with
the other dissyllabic feet. Equally important, on the
other hand, is the care Hopkins took to avoid overload-
ing his trisyllabic feet. Clogged syllables in the light
places of an anapestic foot usually produce a trivial (or
sometimes lumpy) effect rather than, as is often supposed, a slower rhythm, the reason being that the
reader will tend to maintain the metrical pace by hurry-
ing these syllables without regard to their normal expressive or semantic value. Hopkins was aware of this
fact, and it is the explicit ground on which he criticized
Swinburne's trisyllabic verse while defending his own
in *The Wreck,* as we have already seen (he rejected,
that is, such an anapest as "Bedford Square" because of
the excessive weight, for two short syllables, of "Bedford"). Finally, he controlled his tempo by playing off
against the foot unit overlapping phrases that gave him
a frequent slight pause between the two light syllables.
This occurs always after a feminine ending, where the
following line may open with one but never two light
syllables and the anapestic foot is carried over but
broken by the terminal caesura (the device most nota-

ble in preserving the metrical gravity of Shelley's "When the lamp is shattered"), and often within the line, where the phrasing becomes amphibrachic though the ground rhythm remains anapestic. The third line of the stanza quoted, for example, in sense breaks mainly into amphibrachic units, "Take settler / and seamen, / tell men / with women /"; so does the opening of the last line, "Not vault them, / the millions / ." This slight rhetorical pause between the light syllables does much to obviate the anapestic gallop.

Discussion of these refinements need not be further labored because they are obvious enough. They have a great deal to do with the metrical success of the *Deutschland,* however, and, for that matter, more widely with the viability of the anapest for serious verse in English as it was being evolved in the nineteenth century. For this poem they made available to Hopkins a narrative rhythm that moves and is flexible yet is consonant with the solemnity of the theme and that is also capable of modulation without abruptness into a different measure, the new sprung rhythm. At the same time, the delicacy of these adjustments in timing enabled Hopkins to sustain, without falling into uncontrolled acceleration, a more unbroken succession of anapests than we usually tolerate in a measure ordinarily demanding much dissyllabic relief. And the same delicacy, added to the fact that the poem opens with a very different rhythm, has tended to obscure the extent to which this trisyllabic measure prevails throughout the poem. After the stanza already quoted, straightforward narrative continues through five more stanzas that are either predominantly or entirely anapestic, but the measure is far from being confined to the narrative. Often elsewhere it runs for a line or two at a time and very often for half a line or more:

The swoon of a heart that the sweep and the hurl of thee trod
The frown of his face / Before me, the hurtle of hell

To flash from the flame to the flame then, tower from the grace to the grace.

And it crowds and it combs to the fall;

Away in the loveable west, / On a pastoral forehead of Wales.

This rhythm is pervasive, not merely occasional, but obviously it is not the whole story.

At the end of 1875, having received encouragement from his superiors to write a poem on the recent shipwreck, Hopkins set to work after his years of almost complete silence. "I had long had haunting my ear the echo of a new rhythm," he said in a passage quoted earlier; and this statement suggests what one might guess from the poem itself, that the rhythm was first of all something heard mentally, that it originated with his auditory imagination rather than as a deliberate theoretical invention, though theory and other poets' practice of course must have influenced his imagination. And by "a new rhythm," naturally, he meant something else than anapests. His own most carefully pondered description of the rhythm was written some years later in his "Author's Preface," of which the essential statement referable to the *Deutschland* is the following:

> Sprung rhythm, as used in this book [MS B of his poems], is measured by feet of from one to four syllables, regularly, and for particular effects any number of weak or slack syllables may be used. It has one stress, which falls on the only syllable, if there is only one, or, if there are more . . . on the first, and so gives rise to four sorts of feet, a monosyllable and the so-called accentual Trochee, Dactyl, and the First Paeon. . . . In Sprung Rhythm, as in logaoedic rhythm generally, the feet are assumed to be equally long or strong and their seeming inequality is made up by pause or stressing.

By this date (1883 or later), his growing preoccupation with music had led Hopkins to reverse his earlier system of scansion. He now accepted, purely for "convenience," he said, a method analogous to that of the musical bar, beginning every foot with the stressed syllable, regardless of the actual character of the rhythm, which he recognized as in English predominantly "rising" (iambic or anapestic, rather than trochaic or "falling"). All his earlier accounts, and hence those closer in time to the composition of the *Deutschland,* adopted the contrary system and terms, "monosyllables, iambs, anapaests, and fourth paeons," as being most consonant with what the true nature of the rhythm generally is. In the present discussion I have followed this earlier and usually more accurate scansion (see *Letters,* II, 39–41 and elsewhere).

The meter, then, is nonsyllabic, and the stresses, as he noted elsewhere, are in general much more strongly marked than those of conventional verse. So much is clear. On one issue, however, Hopkins was somewhat equivocal, perhaps because he was unable to make up his mind on the point of theory or to analyze satisfactorily his own practice, which, fortunately, seems not to have been injured by the theoretical difficulty. The question is whether or not he conceived his feet to be isochronous and, if not, how there can be rhythm at all, when the alternations of stress in regular English syllabic verse have been discarded, other than the incidental broken rhythms of prose or the shifting rhetorical rhythms of the freest free verse. His own is clearly not free verse (though it has been called that), and he himself insisted that, on the contrary, it was very strict. Yet he invariably avoided calling it isochronous. Verse, he had said in his lectures (*Journals,* p. 267, and cf. p. 289), must have a recurring pattern or "figure" that is "over and above" or "independent of" meaning. By implication this definition excludes free verse, though it would cover the Old English strong-stress rhythm, the recurring figure of which usually consists in a regular sequence of two stresses, mid-line pause, two stresses, terminal pause, with the medial pause bridged by fixed alliteration and the whole four-unit figure repeated, with new alliterative binding, in line after line. The definition covers such a figure as this whether in its original recitation the verse was isochronous, as is now thought likely, or not. But Hopkins's sprung rhythm was not Old English strong-stress rhythm either, though it has been called that and though, some years later, when he learned a little Anglo-Saxon, he described its verse as sprung. In fundamental respects it differs from his, for his lacks both of its fixed elements, the fixed relation between pause and stresses and the structurally fixed alliteration. These are the two essentials of its "figure." In his sprung rhythm, not only is there no fixed medial pause or fixed alliterative pattern, but the terminal pause too may be absent or minimized when the line is run over; and even when it is not run over, in a stanza made up of unequal lines the terminal pause is fixed in a repetitive pattern not with reference to neighboring lines but only from stanza to stanza.

Several times Hopkins comes close to describing his verse feet as equal in duration, but each time, as if deliberately backing away, he inserts an alternative: the feet "are assumed to be equally long *or strong* and their seeming inequality is made up by pause or stressing." Harold Whitehall, in support of his contention that Hopkins's sprung rhythm is and was meant to be isochronous, quotes from this passage the statement that the feet "are assumed to be equally long"; but there he stops, omitting the alternative phrase that conflicts with his theory—"or strong"—which, however, is essential and which Hopkins invariably took care to insert in every statement he made on the subject.[20] He had evidently thought the matter over with care and knew that his metrical feet could not be described accurately as a succession of equally timed beats. Yet he clearly

65

felt the necessity of some sort of equality of measure and therefore seized upon the possibly vague notion of "strength" as a second principle when "length" would not do. "Strength" apparently did not mean simply volume of sound, loudness; it seems to be something more like expenditure of energy, though perhaps even that is too definite. Sometimes, however, whether he knew it or not, length (duration of time but not the "quantity" of classical rules) seems to have entered into the "strength." Once he illustrated "strength (or gravity)" by explaining that *bid* is "graver or stronger" than *bit* (II, 41). It also takes longer to pronounce unless one works hard to make it equally short. More generally, he explained, when a foot consists of only one syllable, its stress is strengthened by the "slack" of the unstressed syllables that might be present but are not, "as though the slack syllables had been absorbed" into the single main one (II, 22). Apparently Hopkins leaned toward an isochronous theory of poetic rhythm but had too accurate an ear not to be aware that in actual fact when a poem is well read the metrical units are not identical in duration and often are not nearly so. He took care of the discrepancy by specifying for his sprung rhythm only that the feet "are assumed" to be equal and by adding invariably the alternative of "strength" to pure duration. Most of Hopkins's statements on this subject, as well as most of his rhythms themselves, can be interpreted on this principle, though his consistency was not absolute.[21]

IV

An isochronous theory of English poetry held literally, in an unmitigated form, is patently impossible. One need only think of the ruinous effect of reading a complex poem as we read some of the simplest nursery rhymes. "One, two, / Buckle my shoe" is indeed strictly isochronous as we usually recite it, but it is composed for the feet, not the head. All sensible metrists take for granted that by "equal time" in poetry—or even, though within much narrower limits, in music—we mean time not in an absolute sense but as apprehended by the mind, and that, further, in verse the meaning of the words is bound to set up counterclaims against rhythmic regularity that do not exist in music. Furthermore, as the exactness of our apprehension of time is affected by the events that occupy it, the meaning of words in verse constantly modifies our actual perception: intervals will seem equal that are not, and vice versa. But there is another important reason for our being satisfied by a far less regular timing in poetry than we require in music, a difference deriving from the nature and origin of the media employed in the two arts. That of verse, language, has its everyday existence ouside the art of poetry in forms that, written or spoken, have no rhythmical regularity to speak of. With the sound of arhythmical language so firmly established in daily life as the norm, any departure from this in the direction of rhythm, even a quite distant approach toward regularity, is instantly felt; and an arrangement of words therefore does not have to be carried far toward regularity to be felt as rhythm. Here the often useful parallels between music and verse break down, for the media of music exist only within the art itself; musical sounds have no norm outside of that art. Poetry, in other words, is fundamentally an alteration of everyday sounds, and our apprehension of it is constantly influenced by implicit comparison with that nonrhythmic norm, whereas in music there is no other norm beyond music itself: not only the art but the medium which it employs is wholly invented and self-contained. Genetically this statement is an oversimplification, since in origin music, dance, and poetry are interwoven; but it is true for Western music as we know it, and as far back as practically known music goes. Instruments—violin, or, for that matter, the pipes of Pan—even the singing voice and musical tones arranged in the diatonic or other scale or mode are familiar only within the context of the art of music, which in the West, with the exception of plainchant, has been strongly rhythmical for many centuries, so that in the arrangement of musical sounds there exists no nonrhythmical norm from which a departure toward rhythm would comparatively be felt as rhythm. This is one (not the only, but perhaps the least recognized) basis for radical differences between musical and verse rhythms.

For an isochronous theory of sprung rhythm to be viable, then, it is necessary only to recognize how slight and how subjective the requirement of regularity must be. Time units may *suggest* equality without arousing the expectation of their ever being really equal. For an isochronous theory of conventional verse also, it is only necessary that we conceive the regularity to be suggested, scarcely ever even approximated as it is in music. Equal timing is the hinted, never the realized, pattern marked off by the stresses. In this sense I believe conventional English accentual syllabic verse, as well as sprung rhythm, is isochronous; or, if so loose a sense of the word "isochronous" is objected to, at any rate the hint of equal timing is an essential component of English verse rhythm.

To suggest equality of time, however, grows less easy as the number of syllables between stresses becomes more variable and where there is not, as there is in Anglo-Saxon verse, a larger fixed rhythm of regularly spaced strong pauses. Sprung rhythm, therefore, if used as the prevailing rhythm of a serious poem and not as an occasional expressive variant, presents several major difficulties. First and most obvious is that of rhythmic clarity: how, in any but the simplest verse, is it possible for the reader to recognize the stresses intended by the poet or to find an arrangement of stresses satisfactory to himself, by which the rhythm is delineated? A second problem (or a different formulation of the first) is that

68

of preserving the suggestion of equal timing, or of any other recognizable pattern if the notion of timing is rejected, when the regularity of a stress-syllabic pattern is discarded. A third difficulty is that of ensuring, in a measure usually having a higher than average proportion of unstressed syllables, against a lightness of texture and acceleration of tempo that would be out of keeping with serious poetry. And a final problem is that of too great a simplicity of the wrong kind, resulting from an absence of tension in the texture and an accompanying loss of certain resources of expressiveness.

Hopkins was aware of and explicit concerning the first three of these difficulties. He explained that, though sprung rhythm like common English rhythm is to be classified as accentual and not quantitative, nevertheless, for excellence in the new rhythm (εὖ εἶναι as distinguished from εἶναι), "great attention to quantity is necessary. And since English quantity is very different from Greek or Latin a sort of prosody ought to be drawn up for it, which would be indeed of wider service than for sprung rhythm only" (II, 39, 41). Other passages in the letters testify to his continued concern with problems of timing; and in practice usually, if not invariably, he was successful in solving the second and third of the problems I have listed, always by paying the most careful attention to his timing. Nearly always, when his rhythm is clear it "feels" right. But it is not invariably clear. That, the first difficulty in my list, he was fully aware of but could find no way of overcoming except by the use of stress marks and other more elaborate symbols to indicate his metrical intentions. He deplored these: they "are always offensive," he told Bridges. "Still there must be some" (I, 189). The dilemma did not suggest to him any fundamental weakness or serious limitation in the new rhythm itself. The last difficulty Hopkins seems to have been only faintly aware of and did not always succeed in circumventing.

Conventional English verse is a more nearly self-reading idiom than sprung rhythm. The pattern establishes the syllables to be stressed or not stressed, and therefore, though the meaning perpetually modifies and not infrequently cancels or reverses the stresses dictated by the pattern, still, when variation is not clearly dictated by the sense, the reader's voice almost of itself knows what to do, and his mind is even assisted in interpreting the meaning by the presence of the known pattern. There are nearly always uncertainties and ambiguities and always tensions in this perpetual counterpoint between meaning and pattern, but they are illuminating and enriching complexities in the hands of a good poet, and they are felt as part of the design itself; they do not suggest mere confusion. Nonsyllabic stress rhythm too can be self-reading in a very simple type of verse in which a sharply marked, literally isochronous rhythm is established, often with the aid of repetitive language. In "Jack be nimble, Jack be quick; Jack jump over the candlestick," the rhythm of the last half is clearly dictated by the exact pattern set in the first, though, reading the last alone, we might not find quite that rhythm in it. In the strong-stress, mechanically timed nursery rhyme, the meaning is killed—which is part of the fun. But this will not do in serious verse, and neither, for this very reason, will realized, as distinguished from suggested, equality of timing, for literally isochronous meter extended beyond a moment or two is bound to kill the meaning by tyrannical distortion or exaggeration.

It is obvious that in sprung rhythm or any nonsyllabic accentual verse in which the rhythm is not set by a rigidly isochronous beat such as that of nursery rhymes and doggerel, the metrical stresses must be dictated by the meaning alone—that is, by the speech stresses— since there is nothing else, no predictable pattern, otherwise to govern them.[22] The main rhetorical stresses of a sentence and the unmistakably subordinate syllables offer no difficulty, but in the use of language there is the very large middle group of sounds which may receive more or less prominence, according to occasion. A particular line may have, say, two unmistakable stresses and four or five other possible ones. In accentual syllabic verse such as our conventional iambic measure, the predetermined pattern offers the key to the choice among these and so creates an ordered line in addition to serving as a guide to meaning and rhetorical emphasis; in sprung rhythm this key is absent and there is no other. In this four-stress line in the *Deutschland* (stanza 34), for example, "The heaven-flung, heart-fleshed, maiden-furled," the meter does not guide the reader in choosing four from the six possible stresses. For a passage of great emphasis, made up of clear contrasts of sound in which all the possible stresses are unmistakably strong speech stresses and the sum of these is the number required by the line, sprung rhythm serves admirably; but for subtler shadings it does not, and an unlikely emphasis which the reader could not be expected to guess cannot be suggested by the meter at all.

Most metrical systems that have given rise to great poetry have been complex themselves or else have been hospitable to rhythmic complexity of one sort or another. The quantitative patterns of classical verse were fairly complicated, and their rhythmic effect, particularly in Latin verse, became still more so through the "counterpoint" of the word accents played off against the quantitative pattern. In English verse the conventional base is extremely simple, but the clarity and steadiness of the base have encouraged, demanded even, the development of the highly complex counterpoint of the rhetorical pattern and the remarkably elaborate, vital interplay between the speech and the metrical patterns to which our poetry owes so much of its beauty. Nonsyllabic accentual verse, including sprung rhythm, does not appear to afford any such interplay, since the metrical pattern has to be created by and consequently is identical with the speech pattern and there is nothing for either to play against. It offers great variety; but variety alone—in this case wide irregularity in the number of light syllables between stresses—is not complex; it becomes so only when organization, some form or pattern, becomes perceptible in it. Hopkins must have had an inkling of this lack himself, for on one occasion he explained that by means of his "outrides" he secured a "strong effect of double rhythm, of a second movement in the verse besides the primary and essential one, and this comes to the same thing or serves the same purpose as counterpointing by reversed accents." [23]

To sum up, then, sprung rhythm, as Hopkins maintained, has over conventional meter the distinct advantages of strongly marked emphasis, naturalness, and flexibility in the placing of accents. Its disadvantages lie in its frequent lack of both rhythmic and rhetorical clarity, which he tried to defeat by means of elaborate markings, and in its lack of subtlety—of rhythmic subtlety from the absence of counterpoint (that is, of any suggested secondary rhythm) and of expressive subtlety from the nondescript status of all except indubitably strong and indubitably weak sounds. The absence of subtlety Hopkins never fully acknowledged. He often defeated it successfully, not to any extent by his "outrides" but by a shift (conscious or not) to conventional meters. This last is a major point to which I have been leading, somewhat tortuously.

v

As Hopkins employed it in *The Wreck*, the "new rhythm" that he called sprung is actually a blend of conventional and sprung rhythm, with the former predominating. The great majority of lines in the poem are metrically conventional, with no more license than Tennyson exercised in his least adventurous verse.

72

Reading through Hopkins's first twenty stanzas, for example, I find an average of fewer than one out of five lines that will not scan, throughout, conventionally; and most of them not only *can* be scanned but are read most naturally so. Yet the general rhythmical effect of the poem is new beyond a doubt. The interesting thing is that it took so little novelty to make it new. The closing stanzas, it is true, are extremely irregular; but it is not these that create the novelty, for the new character is established at the outset. This, in fact, is a large part of the secret. The poem does open with a genuinely new rhythm, and it is a hospitable one. It can retain its character while including a considerable number of conventional units, and these then form a smooth bridge to whole passages in conventional meter. Playing thus in and out of sprung rhythm, Hopkins was able to employ it where its effects are most valuable—for the emphatic, prophetic, oracular passages in the *Deutschland* —and to move easily into regular meter when a smoother flow and finer shadings of rhythm and meaning are wanted. This changing rhythm had been greatly facilitated by the nineteenth-century development of logaoedic-anapestic meter, for that, already flexible in its syllabic pattern, is the main meter of the *Deutschland* when it is not sprung. Another variant, the occasional monosyllabic foot not only at the opening of a line (where it has been common since the sixteenth century, particularly in verse that equivocates between iambic and trochaic movement) but at the end of an iambic line, where it brings two stresses together as we have seen in Swinburne, or elsewhere in the line as it appears in the verse of Arnold's *Rugby Chapel* and *Heine's Grave*—this variant too forms part of the bridge between the pure sprung and the regular rhythms in Hopkins's poem.

Though I have little faith in the usefulness of a numerical analysis of anything so subtle and so subject to unconscious manipulation as poetic rhythm, out of curiosity I made a count, as objective as possible, of the metrical units of *The Wreck,* scanning the whole as sprung rhythm only and employing throughout Hopkins's classification of admissible feet: monosyllabic, iambic, anapestic, fourth paeonic, and the occasional foot of more than four syllables that his system allows for special effects. The count turns out to be distinctive enough, even allowing for a considerable margin of error or disagreement, to shed light on the nature of the verse. The poem is written in a fixed stanza form, with a fixed number of feet in each line, the whole adding up to 1,145 feet in the poem. Of these I count 168 monosyllabic, 363 iambic, 542 anapestic, 50 paeonic, and 22 longer feet. This is the count, give or take a few probable errors due to the uncertainty of an accent and hence a foot, scanned according to Hopkins's principles of sprung rhythm throughout. This, of course, means scanning by his rules for sprung rhythm lines that read naturally as standard meter. About fifty lines open with a pattern which in conventional iambic verse would be regarded as a simple trochaic inversion and which sounds like that kind of opening in Hopkins's lines ("Whether at once . . . ," "Wording it how . . . ," "What was the feast . . . ," etc.). Sprung rhythm having no inversions, a grouping of this kind has to be classified as a monosyllable followed by an anapest. Re-scanning these and similar inversions following a pause as conventional verse reduces the true monosyllabic feet in the poem to considerably fewer than a hundred; it reduces the trisyllabic ones as well and correspondingly increases the dissyllabic feet to almost a rough equality with the trisyllabic, a more normal proportion for respectable anapestic verse. The proportion of paeonic and still longer feet is in effect smaller than the count I have made, for I included even instances in which a syllable would commonly be elided or slurred into the equivalent of a trisyllabic foot: "flower," "shower," "the being with it," "sweet heaven was astrew." Most of the

74

feet of more than three syllables are concentrated to- ward the end of the poem, long after the general rhythm and movement of the verse have been established (I find only seven unelidible paeonic feet and no longer ones in the first two dozen of the thirty-five stanzas).

Whether he was conscious of the fact or not, then, Hopkins created his new rhythm by means, numerically speaking, of very modest departures from what readers of conventional verse were accustomed to. If in thought and style his writing had not been so highly idiosyn- cratic, his rhythm in this first "great experiment" would have presented few problems.

There would have been some, however; and we meet one, squarely, in the first line. The rhythm established in the opening stanza is a slow, evenly measured beat ap- propriate to the solemn, oracular prayer uttered with strong feeling and hence rhythmically intensified—a grave, incantatory rhythm.

> Thóu mástering me
> Gód! giver of bréath and bréad;
> Wórld's stránd, swáy of the séa;
> Lórd of líving and déad;
> Thou hast boúnd bónes and véins in me, fástened me flésh,
> And áfter it álmost únmade, whát with dréad,
> Thy dóing: and dóst thou toúch me afrésh?
> Óver agaín I féel thy fínger and fínd thée.[24]

The fixed metrical pattern of this stanza, which becomes unmistakable later if not here, calls for two stresses in the initial line throughout Part I [25] with the sense usu- ally running over into the second line. Gardner reads the opening with primary stresses on *Thou, me,* and *giver,* and adds a secondary stress on *mas*[tering] and *God.* Both rhythmic flow and meaning seem to me to require a different reading, however, as I suggested in the last chapter, with *Thou* at the opening standing alone and *mastering me* read as a single proclitic epithet of God, the equivalent of *masterful* but altered to *-me* for a reason characteristic of Hopkins's schematic habit of thought, that the theme of Part I has to do not so much with every man's as with the poet's own relation to God.[26] The difference between these two readings, which is more extreme than most disagreements about the scansion of standard verse, illustrates one of the limitations of sprung rhythm already discussed, the fact that the meter cannot illuminate the meaning, and that in fact we often must determine the meaning before we can even guess at the rhythm, though in this particular passage it seems to me that the balance of sound in the first several lines and the initiation, by means of the strongly proclitic construction, of a forward movement —interrupted momentarily but not for long by the following epithets of power—argue in favor of the reading I have suggested. I read the whole stanza without any secondary stresses, with nearly all the main ones very strong and deliberate, and with the light syllables almost disappearing under the weight of the stresses.

The last line of the stanza, in a somewhat different manner from the first, again illustrates the rhythmic and rhetorical ambiguity inherent in sprung rhythm. The six stresses of this line do not make themselves known at a first reading. Five are evident, but *thee* might easily be unaccented (producing only a light rhyme), following as it does the naturally stressed *find*. Subsequent stanzas make the design clear, which is fair enough, since a trial reading of two or three stanzas may be necessary even in standard verse forms. But the line is unsatisfactory, and the strong stress placed by Hopkins himself on the monosyllabic foot *thee* seems to make it more, not less so—unsatisfactory in terms of meaning as well as rhythm because "find thee" seems close to a tautology and certainly redundant, merely filling out the line. It is only when one reads Hopkins's commentary on the *Spiritual Exercises* of St. Ignatius that one recognizes that, though the line may be unduly condensed and for some tastes too anthropomorphic, it is not, after all, redundant. The metrical emphasis on *thee* is heavy and essential; it closes the stanza with a strongly sprung and measured beat. But to feel this we have to know that "the finger of God" translates St. Ignatius' "Digitus paternae dexterae," quoted by Hopkins and interpreted by him as "the works of God's finger," symbolizing the exercise of His power "in operibus," "working in the world" of material phenomena, as distinguished from God's self, God as Love; or, as he put it again, the distinction is between God's *power* and His *essence*.[27] The last line of the first stanza, then, really sums up the whole first division of the poem, and is to be read with heavy stresses throughout, on *Over again,* as well as on *thee*. The sounds will bear these heavy and prolonged stresses, and, once we have got the full impact of the meaning, the sprung close is more expressive and imposing, probably, than standard meter would be. On the other hand, in standard meter, if we do not understand the meaning we still have the ground rhythm to fall back on, whereas in sprung rhythm we have nothing. It is no wonder that Bridges, who probably would not in any event have liked the anatomical image in this passage and who had not the aid of Hopkins's Ignation commentary, bristled. Nevertheless, in spite of a possibly debatable first line and a last one that reads acceptably only when illuminated from outside sources, the opening stanza seems to me great and impressive, as well as new. It establishes the slow tempo, with a beat precise and marked enough to spread something of its character over the succeeding stanzas even when these are for long stretches composed in conventional meter. The sprung rhythm returns, sometimes for only a beat or two, often enough to keep its influence over the whole alive, and from time to time becomes dominant afterward without shock, notably in the opening stanza of Part II and again more and more as the poem draws to its close.

Only in the final stanzas, however, is the new rhythm

exploited with the freedom and carried to the extremes that Hopkins's definition provides for; only here are the monosyllabic, paeonic, and longer feet used with the elastic effects theoretically possible in his system, on anything like equal terms with the regular dissyllabic and trisyllabic feet. To what was said in the last chapter regarding the poetic effect of the close, which fails, as I think, but only in the last two lines, little needs to be added. The stanza that opens the recapitulation,

> I admire thee, master of the tides,
> Of the Yore-flood, of the year's fall,

represents a magnified and intensified return to the oracular address to God in the first stanza, but metrically, as well as in thought, on a much grander scale. The rhythm now is more complex and varied, fuller— literally fuller, since there are a great many more syllables in this stanza—with numerous five- and four-syllable feet and, at the other extreme, one series of five heavily stressed monosyllables in succession.[28] Yet all this variation is successfully held within rhythmic control of the established stanza form. The grave measured beat creates an illusion of equal timing, with an effect more flexible than in the first stanza but no less marked and solemn. Here and in what follows, the lofty tone is maintained consistently (except for the aberration at the very end), technical virtuosity never obscuring but only enhancing the thought and feeling, and transforming it too, for the poetic power transcends the sectarian elements that in a lesser poem might well put off readers of a different faith.

Through most of the intervening stanzas the metrical intention is clear and the rhythm flexible and expressive. Where difficulties occur, they are most often due to indeterminate stresses—too many or too few available for the requirement of the line, with a resulting arbitrariness (Hopkins's if they are marked, the reader's

if they are not) in the choice of stress. The second of
the lines quoted above is typical of these uncertainties.
It is a three-stress line with four possible stressed syllables. I interpret the capitalization and hyphen in *Yore-
flood*, along with shortness of the vowel in *flood*, as a
hint that *flood* is subordinated; stress then falls on *Yore*,
year's, and *fall*. Once the decision is made, this reading
seems satisfactory, for reasons (too complex to be entered into here) having to do with the progression of
vowel and consonant sounds. Elsewhere, however, this
indeterminateness occasionally weakens the rhythm.

Something remains to be said of the stanza itself,
though no problem of critical or technical analysis is
more baffling than that of trying to uncover the secret of
success or failure in the use of a stanza made up of lines
of varying length. In his "Author's Preface," Hopkins
asserted that "it is natural in Sprung Rhythm for the
lines to be *rove over*, that is for the scanning of each
line immediately to take up that of the one before, so
that if the first has one or more syllables [i.e., unstressed
syllables] at its end the other must have so many the
less at its beginning; and in fact the scanning runs on
without break from the beginning, say, of a stanza to
the end and all the stanza is one long strain, though
written in lines asunder." In a note to this passage,
Bridges interprets *rove over* to mean simply enjambment, and his explanation has passed without question.
Hopkins's thought was not quite so simple, however.
Rove-over scansion and enjambment were related but
evidently not identical in his mind, for on another occasion he explained to Bridges how certain kinds of enjambment "help" the "over-reaving" (I, 86), by which
he cannot have meant that they were quite the same
thing. All his poems, the fragment of a verse play and a
few other fragments excepted, employ end rhyme and
a fixed number of stresses to the line, both of which
mark the line as a formal reality, not to the eye only;
moreover, the great majority of his lines are in fact end-

stopped. He did not, either, as a rule wish the rhymes to be minimized in the reading, rather the contrary; sometimes he marked them, even when the sense was run over, for particular prominence; [29] and in a letter telling Bridges how the sonnet *Spelt from Sibyl's Leaves* should be read, he said, "Above all remember what applies to all my verse, . . . that its performance is . . . with long rests, long dwells on the rhyme . . ." (I, 246). The line formation is therefore—and is intended to be—perceptible to the ear as a reality: it is not a fiction. What Hopkins wished to do, I think, was to emphasize, and to avoid letting the line units interfere with, the overriding rhythm and tune of the stanza, its "one long strain," which is not incompatible with the reality of the smaller unit of the line (or, if one objects to "line" as something merely visual, then the units of beats marked off by rhyme and more often than not by the end-stop). He may also have been trying to obviate the unfortunate line-by-line kind of reading all too common even now, and I suppose more so in an earlier period of much schoolroom memorizing and reciting by rote, which would not have been easy for even a sophisticated reader to outgrow.[30]

Characteristically, Hopkins set himself as difficult a task as possible by employing his new rhythm for the first time in a new stanza form of great complexity, in which the lines vary in length from two to six feet and there is no apparent symmetry within the stanza either in the arrangement of the lines or in the rhyme. It has been observed by other writers that the eight-line stanza of *The Wreck* bears some resemblance to that of the Hymn in Milton's *Nativity Ode*. This stanza had returned to notice in *Songs before Sunrise* (1871), where Swinburne employed it in his ode *Blessed among Women* and in the opening strophe and corresponding antistrophe of the *Ode on the Insurrection in Candia,* both poems in which sprung and counterpointed lines, as well as verbal foreshadowings of Hopkins, appear.[31]

The stanza is characterized by the intermingling of short and long lines, with the short predominating at the beginning and the long at the end, the conclusion being a four-stress line followed by an Alexandrine, as in the *Deutschland.* The Hymn stanza, however, is quickly apprehended by the ear, for its initial three-line unit, a rhyming couplet in trimeter followed by a pentameter line, is repeated immediately in another trimeter couplet and another pentameter line rhyming with the first one, and the two remaining lines, this time of uneven length, conclude the stanza with another adjacent rhyme. Hopkins's stanza has no such symmetry in line length, no adjacent rhymes, no rhyming lines of equal length; and his concluding rhyme is five lines distant from its correspondent rhyme. This final one still tells, for it has been heard twice before in the first and third lines, the first being more often than not run over, however, and its rhyme being somewhat dimmed by the enjambment.

To have created a recognizable and satisfying form out of a new rhythm in a stanza such as this must be an almost unprecedented achievement. One can say a good deal about the balance somehow created in the relation of the uneven lines to each other, and about the distribution of pauses and cadences; yet I at least cannot quite tell how such a stanza establishes itself in the mind as a satisfying form, so varied as never to become monotonous, yet always present and always perceptibly molding the smaller rhythmic units into the "one long strain" that Hopkins spoke of (his "one long strain," be it noted, is nothing so simple in form as merely one long sentence). The metrical success, of course, is only theoretically separable from all the other elements of the poem, and for this reason one must be curious to know how the stanza would work and what effects it might be capable of in the hands of another poet, with another theme, perhaps in a different meter. I do not know that it has been tried again. At the very least, this "great metrical experiment" added a fresh resource to English rhythms. Indeed, it may be said almost to have added two resources. For the whole can be roughly described as an anapestic poem in a sprung frame; and it would be hard to find in all the logaoedic-anapestic verse that nineteenth-century poets were developing a poem largely in this trisyllabic measure, of comparable length and seriousness, in which the trisyllabic movement is handled with such skill and acquires such dignity—in which its full potentialities, in fact, are demonstrated.

4

Later Rhythms

HOPKINS spoke of the *Deutschland* as his first venture in a rhythm afterward "perfected." I have treated it, purposely, as rather an end than a beginning because I do not think he ever surpassed it. He went considerably beyond it in verse that is more consistently "sprung," and those later poems are worth study on their own account though in the success of their metrical effects few quite equal the *Deutschland*. Most of the experiments following that poem were governed by the direction already taken, but they do not represent a chronological, step-by-step advance toward pure sprung rhythm. In some poems he carried this rhythm to its theoretical limits, detaching it altogether from conventional meters, but in others he turned back to accepted patterns and in many explored intermediate rhythms. To keep matters clear, the immediate chronology may be briefly summed up.

During the summer of 1876, while the fate of the *Deutschland*, sent off hopefully to *The Month*, was still pending, two occasional pieces were composed, *The Silver Jubilee*, addressed to the Bishop of Shrewsbury, written in June or July, and *Penmaen Pool*, written "for the Visitors' Book at the Inn" sometime during August. Designed for unliterary readers, these are metrically conventional except that in *The Silver Jubilee* the third line of each stanza is given over to a repetition of the rhythm tried out in *St. Dorothea*, the jerky "Whý should this désert bé" formula that had so inexplicably attracted him, employed here with a result no happier than before. *Penmaen Pool* has a pronounced mechanical Swinburnian movement, and is otherwise undistinguished. Two other more characteristic poems were written during that summer but remained unfinished. The first was the quite beautiful and original, but still exceedingly Swinburnian *Moonrise* in long unrhymed alliterative lines of finely timed and weighted anapests: "I awoke in the Midsummer not-to-call night, ׀ in the white and the walk of the morning," which ends, "Parted me leaf and leaf, divided me, ׀ eyelid and eyelid of slumber," with its echo of moonlight and leaves and of the phrase "half divided the eyelids of the sunset" from the *Hendecasyllabics* in Swinburne's *Poems and Ballads* (*Works*, I, 331). After this came an attempt in *The Woodlark* to express a bird's imagined delight in a summer day by an extravagant use of sprung rhythm (with some lines again influenced by the "St. Dorothea" pattern), an attempt that reveals as clearly as any poem could the essential limitations and weaknesses of sprung rhythm discussed in the last chapter. Even with the aid of Hopkins's indications of stress, it is difficult to determine how some of the lines—"So tiny a trickle of sóng-strain" is an example—were meant to be stressed or timed; and, intention apart, no satisfactory, undistorted reading seems possible. Though it is only a draft, incomplete and, according to Bridges' note, made up of "fragments in some disorder," it illustrates the difficulties Hopkins encountered in first undertaking to go beyond the rhythms of the *Deutschland* into pure sprung rhythm. It was abandoned, for whatever reason, and the loss is not great.

These few occasional and unfinished verses, together with a small quantity of other verse in Welsh and Latin, engaged his spare hours while he waited to hear from *The Month* about his long poem. After its rejection, there followed six months of silence broken early in 1877 by the composition of *God's Grandeur* and *The*

Starlight Night, "two sonnets I wrote in a freak the other day," Hopkins told his mother, adding, "They are not so very queer, but have a few metrical effects, mostly after Milton" (III, 144). The modifications of conventional verse in these sonnets are subdued enough to pass unnoticed not only today but in the 1870's as well. Their chief metrical departure is what Hopkins called "counterpointed" rhythm, standard iambic lines in which the stress is reversed twice or more consecutively,[1] so that a new rhythm is played off against, or is "mounted" over, the regular one, which continues on in the mind: "The world is charged with the grandeur of God" and "Generations have trod, have trod" (the superscribed symbol is Hopkins's indication of a counterpointed foot). There are also instances of extrametrical light syllables, usually, however, such as may be half slurred, a common liberty in the relaxed iambics of his contemporaries. The sonnets are marked by his characteristic strangeness, but this lies in the bold imagery and grammatical condensation, not in any pronounced metrical adventures. After these two pieces in standard rhythm sparingly counterpointed, he broke into further experiment.

The precise order of composition of the remaining sonnets of 1877 is uncertain, for Hopkins dated some of them merely " '77" while pinning others to a particular month or day. The metrical experiments which they represent range from those of *Spring,* the effects of which are relatively conventional in spite of what Hopkins called "sprung leadings," to the extremely complicated rhythms of *The Windhover* and *Hurrahing in Harvest.* In attempting to read these and later poems satisfactorily, we are now and then brought up short—balked, in fact—by what had best be discussed once for all, the presence of passages in which Hopkins's rhythms can be described only as eccentric in their arbitrary handling of the relation between sense and meter, passages marked to be read in ways that I think cannot be justified in terms either of rhythm—sprung or conventional or counterpointed—or of any imaginable meaning, however subtle. Like the "St. Dorothea" rhythm, they appear as arbitrary wrenchings of sense for the sake of a desired pattern. It is natural for a reader who values the work of Hopkins to seek some justification for strange readings indicated by the poet, and for a long time it was my own conviction that such justification should be sought and must always be predicated, little success as one might have had in finding it. But certain considerations, one in particular, have altered this conviction, persuading me that now and then —not always but not infrequently either—what appears odd simply *is* odd, must be ascribed, that is, to pure idiosyncrasy. Not that Hopkins might not have been able to produce some sort of explanation—I have little doubt that he could have. But he did not, and, more to the point I think, none that one can imagine is anything but unsatisfactory. The chief warrant for this judgment is indirect; it lies in Hopkins's reading of certain lines, not of his own, but of Bridges' work.

Among the poems in which Bridges employed sprung rhythm, Hopkins admired *London Snow* though its rhythm, he said, "is not quite perfect" (I, 111). He offered a number of suggestions, of which one concerned the third and fourth lines of the following passage:

And all woke earlier for the unaccustomed brightness
Of the winter dawning, the strange unheavenly glare:
The eye marvelled—marvelled at the dazzling white-
    ness;
The ear hearkened to the stillness of the solemn air;
No sound of wheel rumbling nor of foot falling . . .[2]

"I suppose you scan 'The éye márvelled—márvelled at the dázzling whíteness; the éar heárkened to the stíllness of the sólemn aír': this is well enough when seen, but the following is easier to catch and somewhat bet-

ter in itself—'Eye márvelled—márvelled át the dázzling
whíteness; ear heárkened to the stíllness ín the sólemn
áir' " (I, 122). This sacrifice of a stress on the two nouns
eye and *ear* in favor of two prepositions, *at* and *in,*
cannot be ascribed to subtle shades of meaning because here the meaning is plain and simple, it obviously
does not carry hidden subtleties; moreover the meaning
is Bridges', not Hopkins's, and there is no hint that
Hopkins meant to alter it. His "improvement," therefore, seems simply an eccentric metrical preference, a
dwelling in a region of taste inhabited only by himself
(it even sacrifices Bridges' line-encompassing and
meaningful assonance in *eye-white*[ness] and *ear-air,*
which in order to carry past intervening sounds requires stress on *eye* and *ear,* with no compensation but
the more obvious and meaningless ones of *at-daz*[zling]
and *still*[ness] *in*). In this instance—but it is the last
thing one would expect of him—it can be described as
the wrenching of a sprung line back toward more conventional meter, even against the grain of the meaning;
and this, in fact, is what he seems to have done also in
one of his own best-known metrical puzzles, the concluding line of *The Lantern out of Doors.* The earlier
lines of that sonnet refer to men who pass by and vanish
from sight, whose fate one will never know, "and out of
sight is out of mind. [But]"

Christ minds: Christ's interest, what to avow or amend
    There, éyes them, heart wánts, care haúnts, foot
        fóllows kínd,
Their ránsom, théir rescue, ánd first, fást, last friénd.

The marks must be Hopkins's own, and the lines are in
conventional iambic pentameter when read as marked.
Moreover, this final reading of the four words "their
rescue, and first . . ." is a deliberate alteration of an
earlier autograph version in which *rescue* is given its
normal speech stress.[3]
  Hopkins's tendency to lay stresses on such words as

their and *and* has been defended as a peculiarly expressive form of oratorical emphasis, and very likely this may be the origin of some unusual or eccentric stresses (though not in *The Lantern out of Doors*). It cannot be held to justify them indiscriminately, however, not only because poetry is not oratory, but also because that kind of oratory is usually of an inferior sort. We must all be familiar with the second-rate preacher who strives for dramatic effect by laying heavy stress on *in* and *as*, *the* and *their* and *and*, the last especially, enunciated often with great emphasis to hold listeners in suspense till the next profundity is ready (I associate the device with an admonitory, a mark-my-words extension of a forefinger). Naturally, such emphasis is occasionally proper and in spoken language may sometimes bring out a particular meaning or, in the case of a conjunction, may create a genuinely desirable suspense. In written language also it justifies itself when it is an integral part of the fabric of thought and not a specious bid for attention, though it is ideally justifiable, I suppose, only if the stress is evident without typographical aid. Hopkins was aware of this kind of emphasis and employed it from time to time with fine effect. In *Spelt from Sibyl's Leaves* it is so inevitable in its context that the stress marks provided by the poet are almost—though not quite—superfluous. That sonnet, first describing the darkening of evening over the earth, turns then from the physical world with "óur [man's] évening is over us. . . ." This is a legitimate and expressive rhetorical emphasis, for the strong *our* is clearly dictated by what has been said in the preceding lines and what immediately follows. No similar justification for "théir rĕscŭe, ánd" in *The Lantern out of Doors* can be found in the context of that poem any more than it can be for Hopkins's improvement of *London Snow*.

I should not wish to make too much of one puzzle in one poem. Any poet has a right to an occasional wayward choice, and any reader should be ready to allow for his own possible obtuseness in particular instances. But this passage in Hopkins is not unique; there are a good many others like it. It stands therefore as representative of one class of difficulty that must be taken into account—if only to be dismissed explicitly —in efforts to sum up the metrical developments that followed *The Wreck of the Deutschland*. With the *London Snow* episode before him, the critic need not feel obliged to perform somersaults of accommodation and rationalization in order to arrive at a reason for admiring all that appears eccentric.

Many of the other instances resemble the close of the *Lantern* in that they stress an insignificant syllable, most often a preposition. Unlike that line, however, they generally occur in poems avowedly written in sprung rhythm, and here they seem to contravene an unbreakable law of this rhythm, that the sense stress always determines the metrical stress. This is a law, as I indicated earlier, a necessary condition of sprung rhythm, not an arbitrary rule, because there is nothing else that can determine or create the metrical stress if the sense does not do so, a circumstance that makes these departures of Hopkins seem particularly wayward. How he could have failed to be aware of the necessity of this law or how he could have got around it is a mystery, yet one is forced to suspect that he did not recognize it. For example, he deliberately invented a symbol ($\frown$) to represent, in his sprung rhythm, a "pause or dwell on a syllable, which *need not however have the metrical stress*" (I, facing p. 262)—which amounts to a contradiction in terms. *Spelt from Sibyl's Leaves* has ". . . self ín self steepèd and páshed—quíte" and "thoúghts agaínst thoughts ín groans grínd"; Manuscript B of *Hurrahing in Harvest* has "I wálk, I líft up, Í lift úp heart, eýes" and "Wánting; whích two whén they ónce méet"; in *Harry Ploughman* a metrical stress is laid on the second syllable, as well as some sort of lengthening on the first, of "shôuldér"; and in other lines we find "And features, ín flesh, whát deed . . ." and "Them —broäd ín bluff híde his frówning féet lashed! ráced. . . ." Both the stress on *in* and the absence of it on *lashed* where the exclamation point immediately follows are to me particularly incomprehensible. These and certain other instances have caused me to wonder whether Hopkins's ear may have been more conventionally attuned to iambic rhythm than he supposed, for they are all warpings of the sense toward more regular meter. But not all his eccentric markings do this either, though I rather think the majority of them do. In *The Wreck of the Deutschland,* a five-stress sprung line that reads quite smoothly as "Whéther at ónce, as ónce at a crásh Pául" is marked so as to be read "Whĕthĕr át ónce. . . ." At one time I thought—it has been suggested by others also—that certain of Hopkins's stress marks were intended to demonstrate merely the nominal pattern from which the actual spoken reading diverges but were not themselves intended to represent any audible stress. Again, however, as most of these puzzles occur in passages of sprung rhythm, this explanation will not hold, involving as it does a contradiction of the nature of that rhythm, and it would also seem to be disproved by his comments on *London Snow,* where he was clearly speaking of the actual, not nominal, reading.

In one or two passages of this kind I can hear—or fancy I can if I half ignore the meaning—a larger rhythmic and melodic strain in which the distortions play a necessary part; but I cannot hear this in most such passages, and even where I can, the effect is so uncertain and so likely to be subjective that the distortion would seem to me a viable device only if Hopkins could be present to conduct the performance or could have recorded his intended reading for posterity and so make the musical strain perceptible to readers. If this is what he was aiming at, however, in the face of these contrary-to-fact conditions one can only conclude that he was wilfully attempting to make the language into a vehicle that it was not.

In origin, the unnatural stresses may possibly owe something to ritual chants in which there is little relation between the musical and the linguistic or semantic emphasis. In a familiar chant of the Lord's Prayer, for example, the opening "Our Father which art in Heaven, Hallowed" is sung on a single tone, the words being huddled together quickly and unemphatically with no rhythmic stresses at all, while in the rest of the line or strain, "[Hallowed] *be* thy *name*," *be*, as well as *name*, has the strong emphasis of raised pitch, increased volume, and lengthened time value. Even though this should be the origin of Hopkins's arbitrary stresses, however, they cannot be justified by the analogy, for the words of a chant are a familiarly known and accepted ritual to which the worshiper's response is mainly a generalized emotion accompanied by only generalized or half-formulated conceptual thought; moreover for the performance and perpetuation of the *music* of the chant, which contributes greatly to the mood that is induced, a well-defined system of notation exists. In individual poetry, by contrast, the emotional effect depends partly upon conceptual thought and meaningful language heard, read, or spoken with a very different kind of attentiveness, and here unnatural stresses or absence of a significant stress can fracture both thought and mood.

There is one other conceivable explanation of these distortions that is not unlike the foregoing and that might possibly be entertained in view of Hopkins's well-known interest in music. In the setting of songs, for all we may customarily say of the composer's "suiting his music to the words," the melodic, rhythmic, and dynamic form of the music is commonly an adaptation to the mood rather than to the verbal sense of the verse and in fact often contravenes the sense. One illustration will make clear what I mean. In the familiar setting, which I suppose everyone knows, of Jonson's "Drink to me only with thine eyes," the dominant emphasis of this opening line, in complete disregard of the meaning, rests on the preposition *with*, since *with* carries the highest pitched note, extends through two notes of the melody, and begins on the strong beat of its bar. In the second line, "And Í will plédge with míne," musical and rhetorical emphasis coincide. But the fourth line, and again the sixth, are like the first: in the fourth the musically dominant syllable for the same reason as before is another preposition ("Or leave a kiss but ín the cup"); in the sixth it is *from* ("The thirst that fróm the soul doth rise").

This is by no means untypical of song-writing. Melodic line follows its own laws and cannot usually be, or is not usually, constructed in exact correspondence— or, as a composer might put it, in slavish subordination —to the verbal-grammatical-rhetorical design. Now, except perhaps for one or two of the poems intended for song, Hopkins was not writing words to a preexisting melody; but if one can imagine his having had in mind some prefixed inflectional speech pattern that was not a musical tune but that was as distinctively conceived as if it were such a tune—a speech-tune-without-words, that is, strong and clear enough to take precedence over the subsequently conceived *actual* words—then one may imagine his arriving at some such unaccountable stresses as we have seen. This in itself would still be a kind of eccentricity, however, for no means existed of communicating a pattern other than that implicit or latent in the words themselves, any more than the particular melody to which we sing Jonson's lyric is implicit in its words. If the tune of "Drink to me only" had not been composed and communicated through musical notation, it would not of itself arise in any reader's mind spontaneously from the words. I think it not impossible that some metrical puzzles found in

Hopkins should have had this origin, but the specula-
tion—and it can be only that—has no real bearing on
the poems as they exist outside the poet's mind. Whatever their origin, moreover, the stresses that bear no
recognizable relation to the meaning still conflict with
the primary formative law of sprung rhythm. Which
leaves us, with these puzzles, precisely where we were,
and the fact of their unaccountability may as well be
acknowledged.

A second teasing difficulty in Hopkins's meters lies in
the celebrated "outrides," and perhaps I should admit
at the outset that these too have defeated me as often
as not. The "outride" or "outrider" or "hanger" was first
conceived as a variation to be used only in standard
meters, along with counterpoint; but soon Hopkins had
begun to combine it with sprung rhythm; and it had
become a "license natural to Sprung Rhythm" by the
time he came to write the "Author's Preface" (in 1883
or soon after), which contains his most considered account of them: they consist, he said of "one, two, or
three slack [unstressed] syllables added to a foot and
not counting in the nominal scanning. They are so
called because they seem to hang below the line or
ride forward or backward from it in another dimension
than the line itself, according to a principle needless to
explain here." This concluding phrase, not surprisingly,
has exposed his metrical theories to some ridicule, particularly as there is no record of the principle's ever
having been really "explained" elsewhere. His earliest
account tells us little. Writing to Bridges in 1877, soon
after he had conceived it, he spoke of it merely as an
"extra-metrical" but "calculated" effect (I, 45). More
light is shed by a note to *Hurrahing in Harvest,* written
at almost the same time: "Take notice that the outriding feet are not to be confused with dactyls or
paeons, though sometimes the line might be scanned
either way. The strong syllable in an outriding foot has
always a great stress and after the outrider follows a

short pause. The paeon is easier and more flowing." This distinction is clear enough in itself; the difficulty lies in recognizing either its presence, if it is unmarked, or its rhythmical or rhetorical justification where it is marked. The last bit of light is provided by a note, written some ten years later, to *Harry Ploughman* (facsimile of MS, *Letters*, I, facing p. 262). After saying as before that the outride is extrametrical, Hopkins adds that "a slight pause follows *as if the voice were silently making its way back to the highroad of the verse*" (my italics).

Theory apart, at times the special effect of the outride is perceptible, but only on the occasions when the inflectional tune or melodic line of the passage in which it occurs is especially pronounced. It is clear, for example, at the close of *Hurrahing in Harvest* where the mood of extreme elation that pervades the sonnet and that in fact is its true subject, is brought to a close in a line whose inflection suggests a soaring flight, following a boldly sprung thirteenth line:

> The héart reárs wíngs bóld and bólder
>   And hurls for him, O half hurls earth for him
>   off under his feet.[4]

The inflectional shape of the final line as dictated by meaning, mood, and the structure of the sentence is a clear smooth arc, rising to its highest pitch on the word *earth;* and from this line, when it is read aloud, the outrides do seem to hang in "another dimension." They interrupt, without destroying, the arc of the main inflectional pattern, which is characterized as a whole by the symmetrical rise and fall of pitch that creates the melodic line. Their effect derives from abrupt alterations in pitch, emphasis, and timing; but the main determining factor is the change of pitch and volume, the outriding phrases being dropped in as an almost incidental murmur, after which the voice can, as Hopkins said, be imagined as "making its way back" to the main line. But such an effect is recognizable, as I have said, only when the tune of the rest of the line is pronounced and comparatively simple so that one can hear precisely what the voice is making its way back to, and in Hopkins's verse at times this condition is not met; often no sufficiently distinctive melodic shape dictated by the sense or mood of the line is perceptible. Though Hopkins himself may have read such lines with a pronounced inflectional pattern, that pattern is not written into the words and hence, even with the guidance of his looped symbol, the reader is unable to make auditory sense of many outrides.

These are the main difficulties presented by Hopkins's meters apart from the intrinsic limitations of sprung rhythm discussed in the last chapter, and I do not think they can be got around. They affect comparatively few lines, however, and except for those the sonnets of 1877 read well rhythmically, whether they are conventional, counterpointed, sprung, or a combination of all three. They succeed, moreover, not only because Hopkins was —it goes without saying—a fine poet with a poet's ear for the music of verse; for in addition they are marked by a new kind of expressiveness that is often the result of his conscious departures from standard verse. In the opening line of *God's Grandeur*, for example—"The world is charged with the grandeur of God"—written, as he said, in standard rhythm counterpointed, recognition of both *with the* and *grandeur* as decisive inversions induces a considerable pause after *charged* and increases the emphasis upon it (because of the lightness of *with* in spite of its stress), so that the expressiveness of *charged* and of the line itself as a line of poetry is greater than if the same words are read with purely conventional meter in mind, whether pentameter or an easier four-beat unit ("The wórld is chárged with the grándeur of Gód").

Of the more experimental sonnets of this period, the least successful metrically seems to me to be *Hurrahing in Harvest,* in spite of the fine effect of its last line, and the most successful *The Windhover, The Caged Skylark,* and *In the Valley of the Elwy.* This last, composed on a base of standard rhythm but sprung and counterpointed freely, is the simplest, its rhythm smooth and quiet, yet saved from limpness, provided with sinew, and infused with gravity mainly by the counterpointing. With the poet's markings, and perhaps even without them, the reading is self-evident.

I remember a house where all were good
    To me, God knows, deserving no such thing:
    Comforting smell breathed at very entering,
Fetched fresh, as I suppose, off some sweet wood.
That cordial air made those kind people a hood
    All over, as a bevy of eggs the mothering wing
    Will, or mild nights the new morsels of Spring:
Why, it séemed of coúrse; séemed of ríght it shóuld.

Lovely the woods, waters, meadows, combes, vales,
All the air things wear that build this world of Wales;
    Only the inmate does not correspond:

God, lover of souls, swaying considerate scales,
Complete thy creature dear O where it fails,
    Being mighty a master, being a father and fond.[5]

The Windhover and *The Caged Skylark* are written in what Hopkins's notes described as "falling paeonic rhythm, sprung and outriding," a designation that may be thought to commit the theoretical if not the actual rhythmic pattern of these poems to the privacy of his own mind; and indeed, with respect to *The Windhover,* there seems no possibility of harmonizing all his relevant statements with the poem itself. Efforts have nevertheless been made to analyze its rhythm in its author's terms. Father Lahey found a paeonic rhythm but only by disregarding Hopkins's markings and distorting the sense to a degree that even in his freest moments Hopkins would probably not have countenanced (Lahey reads, "kĭng-dóm ŏf dăylĭght's"); Gardner, on the other hand, respected the sense and Hopkins's indicated stresses and outrides but failed to observe that when he had done so, only two paeonic feet remained in the poem, leaving the poet's description of the meter unaccounted for.[6] Probably it cannot be fully explained, but if this is true, the air may as well be cleared by acknowledging the fact. It is conceivable that when the poem was first composed Hopkins had not yet invented his "outrides"; that after he did so he read them back into this poem (altering not the words but the way of speaking them) without quite coming to terms with the change.[7] This is scarcely a satisfactory explanation, but I know of none better; and it is true that in other instances, such as that at the end of the *Lantern* sonnet, he did alter rhythms without changing the words. The problem does not arise in *The Caged Skylark*, which, apart from its outrides, has enough genuinely paeonic feet to characterize the poem.

A consideration perhaps more important than that of reconciling Hopkins's practice with his description of it in these passages is the general question of the success of the rhythm, read as nearly as possible in accordance with his markings; and on this there is little disagreement. *The Windhover* and *The Caged Skylark* suffer scarcely at all from the intrinsic limitations of sprung rhythm. Perhaps *The Windhover* does not quite settle into its stride till about the third line: the second, at least, is somewhat indeterminate, not so much because of uncertain stresses as because, following the preceding line, it lacks an inflectional shape and so the voice if one reads aloud, or the mind if one imagines the sound, does not know where to go. The third line seems to me injured by the poet's explicit charge that *underneath*

97

be read with two stresses and the preceding *level* with none, which seems an unhappy distortion of both meaning and rhythm:

I caught this morning morning's minion, kingdom of daylight's dauphin, dapple-dáwn-drawn Fal-
      con, in his riding
   Of the rólling level únderneath him steady áir, and
      stríding.[8]

For the rest, the rhythm of the poem is so fully expressive that its character cannot be separated from the language and meaning (the poem as a whole is discussed in a later chapter, where the imbalance created by these present carping remarks it is hoped may be restored).

Metrical experiment was carried further in the following spring on the occasion of another shipwreck. When the training frigate *Eurydice* sank in a squall off the Isle of Wight with the loss of more than three hundred men and boys, Hopkins turned from sonnets to a more extended narrative, his first long poem in pure sprung rhythm. It is a strange production, extremely skillful in certain respects, but in the relations of rhythm, rhyme, theme, and tone I think in the end a sad failure. Its widely varied elements decline to fuse, chiefly in consequence of Hopkins's determination to find a more popular style than that of his first wreck. In contrast to the *Deutschland*, *The Loss of the Eurydice* employs a simple stanza, a quatrain rhyming in couplets with a shortened third line. In contrast with the *Deutschland* also, the language has been stripped till it is startlingly bare of adjectives. That gives speed to the narrative but it does not, as it might have done, confer strength or gravity upon the poem. The attempt at a more popular manner is probably also what led Hopkins here into a too facile rhythm, a prime defect in all the occasional verse composed for his unliterary colleagues; and either the same striving or else his inveterate love of ingenuity led him into a predominance of feminine, sometimes trisyllabic, rhymes, the effect of which is even more than ordinarily trivial (if not unintentionally comic), partly because they are so often made up of two words: *beach her* and *feature, captain* and *wrapped in, grind their* and *wind there* are among the less mannered of them. Even in the masculine rhymes there is an occasional grotesque juxtaposition, as when adjacent lines match *God's will* with *sea-swill.* That the rhymes and wordplay are often ingenious only makes matters worse, as do the popular orator's rhetorical questions, heavily planted to dramatize the speaker's answer. Was the vessel loaded with valuable cotton or even gold? he asks in the first of these questions, affording himself a disingenuously naïve opening for his answer: No, immeasurably worse, her cargo was human beings:

> For did she pride her, freighted fully, on
> Bounden bales or a hoard of bullion?—
>   Precious passing measure,
> Lads and men her lade and treasure.

The rhyme *fully on–bullion* would have graced one of the jauntier passages of *Don Juan* but is not much in keeping here. Hopkins was unpredictably subject to these lapses from congruity.

Technically, the rhythm of the *Eurydice* is clear enough for the most part; the effort at simplicity has done that much, and the treatment of the subject does not require subtlety of rhythm. Intermittently the rhythm, the narrative, and the imagery fall into harmony; and toward the end Hopkins's deeply felt longing for the conversion of England raises the poem above its straining for popular appeal and the resultant falseness of tone:

> He was but one like thousands more.
> Day and night I deplore

My people and born own nation,
Fast foundering own generation.

As a whole, however, in spite of very fine poetic passages and passages of remarkable technical brilliance, the style, rhythm, and stanza form of the *Eurydice* were all to prove something of a blind alley. Even the passage just quoted is not fully expressive or inevitable in its rhythm.

From the metrical standpoint chronology appears to be of no significance in the writing of Hopkins's later years. No clear sequence can be traced in the dated poems, and many cannot be exactly dated. For the new plain style initiated in *Andromeda* he returned to conventional meter, and usually, though not always, after that the plain style and conservative meter, elaborate style and much-sprung rhythms go together. In *Andromeda* Hopkins took no liberty that may not be found in the blank verse of *Paradise Lost,* and in most of the later tragic sonnets the verse is almost as conventionally strict.

Metrically, as well as in style, the most extravagant of all the poems is *The Leaden Echo and the Golden Echo,* but to regard this piece in quite the same light as Hopkins's other poems is in some respects a mistake. It seems a pity, too, that this one should so often have been placed in the forefront of his work. He had conceived it as a song, and that is what it is, a choral, probably contrapuntal, song to be sung by maidens in the play "St. Winefred's Well." Evidences of its popularity notwithstanding and in spite of its great virtuosity, it does not stand up quite satisfactorily alone, partly because its rhythm is indeterminate in both stress and timing, and also because few of the lines or rhetorical units are shaped into an apprehensible inflectional pattern. It is not merely a poem that might advantageously be set to music; it really requires music to supply missing elements and mold its form. Hopkins evidently had such music definitely in mind and had in mind, too, that it should be a song of mountain echoes appropriate to the scene of the play. For such a musical setting the extraordinary quantity of repetitive sound —repetition that is too far from the main streams of speech to succeed entirely when the words are merely spoken—would provide an effective basis. Or, to put the problem in other terms, the poem as it stands is so exceedingly artificial as to require the still greater artificiality of an elaborate choral setting to carry it off. Simple poems are often said to make the best songs, and the *Echoes* is far from simple; nevertheless, with the right composer a fine, bewildering, dazzlingly complex composition of language and music might be created from it. Even that echo-pun, the pivot upon which the Leaden turns to the Golden Echo, "despair, despair . . . Spare!" which as speech seems ostentatious or overingenious, with the appropriate music for echo choruses need not sound so.[9]

The rest of the later work of Hopkins falls within the scope of what has already been discussed. Many individual passages are of interest metrically but rather with reference to their expressiveness within their context than as new departures demanding separate attention. There are plenty of metrical ambiguities and uncertainties, and a number of other instances in which theory and practice seem to confound each other, but these are all of a kind already discussed and a separate analysis of each is unnecessary. I shall only add here that, though I have been finding more flaws than beauties in Hopkins's metrical effects subsequent to *The Wreck of the Deutschland*, these have been pointed out mainly for the purpose of illustration. In a great many passages of even the boldest experiment his new rhythms more than justify themselves. Some of these will be noticed hereafter.

Most poets who have employed sprung rhythm since

Hopkins invented it have used it as a variant rather than a prevailing rhythm, and perhaps historically that may prove to be its greatest value. It can be blended with traditional accentual-syllabic verse; and when so used, its limitations can be obviated, as Hopkins obviated them for the most part in the *Deutschland*. His later work I think pretty well explored the possibilities of the rhythm, showing what it can and perhaps quite as clearly what it cannot do.

As for counterpointing in Hopkins's sense, though this was not his original invention, his discussion and prominent use of it have undoubtedly made other poets more conscious of it as a rhythmic and expressive resource. About outrides I am not so sure; I can conceive their occasional effectiveness but must confess never actually to have recognized an instance in the work of another poet.

Any reader attempting to understand Hopkins's metrical practice and theory encounters difficulties, as we have long known. A few of these may be quite insoluble, and many, I am convinced, are at best imperfectly soluble; some of both have been discussed here. The fact that this is so does not warrant our concluding, as some critics have done, that Hopkins merely wrote free verse by ear and then from time to time invented ingenious *ad hoc* rules to provide a cover of legitimacy for irregular practice. There is a degree (but only a degree) of consistency in his statements, a degree also of consistency in his practice, and a degree of conformity between the two. The consistency is probably less than one finds in the writing of most sophisticated and self-conscious poets and especially less than in the practice of most who have written about their prosody.

One or two partial explanations are possible. Some imperfect consistency reflects the poet's temperament, in particular his willfulness set in opposition to his need of submission to rigid control, with consequent difficulty in keeping a balance between the two impulses. This dichotomy, discussed earlier in another context, is of course an individual emotional and extra-rational cause; one can see how it induces a man to wish to have his prosodic cake and eat it too. Another source of difficulty —but it was a very great asset as well—was his interest in music, which throughout this discussion I have been taking for granted. Though he recognized the important differences between the two arts (he thought, in fact, that Coventry Patmore in the *Essay on English Metrical Law* recognized the differences too little), still his own great interest in music led him into constant analogies, comparisons, and borrowings. Musical time, for reasons shown earlier, is relatively strict in the equality of its measures as compared with metrical units in poetry, though both are capable of creating the illusion of, or suggesting, equal timing. Hopkins thought the difference between the two arts in this respect should be smaller than it is: "At least," he said, "there is room, I mean, for a freer musical time and a stricter verse-prosody." [10]

We are apt to forget, however, that our notion of musical time now in the mid- and later twentieth century is greatly changed from that of a century ago. From what we know of it, the style of nineteenth-century musical performance would seem intolerably lax in its rhythms today: now, not only must Bach be performed in fairly strict time, but even the Romantic composers, even Chopin, must be played with a good deal of restraint in the shifting of tempo as well as in other respects. The style of performance that flourished in Hopkins's day would seem to us a wallowing in debased sentimentality: even a distinguished performer would by our standards be thought to luxuriate excessively in a *rallentando;* and a *rubato* would license for him almost anything. No other style was current, and to Hopkins, as to others of his day, this was what musical time truly is. If one adds to this the fact that Hopkins took great interest in plainchant, the one form of Western musc that has little rhythm, we can see how, even with his own highly developed rhythmic sense and his great theoretical interest in it and in timing, his difficulty in making sense out of the subject would be great.

In consequence of all this, I suspect that his own reading of his poems, if it could have been recorded and conveyed over the intervening century, might appall our modern taste, for there can be little doubt that it would have been influenced by prevailing musical style. For example, this style I think must be partly responsible for his "long dwells" (Victorian musicians, especially singers, were exceedingly fond of "long dwells"), for his extravagantly diphthongized vowels (*cûrls, hûrls, shôûldérs*), and for other extreme distortions of normal speech and timing; and I think that this Victorian musical taste, because there was such extreme difference between rhythmic regularity as printed in the score and irregularity as performed, may also have had something to do with the ambiguities in some of his ideas concerning "equal lengths or strengths" in sprung rhythm. He is not to be held responsible for the musical taste of his times, nor even for accepting or embracing it. It does constitute, however, a peripheral "period" element in his work, distantly comparable perhaps to the supposed Elizabethan style of acting, which is not felt to be obligatory in a modern production of *Hamlet;* and we may be justified today in modifying or toning down in our own reading Hopkins's instructions where they seem most extreme, for it would seem to me almost certain that in a small degree even his poetry itself and, to a much greater extent, his instructions about reading it were influenced by this prevailing style of musical performance, so bent upon stretching the limits of form and rhythm for the sake of what was thought to be emotional expressiveness. Hopkins himself nevertheless had a highly developed sense of form; and perhaps all the more because of the circumstances I have just outlined, the larger units of his form were always very firm, and his stanzas do nearly always flow in "one long strain." [11]

5

Roots of Obscurity

METRICS, however, were far from being Hopkins's sole concern. Apart from an epigram or two and a brief fling at the triolet, he never wrote without having something serious to say. Not that he was ever didactic; his aesthetic sense was too sure to allow confusion between poem and sermon. But the distinction of art must be bestowed upon what was worthy; and meaning, therefore, meaning in a translatable sense, was important. At the outset, he shared the general assumption of his day that clarity was a virtue, obscurity a fault; and for some time he was reluctant to acknowledge that his own writing was markedly obscure. Instead, he kept pointing so persistently to obscurities in the writing of others that in the correspondence between himself and Canon Dixon, as well as in that with Bridges, the accusation became something of a shuttlecock, the initial toss with both friends coming from Hopkins. His most original and most often quoted statement of principle on the subject was made not with reference to his own poetry at all but in connection with a sonnet sent to him in 1879 by Bridges, the second quatrain of which seemed to him "dark." "One of two kinds of clearness one shd. have," he then announced, "either the meaning to be felt without effort as fast as one reads or else, if dark at first reading, when once made out *to explode*. Now this quatrain is not plain at first reading nor, if I am right in my taking of it, did that meaning explode" (I, 90). A year or two later the idea reappeared, this time sounding even more like a comment on his own style projected upon that of Bridges: "Your strange poem 'When from the book' I could not come to like. I found it *very* hard to understand and totally unexplosive. . . . The difficulty is caused in great part by the want of connecting particles. . . . It takes away ease and flow and charm" (I, 125). For himself, however, he required a loophole. "Obscurity I do and will try to avoid so far as it is consistent with excellences higher than clearness at a first reading" (I, 54). In actual practice, mending an obscurity seems nearly always to have required a sacrifice of other excellences that he was unwilling to make: he rarely revised a poem for this purpose, and ultimately he settled upon the notion of providing his poems with prose paraphrases as a means of getting round the difficulty, though this plan was never systematically carried out. One thing, however, throughout all that he said on the subject, is certain: he wished the reader ultimately to understand and not to ignore his literal meaning.[1]

Not his attitude toward it, however, but his obscurity itself is our present concern, and as Bridges was the first to describe its sources, his analysis is the starting point. His preface to the notes of the first edition of Hopkins's *Poems* pointed to what he saw as the three main sources of difficulty, all of them either grammatical or verbal. They consisted of the omission of relative pronouns, the ambiguous placing of identical forms (i.e., forms that are the same for noun and adjective or noun and verb, etc.), and homophones, the last two being ambiguities of somewhat the same sort. Whether Bridges' subsequent quarrel with the English language itself on exactly these grounds originated in his quarrel with Hopkins's obscurities or not, they were at any rate so clearly connected in his mind that one is tempted to regard his later essays on certain linguistic problems as a posthumous continuation of his war on Hopkins's practices. His long tract for the S.P.E., *On English Homophones*, which appeared the year after his edition of Hopkins's *Poems,* was uncompromising: "The more homophones there are in any language, the more faulty is that language as a scientific and convenient vehicle of speech," and English, he observed, is peculiarly overloaded with them. In an earlier paper, "The Glamour of Grammar," he had commented on the other two sources of ambiguity: "The colloquial omission of the relative pronoun, which is now so common even in our highest-aimed poetry and prose, needs to be warned against, for it tends to make nonsense-groups of words." To him, linguistic clarity was a requirement both practical and aesthetic. He did not rule out, or eschew in his own writing, subtle and complicated thought that for its accurate expression requires complicated and sometimes obscure language: his own poem *Narcissus,* for one, is not more easy to make out than most of the difficult passages of Hopkins. But purely verbal or syntactical ambiguities he thought were avoidable, and he remained severe upon Hopkins for indifference to such defects in the language and for failure to circumvent them.

The problems are not quite what they seemed, however, when Bridges named as "the one chief cause" of obscurity in the sentences of Hopkins "his habitual omission of the relative pronoun," for once that idiosyncrasy had been pointed out, it was easily recognized. Like most of his grammatical liberties, it is simply an extension of an accepted idiom, in this instance the idiom by which a relative pronoun in the accusative case is commonly omitted: the man [whom] he killed; the day [on which] he died. Hopkins's liberty consisted in extending the practice (with sixteenth-century but little modern precedent) to the nominative: "O Hero [who] savest," "creep, / Wretch, under a comfort [that] serves in a whirlwind." The obvious purpose, as Bridges noted, was condensation: Hopkins wished to reduce mere connective words—indeed, all the merely mechanical part of language—as nearly as possible to the vanishing point. As all the unusual instances of his omission of the relative pronoun have been identified and are now well known, this liberty no longer presents difficulty to any but the very newest reader of Hopkins. The real problems now lie elsewhere, mainly in the other points raised by Bridges but also in one or two kinds of syntactical ambiguity that he and others overlooked.

"In aiming at condensation," Bridges had said in his preface, Hopkins "neglects the need that there is for care in the placing of words that are grammatically ambiguous." The criticism was made not on puristic grounds but "because such ambiguity or momentary uncertainty destroys the force of the sentence." He illustrated both this and the preceding license by the line "Squander the hell-rook ranks sally to molest him" (*The Bugler's First Communion,* stanza 5), where *sally* may be momentarily taken in two or three ways. In most passages of this sort in Hopkins the difficulty *is* only momentary, though it sometimes recurs on subsequent readings. In *The Soldier,* an opening question, "Why do we all, seeing of a soldier, bless him?" is answered, ". . . the heart . . . fain will find as sterling all as all is smart, / And scarlet wear the spirit of war there express." Here *as, sterling,* and *wear* are all syntactically ambiguous momentarily. They can be sorted out (*sterling* an adjective parallel with *smart, as* an adverb of comparison, *wear* a substantive); but because they are combined with an inversion of normal word order, this reader, at least, finds it necessary to unwind the sentence consciously at each reading: it does not of itself remain unwound. The point made by Bridges, that even the *momentary* uncertainty "destroys the force of the sentence," is in such a passage as this obviously valid. In another much better poem than *The Soldier,* one half line, "lashes lace, lance, and pair" (*That Nature is a Heraclitean Fire,* line 4), is slightly weakened, or so it seems to me though there is no substantial or lasting ambiguity, by the fact that four of its five words may be either substantives or verbs. The first, one realizes almost at once, is a substantive, the others, verbs— "Shivelights and shadowtackle in long lashes lace, lance, and pair"—yet for a moment the reader has a sense of being adrift without landmarks. One scarcely realizes how much in the way of sinewy strength the mere machinery of syntax affords in English style till one finds it so reduced. Usually, in the writing of Hopkins, the gain in condensation is worth the loss, but I do not think it invariably is.

Occasionally Hopkins employed a similar syntactic ambiguity not for the sake of concentration but as a conscious onomatopoetic device, a sort of grammatical onomatopoeia that involves a play on words, expressing tortuosity by means of tortuosity or punning, in order that the meaning should, to employ his own word for it, "explode." At the end of *The Sea and the Skylark,* what at first seems mannered as well as obscure does, on later readings, explode:

We, life's pride and cared-for crown,

Have lost that cheer and charm of earth's past prime:
Our make and making break, are breaking, down
To man's last dust, drain fast towards man's first slime.

Our make (our kind, mankind) and that which we make (industrial society, "this shallow and frail town" of the preceding lines) break and are now in the very process of breaking, down to man's last dust, to his first slime. (The paraphrase should be superfluous, but the passage has puzzled numerous readers.) [2]

The homophones of which Bridges spoke are more frequent than one is likely at first to notice, for they draw attention only when they raise problems of interpretation and this is not in fact very often. The most celebrated of Hopkins's homophones, however, the word *buckle* in *The Windhover,* set off one of the most heated and most wayward debates in modern criticism, one that no doubt would have astonished Hopkins, who I imagine thought that poem perfectly clear. But discussion of it will have to wait. Another, in *The Wreck of the Deutschland,* still puzzles me though it too has been plentifully discussed.

I whirled out wings that spell
And fled with a fling of the heart to the heart of the Host.

Here there are two possible kinds of *that,* as well as two of *spell:* the meaning must be either *during that period of time* or else [wings] *which spell* something. The real difficulty here is that neither reading is satisfactory: the first is too colloquially undignified for its context and the second is forced, pretentious, and scarcely English when *spell* is used without an object. Neither has much relevance, and both therefore seem dictated by the rhyme; yet no other reading seems to be available.[3] The effect, either way, is of a clumsiness uncommon in Hopkins. The phrase is not in a key position and is quickly passed over, but it would be more quickly and painlessly passed if the reader were not momentarily tripped by the ambiguity. Fortunately, there are not many obscurities of this kind in the poems.

Inversion of the normal word order is not exceptional even in modern English poetry, despite the missionary effort toward "natural" language on the part of such writers as William Carlos Williams. Though now so often decried, its value for emphasis, for tight linking of thought, and for balance, as well as for sheer variety, has been too great for many poets to forgo willingly. The loss of inflection in English imposes some limit on the order of words, but what this limit is felt to be has always varied. At one time Hopkins considered himself exceptionally restrained in the use of inversions in his verse: "By the by, inversions—," he wrote to Bridges in a letter of 1879, "As you say, I do avoid them, because they weaken and because they destroy the earnestness or in-earnestness of the utterance. Nevertheless in prose I use them more than other people, because there they have great advantages of another sort. ["Meant to write I have every day for long," he once wrote in a subsequent letter, possibly but not certainly with a jocular intention (I, 135)]. Now these advantages they should have in verse too, but they must not seem to be due to the verse: that is what is so enfeebling (for instance the finest of your sonnets to my mind has a line enfeebled by inversion plainly due to the verse, as I said once before . . .). As it is, I feel my way to their use. However in a nearly finished piece I have a very bold one indeed" (I, 89).

Hopkins came to use more than one "bold" inversion, and by and large they contribute in no small measure to his obscurity, particularly when, as often, they accompany other sources of difficulty. He did for the most part avoid those that would read as if they were dictated by the rhyme, and in fact generally avoided any that might sound smooth; his were apt to be violent dislocations: "Patience who asks / Wants war, wants wounds" is one of the milder of them (in "Patience, hard thing"). The opening of the earlier *Peace*, which, judging by the date of its composition, may be the "very bold" instance referred to in his letter,[4] contains inversion within inversion and followed by inversions, all of which, together with the metaphor, produce a startling but not altogether satisfactory effect, for they tend rather to impede the movement and cloud the metaphor:

When will you ever, Peace, wild wooddove, shy wings
    shut,
Your round me roaming end, and under be my boughs?

In such a passage as this, though no difficulty of interpretation is involved, the effect on the reader is of willful, even perverse singularity and not of power or intensity. Experimental inversion and complicated involutions of word order reach their extreme limits—beyond which I think it must be impossible to go and still remain technically, or nominally, within the limits of accepted grammatical law—in two late sonnets, oddly enough though perhaps not unintentionally, the two poems in which Hopkins undertook to deal most explicitly with the common man, the English (or Irish?) laborer, *Tom's Garland: upon the Unemployed* and *Harry Ploughman*. These, the most involved things he ever wrote, are full of brilliant, vivid images and phrases; but the images are embedded in a syntax almost beyond disentangling, and the extreme mannerism of style becomes ultimately a distraction. Often elsewhere, however, inversion became a source of strength and distinction in Hopkins's style, as will appear later on, particularly in the discussion of certain of the "plain" sonnets.

There are other sources of obscurity, both in the writing of Hopkins and in the English language generally, at least one of which it is surprising Bridges should have failed to remark, for it is as common and as deeply rooted in the nature of language and thought as any that engaged him. It occurs sometimes in Hopkins's poetry and with great frequency in certain parts of his prose.

When Hopkins wrote in verse of "the past-prayer, pent in prison, / The-last-breath penitent spirits" (*The Wreck of the Deutschland,* stanza 33), it is not quite clear, though it is relatively immaterial, whether he was speaking of three distinct groups or of two or one, or whether the words correspond to an indecisiveness in his own mind about the number, for the modern schoolroom precept requiring identical phrasing of parallel groups of words was not a prescribed custom till very recently and application of it will therefore not resolve a nineteenth-century obscurity. And similarly, when he wrote in prose concerning Parmenides, "His feeling for instress, for the flush and foredrawn, and for inscape is most striking" (*Journals*, p. 127), the syntax is again ambiguous. Do "the flush and foredrawn" define "instress," or do they describe certain aspects of it, or are they together the second of three separate things for which Parmenides had feeling? Still bearing in mind the absence of today's rule, there is no way of knowing the answer unless we already know what "instress" is and what particular sense of "flush" and "foredrawn" the writer had in mind. Determination of the meaning is made no easier by the fact that, whatever sense of the words is intended, it is clearly metaphorical. When Hopkins wrote, "There is a degree of effort, pain, weariness to which [the mind] yields" and "[the mind] has a finite insight, memory, grasp of apprehension, power of calculation, invention, force of will" (*Devotional Writings*, p. 124), we do know that these are lists of different things, but we know this not from the syntax but by commonsense understanding of the qualities listed. On the other hand, when he wrote, "Nothing can in the order of time or even of nature act before it exists or exercise function and determination before it has a nature to 'function' and determine, to selve and instress with" (*Devotional Writings*, p. 125), do "selve and instress" mean exactly the same thing, respectively, as "function and determine"? and if so, why are the words added? Or are we being told something new about the first two words, and if so, what? Or, again, are the latter two an expression of indecision or indeterminateness in Hopkins's own thought? Often, certainly, such passages represent the groping after an elusive thought: a first attempt at formulation is followed by a second, aimed at greater precision but without such conviction of having hit the mark as would move him to cancel his first shot. We must all have written in this way at times, and from this point of view such parallel constructions may conceivably be regarded as a positive resource for

113

the conveying of indecisive thought. Whether for better or worse, at any rate, a vast potential for undefined meaning must be seen to reside in this class of syntactic construction.

These observations, not, certainly, novel to professional students of language, arose with particular vividness during a rereading of the prose of Hopkins and a subsequent return to the poetry, for one becomes aware during the course of such reading that his obscurities are not confined to poetry, yet it is equally evident that when his primary intention was to communicate, Hopkins communicated unfailingly. His letters are unexceptionably clear, no matter who the correspondent or how abstruse or technical the subject. Though in writing to Bridges and others about poetry or metrical questions, he sometimes stopped short of the full explanations that we should like to have, nevertheless as far as they go, and in the language itself, there is almost never anything obscure. His sermons, too, are models of clarity if not always of suitability for his audience. On the other hand, his journals and spiritual notes can be at least as obscure as his poetry and are sometimes more so.

For the difficulty of the prose, two main causes are responsible, causes different from those usually dwelt on with reference to the poetry. One is the frequency with which Hopkins employed words in new or unusual, ultimately often in private, senses, together with certain coined words, few but generally used at key points and troublesome when they occur. The other is what has just been described, the ambiguous use of appositional and other indeterminate parallel constructions. Either alone may be troublesome; combined, they are likely to defeat the reader altogether. And they are sometimes additionally complicated by out-of-the-way metaphors.

His journals, when they are more than simply records of comings and goings or notes recalling that the day was "fine" or "dull," are largely given over to extended observations of nature. Usually they attempt to describe literally some appearance of tree, sky, or water with the utmost exactness, in the utmost detail, and with almost exclusive concentration upon form or design. Color also interested him but most often as serving to define form. The resulting descriptions sometimes open our eyes as Charlotte Brontë said *Modern Painters* opened hers; they are obviously Ruskinian though always directly observed, never merely imitative. On the other hand, however exact the account may have been for himself, it is often neither clear nor vivid to a reader. For example, he observed the forms of different kinds of trees and on one occasion made the following note:

Oaks: the organisation of this tree is difficult. Speaking generally no doubt the determining planes are concentric, a system of brief contiguous and continuous tangents, whereas those of the cedar would roughly be called horizontals and those of the beech radiating but modified by droop and by a screw-set towards jutting points. But beyond this since the normal growth of the boughs is radiating and the leaves grow some way in there is of course a system of spoke-wise clubs of green—sleeve-pieces. And since the end shoots curl and carry young and scanty leaf-stars these clubs are tapered, and I have seen also the pieces in profile with chiselled outlines, the blocks thus made detached and lessening towards the end. However the star knot is the chief thing: it is whorled, worked round a little, and this is what keeps up the illusion of the tree: the leaves are rounded inwards and figure out ball-knots. Oaks differ much, and much turns on the broadness of the leaf, the narrower giving the crisped and starry and Catherine-wheel forms, the broader the flat-pieced mailed or shard-covered ones, in which it is possible to see composition in dips etc on wider bases than the single knot or cluster. But I shall study them further.

Which he did, announcing eight days later, "I have now found the law of the oak leaves." (*Journals,* pp. 144–146, 364n.)

The meaning of this passage, written, one must suppose, for his own benefit, Hopkins was obviously under no obligation to make plain to anyone else. Its significance now lies in what it reveals of certain habitual modes of thought and expression. In it he was attempting by analytical description to find out, as well as to record, the characteristic visual form of oak trees. A reader almost certainly will be lost—even a botanist, director of the Botanic Garden at Cambridge, when consulted by the editor of the *Journals,* confessed to being lost. For though the writing at first glance seems painstakingly literal, not only is the welter of detail too great to be comprehensibly ordered in the temporal consecutiveness of language, but the detail itself, in spite of the sprinkling of geometrical terms and the literal air, is more metaphorical than at first appears and the metaphors are to a large extent private. "Brief contiguous and continuous tangents" may not be obviously metaphorical, but the apparent contradictions among four of the five words are hard to resolve in any literal sense or into any visual equivalent; "a system of spokewise clubs of green—sleeve-pieces" is obscure (at least to me) for lack of certainty about the sense—that is, first the literal sense and then its figurative application —of "sleeve-piece" in relation to "clubs," though the latter alone might have been clear. And similarly throughout the passage: "blocks . . . detached and lessening towards the end," "Ball-knots," "Catherine-wheel forms," "Flat-pieced mailed or shard-covered ones." If one can guess at some of these separately, one can still scarcely place them with reference to each other.

116

So the journals run, with many flashes of vivid, precise, and at the same time imaginative observation, along with passages that lose the reader in the detail or through employment of words in uncertain senses, both literal and figurative. The characteristic difficulties of the descriptive notebooks are more often verbal and metaphorical than syntactic. In the spiritual notes the verbal ones remain but are complicated, sometimes disastrously, by equivocal coordinate syntax. In their present form these notes too must be regarded as private writing, though they are much less so than the descriptive notes, for the greater portion of what we have consists of the rough draft of a commentary on the writings of St. Ignatius for which Hopkins had hope of eventual publication. This writing is of interest to the lay reader mainly for the light it sheds upon images and certain doctrinal passages in the poetry and upon the meaning of terms that are of key importance either in the poetry or in his discussions of art, aesthetic form, nature, rhythm, and his poetry. If it were less obscure, it would provide more of this illumination.

Of particular terms, the two that immediately come to mind as being most closely bound up with both his aesthetic and his religious thought are *inscape* and *instress*, both words of his own invention. The meaning of *inscape* can be determined with some degree of confidence—only, however, because Hopkins took care to define it once in a letter specifically addressed to an actual reader. "But as air, melody," he wrote to Bridges, "is what strikes me most of all in music and design in painting, so design, pattern or what I am in the habit of calling 'inscape' is what I above all aim at in poetry." He added that "it is the virtue of design, pattern, or inscape to be distinctive" (I, 66). From this clear-cut statement, in which the coordination does not appear to admit of any ambiguity, it is possible to see what Hopkins meant by the term, which he had been using since his undergraduate days at Oxford. Essentially, inscape is little different from what is commonly called organic form, being a form or design the external character of which is determined by, and exhibits the distinctive, individual, internal character of, either the object or the artist (creator) or both. "Organic form," if he knew the term, might not have been satisfactory to him because its explicit emphasis on one aspect, the "living" character, of such form tends to obscure its second aspect, which is nevertheless implicit in the concept, distinctiveness. *Inscape*, then, may be roughly described as organic form with emphasis on the individuality implicit in the organic. Though the term itself does not occur in Hopkins's poetry, his preoccupation with what it represents is an underlying principle in all his work: the particular word scarcely matters, but that he felt so strongly about the concept that he had to invent his own name for it is significant.

The term *instress* presents a more difficult problem. It occurs twice in the poems (in stanza 5 of the *Deutschland*, a passage discussed in chapter 2; and in stanza 2 of *The Handsome Heart*) and many times elsewhere, appearing as both verb and substantive, in religious contexts and with reference to natural beauty. Sometimes it seems to be a property of the object; at other times it appears as the effect of the object on the human or supernatural being; and at least once (at an early date, 1866) there appears to be a confusion between subjective and objective: "From the top the lake of Brienz was of the richest opaque green modulated with an *emotional* instress to blue" (*Journals*, p. 176; my italics). Always the term has something to do with emphasis, but beyond that I can be sure of no single, consistently maintained meaning. Hopkins never defined it for the benefit of another reader as he did *inscape*, and he uses it peculiarly often in parallel or coordinate constructions that are apt to sound like uneasy strainings after either a more accurate or perhaps a more intense expression: "all that energy or instress," "the stamp, seal, or instress," "this song of Lucifer's was a dwelling on his own beauty, an instressing of his own inscape" (*Devotional Writings*, pp. 137, 139, 200–201). These are among the clearest uses of the term and probably also the most nearly alike in meaning. It will be noticed that they all occur in appositional syntax that has somewhat the look of a definition; yet neither the ostensible purpose nor the actual result quite amounts to an informative definition for the enlightenment of a reader other than himself.

The foregoing summary discussion has been introduced not primarily to provide a gloss for the particular vocabulary of Hopkins's prose writing but rather, or at least primarily, as a means of inquiring into the nature of his obscurity and the ways in which it varies in the different classes of his writing.[5] It was said earlier that when his primary intention was to communicate, Hopkins wrote with habitual clarity; and it is certain, too, that as a poet he did not choose to write private poetry. The gap, nevertheless, between his particular characteristic creative will and most readers' ability, at least without considerable effort, to follow him has always been a wide one; and the gap is not fully accounted for by the ambiguities of vocabulary and syntax that have been under discussion. In addition to, and indeed underlying these, were the deeply rooted eccentricities of thought, feeling, and what without implying anything mystical may be called "vision," such as led to the parallel drawn earlier with Blake; and it is all these things together that make Hopkins's poetry difficult.

Now and then the particular character of his imagination or his particular mode of thought and feeling leaves the reader so uncertain that the whole drift of a poem becomes ambiguous. *The Starlight Night*, for example, though it seems a relatively clear and simple sonnet, has been read quite plausibly in two very different and incompatible ways. As this poem exhibits more than one of his characteristic types of obscurity, it may stand

here as a single illustration of some of the problems that
have been discussed.

Look at the stars! look, look up at the skies!
  O look at all the fire-folk sitting in the air!
  The bright boroughs, the circle-citadels there!
Down in dim woods the diamond delves! the elves'-eyes!
The grey lawns cold where gold, where quickgold lies!
  Wind-beat whitebeam! airy abeles set on a flare!
  Flake-doves sent floating forth at a farmyard scare!—
Ah well! it is all a purchase, all is a prize.

Buy then! bid then! —What? —Prayer, patience, alms,
     vows.
Look, look: a May-mess, like on orchard boughs!
  Look! March-bloom, like on mealed-with-yellow
     sallows!
These are indeed the barn; withindoors house
The shocks. This piece-bright paling shuts the spouse
  Christ home, Christ and his mother and all his
     hallows.

About the central thought there is no question: the
beauty of the night, beauty in the concrete world, may
be fully possessed and enjoyed only if one is devoted
to the spiritual values of Christ, for they are the true
meaning of beauty in the material world. There may be
different theological formulations, Thomist or Scotist,
of the relation between matter and spirit, but the differences do not count for this poem, since the metaphor
that expresses the relation—the barn as material beauty
and the grain as the spiritual—is loose and inexact
enough to be inclusive. "The heavens [or heaven and
earth] declare the glory of God," in short, is the theme.
The problems thus involve only the concrete picture,
but they involve almost the whole of that. What we are
given is a series of visual images, some or all of which
must be metaphorical or even doubly metaphorical, set

forth in a series of coordinate grammatical constructions. As in the prose description of oak trees, a main difficulty is that of matching the metaphor with its literal, visual equivalent in the absence of syntactic guideposts or of the visual clarification afforded by a photograph. Here Hopkins himself is not struggling to make out something. He knows what he is looking at, and the reader is obviously expected to see it too, exactly; what is more, the separate images, almost without exception, are clear and vivid in themselves. Yet what they correspond to, the whole primary scene, in fact, is ambiguous, for we cannot be certain whether throughout the poem we are looking exclusively upward at the night sky, or whether we are looking both upward and all about us, taking in the whole scene of sky and earth. The first three lines clearly describe the starry sky, and the highly imaginative metaphors there need no comment; but with the fourth line possible readings diverge.

The more literal may be taken first. According to this, "Down in dim woods" brings the eye down from "there," the sky, to the starlit earth: woods with a diamond-like scattering of starlight through the leaves; grey lawns where the dew reflects gold starlight; and trees blown by the wind all variously transformed by this light. The whitebeam, the underside of whose leaves is whitish or silvery, shimmers in the wind and starlight; the aspens' ("airy abeles") individual leaves, each set crosswise on its long slim stalk, flare in all directions, catching innumerable lights.[6] The next line, however, "Flake-doves sent floating forth at a farmyard scare!" is ambiguous under either reading, for in either case the question is whether the doves are actually present in the scene, or whether they are a metaphor describing motion in the trees of the preceding line; the line may thus be literal, except for the metaphor of "flakes"—a flock of doves scattering "as if" they were "flakes"—or metaphorical, blown leaves in a gust, fanning out like

121

doves that resemble flakes: the ambiguity lies, once more, chiefly in the indeterminate coordinate syntax. The two lines of the sestet in which, after the hortatory interruption, the natural description is resumed, are clear enough in themselves and according to this first reading are a further description of trees to which starlight lends the illusion of bloom, whitish like that of an orchard in May or dimly tinged with yellow ("mealed-with-yellow") like willows in March.

According to the second reading of the poem, the eye of the beholder remains fixed on the sky throughout, and all the descriptive detail is simply a series of fanciful images suggested by the night sky and the stars without reference to any surrounding scene. In this reading "down in dim woods" refers to the depths of the sky; "the diamond delves! the elves'-eyes" are the stars seen against the dark of night; the "grey lawns" are again sky; and "gold," trees, "May-mess," "March-bloom" are all successive fanciful epithets for stars or the Milky Way. "Set on a flare" in this reading is brightness of stars, not movement of aspens, but the doves remain ambiguous—stars that are like dovelike flakes (or flakelike doves), or stars like leaves blown like a flock of (flakelike) doves. Now all this explanation sounds slightly absurd; but still these are two extremely different readings, and the choice matters because the images are presented with such vividness that we cannot read the poem as a verbal structure only; we are forced to apprehend some imaginative visual structure. But which is that structure? [7]

Though the second reading, by which all the imagery is seen as referring to sky and stars, is apparently the widely accepted one,[8] it is not the one that comes to me naturally; I have not altogether persuaded myself that it represents Hopkins's meaning and am inclined, though with great uncertainty, toward the first, partly, no doubt, from simple preference—read so, the poem seems less fanciful and more imaginative—but partly also because it is more in keeping with the modes of thought characteristic of Hopkins. His passion for the exact reality of appearance in the physical world generally governed even his strikingly imaginative images and epithets; it did not ordinarily permit him to let fancy roam as freely and as far from the visual actuality as it does if we are meant to see the sky or stars successively as woods, elves'-eyes, lawns, poplars and other trees in wind, startled doves, and flowering orchards and willows. It is the succession of these varied and farfetched images even more than their separate character that makes them, in this reading, seem self-indulgently fanciful rather than imaginatively exact, as Hopkins customarily strove to be. Yet one cannot say that he might not once have indulged in this kind of fanciful ingenuity.

Besides the large ambiguity embracing the whole scene of the poem, *The Starlight Night* contains verbal and syntactic obscurities that illustrate other problems discussed earlier. The word *flare,* as I have indirectly noticed, belongs to the class of homophones that Bridges found to be such frequent stumbling blocks: it may be read as either fire or movement. This particular homonym need not be disturbing in its context, however, because the two senses of the word are not mutually exclusive: the flare of a torch suggests both brightness and windblown motion, and so does the flaring motion of shiny poplar leaves that gleam, as well as move, in starlight. The mind of the reader can therefore entertain both images without a sense of conflict or confusion, and it matters relatively little which he takes to be dominant. Typical of the obscurity due, in Bridges' terms, to "neglect" in the placing of grammatically ambiguous words are those in the fourth line, "the diamond delves." Subject and verb, or adjective and substantive—either is possible, both make slightly odd sense. Taken alone, the first reading is preferable to one that requires a double grammatical transformation, first that of a noun (*diamond*) into an adjective and then of a verb (*delves*) into a noun. But as the simpler reading violates what appears to be a parallel series without verbs (*elves'-eyes, lawns,* and so on), one must, I think, be driven to this second unlikely alternative.[9]

These ambiguities, together with the uncertainty concerning the doves (the question of whether they constitute a fourth independent image in a parallel series or are in descriptive apposition with the third), illustrate something of the texture of obscurity in Hopkins's poetry; and it should be evident too, from these examples, how often the obscurity is associated with the coordinate grammatical constructions that cause difficulty in his prose. In another writer these constructions would be much less apt to give trouble, simply because the meaning of a poet whose thought and feeling run in more central channels, channels more similar to our own, can often be recognized or easily guessed, even when the syntax is indeterminate. Ultimately we come back, therefore, to strangeness in the temperament and vision of Hopkins himself; it is this most of all that from time to time prevents our following him. The man who in his journal described the sky of a beautiful bright day that had given him pleasure as "that fleshy blue sky" (*Journals,* p. 235), whose love of inscape led him so far as to admire the "melodious lines of a cow's dewlap" (*Journals,* p. 171), and who wished to read Bridges' lines in *London Snow* with such distortions as we have seen—a man whose essential oddities of eye and ear drew him to such borderlands as these must pass beyond the reader's horizon at times. In some degree, though not fully, Hopkins was aware of his difference from other people, and in the well-known statement to Bridges defining inscape, part of which has already been quoted, he took account of it in his own terms. "No doubt my poetry errs on the side of oddness," he wrote. But inscape was what he above all aimed at. "Now it is the virtue of design, pattern, or inscape to be distinctive and it is the vice of distinctiveness to become queer. This vice I cannot have escaped" (I, 66). In later years he felt that what he needed, to be "more intelligible, smoother, and less singular," was an audience (I, 291). But the argument was circular: without less singularity there could be no contemporary public audience.

It would be wrong to overemphasize the temperamental "queerness" of Hopkins. If he were only queer, his poetry would never have touched us; and many of his particular virtues as a poet—originalities of thought, imagery, and rhythm—are bound up with this strangeness quite as much as are the occasionally unassimilable mannerisms. Nevertheless, recognition of the sometimes private character of his world is necessary if we are to avoid serious misrepresentations, for we have to be constantly aware that our own insights are not necessarily relevant in dealing with his poetry.

6

Bridges and the Two Styles

ROBERT BRIDGES was the first literary reader of Hopkins's mature poetry, as well as, nearly half a century later, its first editor. Until Hopkins's death in 1889, the relation between the two friends was important for both, and their influence upon each each other's work remains important for us. Though in this connection justice has been done Bridges by a few writers on Hopkins and perhaps more than justice by a smaller few, on balance something is still owing to him, for he has been subjected to bitter criticism ever since Hopkins's fame began to rise some thirty or more years ago. Even the appearance in recent years of a carefully weighed book given over entirely to the relations between the two men [1] leaves unmade, or incompletely made, points that are significant, and not for biographical reasons alone.

With reference to Hopkins, the most substantial complaint against Bridges has been directed at the critical account with which he introduced the poems to the public in 1918, an account in which considerably more space is devoted to the faults than to the virtues of the poems. Long before that date, Bridges had let it be known that when he came to publish the poems he wished, so far as possible, to disarm hostile criticism by himself anticipating all that could be said against them. Doing so he hoped would minimize the shock they were bound to cause; but he also wished the public to recognize that he was publishing them not in the blind partiality of friendship but upon a clear-sighted critical

126

judgment of their worth, faults and all. Perhaps he leaned over backward too far in dwelling on these; certainly the emphasis is disproportionate if his essay is to be judged by what we think today, though the early reviewers saw no unfairness.[2] If, as may be, acceptance of the poems would have been hastened by fuller praise and briefer blame on the editor's part, it is a pity he was not more generous with the praise. But no one now can know what the result would have been at the time; and if his estimate of the probable public response was faulty and in the retrospective view his critique hypercritical, his reasons for what he wrote were not, at any rate, wholly ungenerous.

The name of Bridges has already cropped up frequently in these pages; it remains now to go back to earlier and more important considerations, particularly to those bearing upon the character and value to Hopkins of the friendship during his lifetime and still more particularly to the question of Bridges' value to and influence upon Hopkins's poetry. What is to be said here constitutes, therefore, in the main a kind of slant preface to the discussion of poems which Hopkins came to write in two widely disparate styles.

Whatever else may be said, all who have written about Hopkins and more especially all who value his poetry owe an enormous debt to Bridges. So much has been duly, if sometimes grudgingly, acknowledged. Had the two men never met, or had their friendship not been renewed and maintained as it was, under difficult circumstances, the poems could easily have been lost sight of entirely or have perished. This nearly everyone knows. Bridges has nevertheless been taken to task on other counts besides that of churlish editing; he has been charged with undue delay in waiting for nearly thirty years after Hopkins's death before publishing the poems and with grossly inadequate appreciation of them during Hopkins's life as well as afterward. C. C. Abbott replied to the charge of delay by printing figures for the sale of the original edition of 1918, which consisted of 750 copies. Fifty, he reported, were given away; 180 were sold during the first year and 240 in the second; "then an average of 30 a year for six years, rising to 90 in 1927," the last 4 being disposed of in 1928 (I, xx, n. 2). Obviously, the world was not over-ready for the poems of Hopkins even in 1918 and even though Bridges had done something to prepare a public by presenting a handful of them, chiefly in Alfred H. Miles's anthology *The Poets and the Poetry of the Century* in 1894 and in his own *The Spirit of Man* some twenty years later.

Yet the question of Bridges' motives is not quite as simple as these figures suggest. Immediately after the death of Hopkins, he did plan to publish the poems and to write a memoir to go with them. In the eighties and nineties a memoir would have been expected, indeed almost necessary, in introducing to the public any such unusual work by a dead and unknown writer. But Bridges could scarcely have written that memoir. He was an outspoken man; he detested Jesuits; and he detested, or at least deplored, in Hopkins what he regarded as a wasted and unhappy subjection of himself to their rule at the expense of his creative powers. The strain of attempting the impossible shows clearly in the very brief biographical introduction that he wrote to accompany the selections from Hopkins in Miles. Furthermore, Bridges disliked the extreme or the outlandish, and indisputably in those early days Hopkins's poetry was, with whatever virtues, extreme by any reader's standard and sometimes outlandish. Finally, Bridges was something of a missionary and reformer in the world of letters, not only in his well-known plans to reform English spelling and diction but also, and of more importance, in his desire to see new rhythms introduced and accepted in English poetry. As he did not wish these brought into disfavor by accompanying eccentricities, his eagerness for immediate publication of Hopkins's poetry underwent a change.

I should myself prefer the postponement of the poems till the memoir is written, *or* till I have got my own method of prosody recognized separately from Gerard's. They are the same, and he has the greater claim than I to the origination of it, but he has used it so as to discredit it; and it would be a bad start in favour for the practice we both advocated and wished to be used.[3]

This is harsh and arrogant today; it would not have seemed so when it was written in 1890, nor would the further explanation in the same letter, "Readers would not see that the peculiarities of his versification were not part of his metrical system, but a freakishness corresponding to his odd choice of words." In 1890 this statement too would have been simple truth in the view of even a sympathetic reader of Hopkins. It was in 1890, and is even now, an "odd choice of words" to describe, for example, the giving of first communion to a boy as "forth Christ from cupboard fetched, how fain I of feet / To his [Christ's] youngster take his treat" (*The Bugler's First Communion*). "Odd" is indeed rather a restrained epithet for the expressions [*Christ's*] *youngster* and *treat* and later in the same poem, *Christ's royal ration* for the Eucharist; and the unreal Saxonism in which the epithets are embedded is scarcely calculated to soften the oddity. As there are numerous other passages in Hopkins's poems that are equally "odd," the truth of Bridges' statement is undeniable, however unwelcome to the devotee. Its tone, nevertheless, does reflect an imperfect sympathy and makes plain that for Bridges other interests in his life could take precedence over devotion to Hopkins's memory. Perhaps this is a pity, but it is not villainy. Nor is it by any means the whole story.

Two influential modern critics have seen only this side of the matter and have castigated Bridges unmercifully for it. F. R. Leavis, contemptuous of Bridges on all counts and equally as poet, critic, and man, characterized his taste as "prim donnish conventionality," a product of "the academic mind" as impervious to greatness as Johnson's was to *Lycidas* but more despicable on other scores, a poet, moreover, whose interest in poetic technique deserved only to be lumped with his interest in spelling. Between Hopkins and Bridges, Leavis could see the latter as offering nothing of value but only "constant incomprehension and discouragement." [4] In a similar vein Sir Herbert Read wondered what possible basis there could have been for the friendship unless the attraction were purely "instinctive, even physical." "How otherwise," he asked, "could Hopkins tolerate the conceit, the pedantry, the cruel lack of perception" that were all Bridges had to offer in return for Hopkins's endearing virtues.[5] The letter of Bridges to Mrs. Hopkins from which, not wishing to present one side of the controversy only, I have quoted would have reinforced the indignation of these and other critics hostile to Bridges had they known it when they wrote.

Yet an examination of the evidence does not suggest that Bridges was by any means merely the obtuse or meanspirited friend pictured by Leavis and Read. It shows, on the contrary, that in spite of extreme temperamental differences Bridges valued Hopkins's work highly though with many qualifications, and it suggests also that he was a major influence upon the creation of some of the finest of that work. What needs to be noticed first, though, is that the relationship, both personal and literary, was a rewarding but difficult give-and-take affair and that it was Hopkins, not Bridges, who set its critically unsparing tone.

Next after the religious preoccupations of Hopkins and his passionate love of natural beauty, the greatest resource of his mature creative life, as far as is known and as even Leavis acknowledges, was this long friendship. Because the intimacy of their undergraduate days had been broken by his conversion to Catholicism and communication during the next few years had been desultory and strained, then for a time broken altogether, his first great original step, resulting in *The Wreck of the Deutschland*, was taken in literary solitude, independently of Bridges and of all other contemporary influences except those that came through reading. The rejection of this poem by *The Month*, however, in spite of the friendly disposition of its editor, Father Henry Coleridge, who was Hopkins's oldest friend in the Jesuit order, seriously disappointed and discouraged him. Apparently it silenced him also until, unconnected with these events, some six months later (early in 1877) and after a two-year interval in their correspondence, a letter arrived from Bridges with a promise to send him *The Growth of Love* (the early pamphlet edition consisting of twenty-four sonnets) and a pamphlet collection of Bridges' Latin verses. Even before the poems arrived, the letter itself appears to have revived Hopkins's creative energy, for within a day or two of its arrival he wrote the first draft of the sonnet *God's Grandeur* and the next day answered Bridges' letter and wrote another sonnet, *The Starlight Night*, though as yet he said nothing to Bridges about his own writing.[6] The pamphlets, when they came, elicited from him an extraordinarily long letter (dated April 3 but written over a much longer period of time, it extends to eight printed pages) in which he entered into a detailed criticism of Bridges' verses (I, 32–40). This letter marked the active beginning of their critical exchanges, though in the meantime another had come from Bridges with a stimulating discussion of Milton's rhythms and of his own (Bridges') experiments with Miltonic rhythm. All this was a great refreshment to Hopkins after the ten-years-long drought of literary exchanges. Replying in his letter of April 3, he now disclosed that he too had been writing verse and experimenting with new rhythms; he promised to enclose the two recent sonnets.

131

During that spring, summer, and early fall of 1877, still under this renewed stimulus from Bridges, Hopkins composed ten of what are among his best-known sonnets, a considerable output for him at any time of his life. The tone and length of his long letter, the circumstances—it was written during a period when he had scarcely any leisure and was, besides, exhausted and half ill—reference in other letters to their talk when they met that summer, and the flurry of poetic production—all testify to the importance for the creative side of Hopkins's life of this renewed, and renewing, friendship. He badly needed encouragement, and, along with criticism, he now received it from Bridges. Without this stimulus, the chances would seem very considerable that, after perhaps trying out a few more pieces in his new style and finding them rejected for publication, as they would be sure to be, Hopkins would have sunk once again into a silence that he would break only to write more of those occasional verses of his that most readers now prefer to forget. They were a poetic compromise which I think he would have been driven to make more of if Bridges' audience of one had failed him and he had continued to write at all.

Inglorious Miltons may be mute from other causes than poverty or village ignorance; and in both the temperament and the circumstances of Hopkins many forces conspired against his work as a poet. His asceticism might again, as in the past, have forbidden as self-indulgence writing that had proved unacceptable and could therefore offer no justification for existing except his own satisfaction. Even without a deliberate act of renunciation, the ascetic was always in danger of stifling the creative side of Hopkins in the absence of a counterinfluence, for as his letters make abundantly evident, he was a man who needed the encouragement of some reader or the hope of readers to stir his constantly overtaxed energy, living as he did in a chronic state of physical and psychic exhaustion. His letters confess his need of an audience, and indeed, though this was conscientiously subordinated to the claims of his religious dedication, they make clear also his longing for fame. It is very likely, therefore, that Bridges not only preserved the physical texts of the poems for posterity but preserved the poet too as a producing poet. He was no makeshift, no mere better-than-nothing audience either; nor was he a friend who read the poems condescendingly or out of friendship alone; he read them with admiration. Indeed, Leavis and Bridges' other detractors to the contrary notwithstanding, I am not at all sure that Victorian England could have provided for Hopkins's particular kind of poetry a better or more perceptive audience, whether for encouragement or criticism; to think otherwise is to project our own taste backward by a century.

The character of the correspondence between the two friends has been a good deal misapprehended. It was a two-sided affair, but because one side only survives, it has been seen out of focus, Bridges being seen as harsh and uncomprehending, Hopkins as all "frankness, humility, and grace." Humility, yes, no doubt, and grace certainly; still Hopkins was made up of about equal parts humility and arrogance, as the letters plainly show.[7] In their critical exchanges, the blows as well as the benefits were mutual, and for all that has been said about the severity of Bridges' strictures on his friend's poems, it may be doubted whether Hopkins received many more blows than he dealt. At any rate, he dealt the first, along with praise, in that long letter of April 1877, which established a tone of critical frankness for the subsequent correspondence. In it he expressed admiration for the poems Bridges had sent: "The sonnets are truly beautiful, breathing a grave and feeling genius, and make me proud of you," he wrote; but then at once, with an arrogance equal to any Bridges afterward exhibited, he began to find fault unsparingly, and to rewrite Bridges' lines for him—no small liberty to take with another man's verse. After parenthetically noting that Bridges always had been and still was "given to conceit," he proceeded to the fifth sonnet,[8] which he liked best though its thought was derivative, it had a "weak" third line—"you mean something more like . . . ," and "the barbarous rhyme of *prow* and *show*" was utterly deplorable. In another "the personification is wrong"; he proposed altering (for the worse, I think) two lines of the fine sonnet "O Weary Pilgrims"; [9] a line of another "ought to be"— and there follows his rewritten version. Still another sonnet is "weak"; its "rhythm is not expressive, it only halts"; and another contains a line that Hopkins "cannot understand at all." In this manner he went through the series, noting that he had not yet "studied" the poems. But he closed his critique with praise of their beauty and their "manly tenderness" and "flowing and never-failing music" (I, 33–39).

From this time on, Bridges continued to send his poems to Hopkins for criticism; and Hopkins, though nearly always praising them, continued to expend the greater part of his attention on their faults and on suggestions for amendment. "Could you not end something like . . . ," he would say. Or, "a lovely poem. But nevertheless I must tell you that the first verse appears to me to be faulty. . . . *Silence!* shd. be *Hush, hush.* . . . in the last verse I should prefer . . . ," and the meaning of the whole, he complained, is impenetrable. Elsewhere he found "a certain failure in the blank verse," and there are too many echoes of Milton, Tennyson, Gray, and Surrey. "Otherwise the piece is beautiful and full of music. The meaning is bad." Lines are "commonplace" or "feeble and downright padding"; and "the vulgar verses about Anne leave a bad taste." [10]

At one point the severity was enough to discourage Bridges altogether. "One thing you say in your last is enough to make me quite sad," Hopkins wrote, some two years after the revival of their correspondence.

"You ask whether I really think there is any good in your going on writing poetry. The reason of this question I suppose to be that I seemed little satisfied with what you then sent and suggested many amendments in the sonnet on Hector. I do still think"—and even now he was off on further "amendments" before he could pause to reassure Bridges of his admiration (I, 93 ff.).

The supposition that the criticism of Hopkins's poetry conveyed in the lost letters of Bridges was very different in tone from this—that it was wholly, or even predominantly, discouraging—rests upon a superficial reading of these surviving letters of Hopkins. Particularly, a reader such as Leavis, approaching them with a fixed dislike of Bridges, easily forgets that what each correspondent almost inevitably picks up and dwells upon in reply to mingled praise and disapproval, especially if he is, as Hopkins was, rather a stubborn man, are the objections to be answered, the difficulties to be explained away, the defense, in general, of what he has done. Careless or biased readers, encountering all these defenses in Hopkins's letters, overlook evidence that should create a much different picture. A letter about his poem *The Loss of the Eurydice,* for example, takes up seriatim twelve different questions or objections that Bridges had raised, and a reader may easily notice the two or three pages given over to answering these and fail to notice the single sentence that precedes them: "It gave me of course great pleasure to read your words of praise." Later, in the midst of a long criticism of Bridges' *Ulysses,* it is easy to miss the remark, "It is too bad that I shd. so abuse *Ulysses* after your encouragement of *St. Winefred*"; or elsewhere to miss his brief acknowledgment of "a very flattering and endearing" letter.

More evidence comes indirectly when we learn, still from the letters, of Bridges' having discussed Hopkins's work with Pater, of his wish to show the poems to Andrew Lang and other friends, and of his proposal to draw public attention to their existence through Edmund Gosse, who had seen and liked them. As Bridges praised them in very high terms to others, I cannot imagine his having withheld this praise from Hopkins himself. R. W. Dixon once wrote to him, "Bridges struck the truth long ago when he said to me that your poems more carried him out of himself than those of anyone." [11] A poet could scarcely hope for much higher praise than this.

Hopkins's new rhythms had very early aroused interest in Bridges, who had begun by parodying that of the *Deutschland* (I, 44) but within a year was asking permission to try it out seriously in poems of his own. Subtle and fastidious as his ear was, he could hardly have paid Hopkins a higher compliment, as Hopkins did not fail to know. "I forgot to answer about my metres (rhythms rather, I suppose). Do by all means and you will honour them and me" (I, 55). This on a postcard was his pleased reply to the request. The result appeared early in 1879 in a group of four poems, of which now the best known are *A Passer-By* and *The Downs*. When others were included the following year in *Poems, Third Series*, Bridges added a note describing briefly the new prosody and closing with the acknowledgment: "The author disavows any claim to originality for the novelty: this is almost entirely due to a friend, whose poems remain, he regrets to say, in manuscript." Dated "Christmas, 1879," the note stood as Bridges' Christmas present to Hopkins, the first public notice of his mature work (the omission of his name was by his own wish, for reasons connected with his profession). Bridges' poems in the new rhythm did not satisfy Hopkins, however. "They do read tentative, experimental," he said. "I cannot well say where the thought is distorted by the measure, but that it is distorted I feel by turning from these to the other pieces, where the mastery is so complete." He was especially hard on *A Passer-By*, now one of the more admired of

Bridges' poems. "*The Passer By* in particular reads not so much like sprung rhythm as that logaoedic dignified-doggrel one Tennyson has employed in *Maud* and since": this was his sole comment on the poem (I, 71).

Obviously, with the most friendly will in the world, and each with fine critical sensibility, two men of such opposite tempers were bound to fall somewhat short of perfect appreciation of each other's work, and both —not Bridges only—did. But that the latter was by no means grossly obtuse is still further shown by the time and care he bestowed upon the poems as well as the manuscripts of Hopkins through the course of many years. As his preface to the notes of the edition of 1918 informs us, he kept and pasted into a notebook each poem as it came to him and later made a careful copy of all the final versions. A year after he had first read *The Loss of the Eurydice*, he was again asking Hopkins about certain passages. In 1882–83 he was restudying the poems with some thoroughness, asking questions from time to time about earlier as well as current work. It was at this time that he elicited from Hopkins an extended explanation of certain parts of *The Sea and the Skylark*, which was then more than five years old (I, 163–164). Through Hopkins's replies we trace his subsequent, and sometimes repeated, study of *God's Grandeur*, the sonnet on Henry Purcell, and even the poem that he had once said he would not "for any money" read again, *The Wreck of the Deutschland* (I, 168–182 *passim*). This he was studying further and discussing in correspondence seven years after it had been written. Copies might have been made and kept by Bridges merely out of friendship, but such close and repeated study of the poems as this was a high critical tribute and beyond question a great encouragement.

During the first summer after their resumption of correspondence in 1877, opportunity had arisen for meetings in which poetry, metrical theory, and music were discussed. By that time Bridges had copies of several sonnets of Hopkins. What he at first thought of them is not recorded, but he must at least have respected them, since from the start he preserved them with care and after the visits Hopkins felt sufficiently encouraged to send him the rejected ode on the *Deutschland*. This we know he did not like. The record does not show whether he found anything at all to praise; in the letter defending it Hopkins mentions only censure, all of which he rejected. The criticism was "bilgewater," he said, and, half concealing his hurt, proceeded with a jocular explanation of the appropriateness of this nautical term (I, 44, 46, 50).

Yet, resented occasionally and frequently rejected though it was, Bridges' criticism was not without effect. Coming on top of Father Coleridge's refusal to print the first shipwreck poem, it was partly responsible for the altered style of the second, *The Loss of the Eurydice*, written during the following spring. In this one Hopkins tried for something more acceptable, both to Bridges and to a possible wider public; the result was a treatment and style intermediate between that of the *Deutschland* and the "popular" one in which he was so ill at ease. The new poem, he said, in contrast with his ode was "short and easy"; it contained proportionately more narrative and less "discourse"; and he hoped Bridges would like it. Bridges did, while as a matter of course taking exception to certain phrases and images. Because it was much less obscure than the *Deutschland* and no doubt still more because its theme and treatment were less sectarian and therefore less personally distasteful to him, he could value it as he could not the earlier work. But *The Month* would not publish the *Eurydice* either.

Even before the rejection of his second "wreck," however, Hopkins had, not without regret, pretty much settled for an audience of one, Bridges, with the addition not long afterward of R. W. Dixon, who became an admiring, not in the least critical and consequently less useful and challenging, reader. "I cannot think of altering anything," Hopkins had written in reply to Bridges' "bilgewater." "Why should I? I do not write for the public. You are my public and I hope to convert you" (I, 46). In spite of this uncompromising reply, he did listen to Bridges' criticism; that became evident a year or two later when he wrote, evidently in response to something indirectly flattering or encouraging: "No doubt my poetry errs on the side of oddness. I hope in time to have a more balanced and Miltonic style" (I, 66). Milton was a frequent topic between them. The continuation of this passage, often quoted in other contexts, has obscured the importance of this opening statement. Bridges' sonnets in *The Growth of Love*, Hopkins had said in recommending them to his family, were "designedly written in Miltonic rhythms but not violent like mine" (III, 146). The "hope" of a more chastened style soon became a resolve of which the first outcome, a few months later, was the sonnet *Andromeda*.[12] "I enclose a sonnet," he informed Bridges, "on which I invite minute criticism. I endeavoured in it at a more Miltonic plainness and severity than I have anywhere else. I cannot say it has turned out severe, still less plain, but it seems almost free from quaintness and in aiming at one excellence I may have hit another" (I, 87).

Andromeda was not an isolated venture. In the verse written after Hopkins entered the priesthood, three styles are distinguishable. Most familiar, as well as most striking, is the elaborate baroque style that reached its ultimate limits in *The Leaden Echo and the Golden Echo* and certain of the later sonnets but that is also the prevailing style of *The Wreck of the Deutschland* and the sonnets of 1877. Beside it stands the plainer and usually less obscure style best known in the "terrible" sonnets. The third, though not chronologically the last, is that referred to before, in which Hopkins tried to strike a popular devotional note and which appears mainly in the occasional pieces composed with his pious but unliterary daily companions in mind. As he was temperamentally unfitted for popular writing of any kind, these last pieces are all more or less embarrassing failures. He was aware of his inaptitude for this kind of writing, though in spite of his better judgment he retained a half-apologetic affection for certain of the occasional verses. Concerning two of them he told Bridges: "I am not surprised at your not liking the May Magnificat, which has about it something displeasing to myself. But the Silver Jubilee I do not regret: it seems to me to hit the mark it aims at without any wrying. Both of course are 'popular' pieces, in which I feel myself to come short" (I, 77–78). For serious literary purposes Hopkins remains, therefore, a poet of two styles, styles readily distinguishable, indeed markedly differing in their extreme forms though often merging into something intermediate. Both, it goes without saying, bear the common signature of his highly individual modes of thought and expression.

With the development of the first of them, as we have seen, Bridges had nothing to do except that his criticisms appear ultimately to have discouraged Hopkins from pushing it to greater extremes than he did: "It is plain," he at last wrote, upon learning that *Tom's Garland* had defeated the combined wits of Bridges and Dixon, "I must go no farther on this road" (I, 272). On the other hand, without the stimulation and encouragement derived from the letters and talk of Bridges and without also the intimately known challenge of the latter's poetic achievement in so much more restrained a style, joined with his castigations of extravagance, it is unlikely that the poems in the plainer style would ever have been written at all.

Hopkins did, as I have said, wish to write poetry that would be acceptable and that would have some kind of influence in the world. In the *Eurydice*, therefore, he had avoided theology and other "discourse," emphasizing swift narrative, adopting simple catchy rhythm and rhyme, to a considerable extent writing down to his conception of a poetry-reading audience but still not eschewing any of his favorite ingenuities or native idiosyncrasies. Here he was making, I think, nearly all the wrong compromises. The plain style that he subsequently developed was not one of compromise at all but followed upon his vivid awakening to a different kind of excellence, one that had not earlier fired his imagination but that gradually came to do so, mainly through the dialogue with Bridges. Though he had no intention of abandoning his baroque style altogether, he did feel challenged to prove, both to Bridges and to himself, that in order to be original he did not need to be "queer," that he could create something genuinely distinctive out of resources that other poets have found sufficient—in short, that he was capable of producing work of high poetic quality in a central, relatively unmannered style. This challenge originated with Bridges and probably would never otherwise have arisen spontaneously in Hopkins's own imagination. It was largely through high and affectionate respect for Bridges' more classic poetic ideal, made vivid to him largely through Bridges' eyes—and through talk of Milton—that a somewhat comparable ideal arose in his own mind. The new style had nothing to do with any direct imitation of Bridges' own poems, but the challenge coming through him was, as I see the matter, its origin.

It has been customary to set off the later "terrible sonnets" as a separate group stylistically because of their close relationship in mood and theme as well as date; but their origin was earlier. From the date of *Andromeda* (August 1879) on to the end of his life, Hopkins pursued these two distinct styles, the one a continuation and further elaboration of the style that had characterized most of *The Wreck of the Deutschland* and the sonnets of 1877, the other this more chastened manner in which the last—as it happened, his last completed poem—was the fine sonnet to Bridges himself. Bridges was his main living link with the literary world, and his influence undoubtedly helped to keep Hopkins's poetry within, if only distantly within, speaking range of that world, yet it also helped preserve it from aesthetic cheapening—"cheapening," that is, in the sense in which his occasional pieces were cheapened, paradoxically, by his own lofty devotional spirit which could sometimes anaesthetize his taste.

From the beginning of 1877 to the end of Hopkins's life, then, dialogue between the friends continued, affectionate, admiring, and tough, each scarcely controlling his impulse to make the other over in his own image. Since the historic friendship of Wordsworth and Coleridge, there has hardly been such another creative friendship between poets or, for that matter, one so improbable. Opposed as they were in temperament and belief, Bridges detesting Catholicism and more particularly Jesuits, and Hopkins irresistibly impelled, though with little hope, to lecture Bridges on his immortal soul and officiously, as Bridges felt, to urge upon him prayer and almsgiving, both men willful and neither noticeably tolerant, still something common—integrity, personal charm among other things, but perhaps above all a love of poetry—preserved their mutual affection; and, what is of more importance to posterity, as poets each benefited measurably from their long association.

For the purpose of these chapters, the relevant benefits are those gained by Hopkins, and they consist of —to sum up once more—first, encouragement (amply if sometimes indirectly established by the surviving letters), which was a large and perhaps even a determining factor in his continuing to write at other than an unsuccessfully "popular" devotional level after *The Wreck of the Deutschland;* [13] and, second, criticism, some of which from the vantage point of nearly a century later appears illiberal but some of which at any date can be justified and which did, in any event, bring vividly before Hopkins's attention certain kinds of excellence that had not been vivid to him before and that were not those he could have found in the work of older or then more famous contemporaries—not in Tennyson or Browning, Swinburne, the Pre-Raphaelites, or even Arnold—and which led to development of the second, "plain" style that some readers now value more highly than any of his other work. These are our debt to Bridges as far as Hopkins is concerned, in addition to the preservation and ultimate publication of the poems themselves.

7

Three Baroque Sonnets

THE BAROQUE STYLE of Hopkins springs in some measure out of elation, elation arising from a sensuous response to beauty in nature, from a heightened spiritual awareness or insight, or even from "the roll, the rise, the carol" of poetic creation itself. It was his most native style, however, and it therefore offered itself to him as well for other than descriptive subjects and ebullient moods. The expansiveness that it involves he could permit himself to indulge provided the opposite side of his temperament were satisfied by severe thematic structure and subjects of single-minded dedication. This is the combination of elements that appeared in *The Wreck of the Deutschland,* and even there, in spite of the solemn and tragic materials, a spirit of elation is felt, not only in the triumphant close, but as an influence pervading the style throughout. Afterward, in poem after poem, elation and a kind of energy to which it gives rise spring into a fountain that falls in a shower of words. This impression is produced by the short poems so often that it comes to seem almost a formula. It is not a formula, however, but a *form,* originating in a particular mode of experience; and, to force the fountain image further, the shower ends its fall each time in a pool of thought infused by emotion, bright or dark-shadowed as may happen. It is this mercurial shape into which his experience forms itself that, among other differences, sets off much of the poetry of Hopkins from that of such another sensuous poet as Keats, who is never elated to the same degree, or at any rate whose elation, in his mature work, is never the main initiating force but is woven into the fabric of varied experience.

The Starlight Night is the prototype of this form in Hopkins. What "I" saw just now—today or tonight—its immediacy, its beauty, moves the emotions; and as this spontaneous feeling begins to cool into thought, from the cooling is crystallized out one or another statement, still infused with feeling, of spiritual significance reflecting an abiding faith. These poems are nearly all two-part sonnets, a form readily corresponding to these two stages of an experience, and they are all simple in the broad outlines of their thought. What I refer to as their baroque character is closely involved with their outward-turned energy and their spirit of elation, making itself felt through diction and syntax, indeed through the whole texture of the language. In Hopkins's last years, the form as well as the mood changed somewhat, yet fundamental likenesses remained. They may be seen most clearly by looking at individual poems directly, and for this purpose three of the greatest sonnets will serve best. As I do not wish merely to ride the hobbyhorse of the "baroque," however—single-valued answers to critical questions being always partly wrong, always producing distortion—the attempt will be made to examine these poems in the round, as poems, from here onward leaving the definition of their style sometimes to take care of itself.

I

Few if any English sonnets have been subjected to as much critical exegesis as has *The Windhover;* [1] yet, for all the ingenuity displayed, there remains at the heart of most of the discussions with which I am familiar an inconclusiveness, really a central fog that belongs, or so it seems to me, to the interpreter and does not answer to anything in the poem itself. The critical confusion may be traced in part to the circumstance of this poem's having been one of the earliest of Hopkins to receive concentrated attention. Interpretation began during the 1920's and 1930's, at a time when the novelty of his style still had our best critical minds more than half paralyzed with shock. Everything looked obscure; and, in consequence, everything was looked for except the simple and the obvious. False scents started during those years have continued to obscure many views of this poem. As the center of confusion lies in the numerous accounts of its literal statement, it is there that I shall begin; and on this literal meaning, as I may as well acknowledge to begin with, I am disposed to be dogmatic.

The Windhover conveys one logically and poetically possible central meaning, and only one in which all the parts of the poem and all the images find a place. Belt buckles and buckles in armor are not part of it; they belong to some other poem, by some other poet, "in another country." An important critical premise is involved.

The Coleridgean "reconciliation of opposites," I. A. Richards's "equilibrium of opposed impulses," Empson's "pregnant ambiguities," the more general "unification of the diverse"—these, or this, for they have the same psychological root and are substantially the same thing, is a principle made up of two terms, of which the first can be neglected no more properly than the second. Juxtaposition founded on the alphabet is insufficient to produce "reconciliation," a conception of which Richards's term "equilibrium" already represents a certain weakening; subtlety and rewarding complexity are not to be bought with a simple pun dignified under the name of "pregnant ambiguity." Not only this, but alternation in the mind of the reader, or indeterminate shifting between one meaning and another not congruent with it, accomplished in however generous a spirit of compliance with the poet or of mediation among his interpreters (or, as may sometimes be, out of caution about taking a stand) does not constitute "unification."

Ambiguity may, and does, have positive values, may provide durable aesthetic satisfaction, but only when the diverse or opposed elements are *significantly* and *actively* and in some depth "reconciled" in the imagination or thought. The ambiguities must even, I think, be such as can be entertained by the mind simultaneously and not merely by turns. Otherwise the result is apt to resemble those ingenious pictures one used to see that by trick showed you from one angle a tree or landscape but, turned another way, represented a nude figure or perhaps the devil himself. To observe that such-and-such a word—*buckles* it is in *The Windhover*—or this line or that image may mean either x or y and to conclude without more ado that it therefore means both is to ignore the requirement of *meaningful* reconciliation, which occurs only if something within the poem transforms x and y together into a Z, or when a new enrichment of meaning x is produced by the presence of meaning y. Otherwise one is merely seeing double.

In a letter of 1883 to Mowbray Baillie, Hopkins wrote of a discovery he believed he had made concerning the presence in the lyric passages of Greek tragedy of what he called an "overthought" and an "underthought," the first being, roughly, the paraphrasable, overt meaning, the other "the underthought, conveyed chiefly in the choice of metaphors etc used and often only half realised by the poet himself." The unusual feature of this observation is Hopkins's conclusion that the underthought does not "necessarily" have a connection with "the subject in hand" though usually it has and usually it is "suggested by some circumstance of the scene or of the story." He rephrased the idea: "Perhaps what I ought to say is that the underthought is commonly an echo or shadow of the overthought, something like canons and repetitions in music, treated in a different manner, but that sometimes it may be independent of it. I find this same principle of composition in St. James' and St. Peter's and St. Jude's Epistles, an undercurrent of thought governing the choice of images used" (III, 252–253). These terms have been applied back to Hopkins's own poems by writers who use them as a warrant for reading into an ambiguous passage two or more meanings even when these are mutually irreconcilable. Todd Bender [2] recently discussed Hopkins's theory as an anticipation of later critical interpretations of the odes of Pindar and then applied it back to the study of *The Wreck of the Deutschland;* others, without going into the classical questions, have applied the two terms to various other poems, including *The Windhover.* Hopkins's theory, however, belongs to the Dublin period, when his profession took him back to the study of Greek literature; it was a new discovery to him then, and it seems pretty clear that it did not occur to him at that time even in retrospect that he himself had written in this way.

Though it had not been noticed much in criticism earlier than the present century and might therefore have struck Hopkins as a new discovery, a continuing image pattern *connected* with the theme of a poem (as he says it usually is) is certainly no novelty, whether its relevance to the theme is explicit or is brought about through submerged metaphor. The latter may be anything from the heavenly stars and storms in Hopkins's own *Deutschland* (storm is literally present but stars are not) to the employment by Herrick, as an example, in *Corinna's Going A-Maying,* of a scattering of religious images in a poem assuredly not religious. But even this latter is not really unconnected with the subject. Though a metaphorical image pattern brought in from outside the immediate frame of reference, it is used to confer a half-ironic, half-serious blessing upon the subject itself, for the submerged metaphors of that poem are a way of saying that, in the mood of May Day morning, the life of nature and the senses is for the moment all the religion one needs.

If this is what Hopkins really meant by the occasional underthought *un*connected with the subject, that is well and good; and I rather imagine that perhaps it is. His one illustration, from Aeschylus, as well as that brought forward by Bender from Pindar, falls into this class of connection by means of submerged metaphor or metaphorical association. If he meant *really* unconnected, however, I think he was wrong; the principle will not hold as an aesthetic principle, and it is also inapplicable to his own work. Now it is true that a single image may be brought in from outside the theater of discourse that is relevant to a passing moment in the progress of a poem but unconnected with the theme as a whole. Nothing, in fact, is more common: Hamlet has his "sea of troubles" without his play's having to be the watery *Tempest;* the "sour scythe" and the sloe are images of this sort in the *Deutschland.* However, if there is introduced a *continuing* pattern of recurrent images related to each other but not to the subject of the work, this pattern sets up competition; the secondary thread of discourse breaks the essential unity of the poem unless the two can be brought into a meaningful harmony, which means that some connection is felt to exist. Counterpoint in music may bring together two different melodies, but only provided they have significant harmonic points in common, or, more exactly, a common harmonic foundation; two record players sounding out simultaneously with different chance-chosen pieces may be said to produce a happening but it is not counterpoint. The parallel here with poetry is an exact one.

Hopkins may not have thought out or expressed quite fully his discovery when he defined his new terms "overthought" and "underthought." They are nice terms and might well be adopted more widely for critical use; but I do not conceive them as telling us anything new

149

about his own or other poetry, and we need to know what we are going to mean by them, for the terms themselves do not answer the question of what relation, if any, we are going to predicate between two strains in a poem when we conceive that two strains may be present.

In his own poetry, Hopkins was more than willing to employ a pun when its double meaning might be "to one thing" significantly "wrought" but not when two meanings fractured a poem or scattered it on the wind or could be contemplated in the reader's mind only by turns. In *The Windhover,* to return to the specific instance, the instinct of critics to hover around the word *buckle* is nevertheless sound, for that word is the structural center of the sonnet, the pivot on which it turns.

I caught this morning morning's minion, king-
  dom of daylight's dauphin, dapple-dawn-drawn Fal-
    con, in his riding
  Of the rolling level underneath him steady air, and
    striding
High there, how he rung upon the rein of a wimpling
    wing
In his ecstasy! then off, off forth on swing,
  As a skate's heel sweeps smooth on a bow-bend: the
    hurl and gliding
  Rebuffed the big wind. My heart in hiding
Stirred for a bird,—the achieve of, the mastery of the
    thing!

Brute beauty and valour and act, oh, air, pride, plume,
    here
  Buckle! AND the fire that breaks from thee then, a
    billion
Times told lovelier, more dangerous, O my chevalier!

  No wonder of it: shéer plód makes plough down
    sillion

150

Shine, and blue-bleak embers, ah my dear,
   Fall, gall themselves, and gash gold-vermilion.

Something buckles and something breaks through.
This is the explicit central statement. Readers who
buckle belts often neglect its second half though Hopkins capitalized the AND between the parts. It is neither
armor nor belts that *buckle* or *break,* nor is it the insignificant bicycle wheel that Empson found mysteri-
ously compatible with military buckles. The images suggested are of an altogether different order of magnitude.
Deck or bulkhead or plates of a ship buckle before fire
breaks through; walls of a building or tower buckle before they crash or burn. In *The Windhover,* the subject of *buckle* is explicit: Brute beauty, valor, and act,
air, pride, and plume—universals, that is, abstracted
from the concrete substance of the preceding lines so as
to stand now for the whole of natural creation seen in
its aspects of beauty and mastery. This world of natural
beauty and power "buckles"—collapses—and *the fire* of
the spiritual world, more specifically, of Christ, *breaks*
through. This is the climactic statement, made (so at
least it seems to me) with unmistakable directness.
Buckle and *break* control all the sestet as it subsides
from the climax of spiritual illumination to the everyday imagery of the conclusion.
   The Windhover is thus one of several variations on a
theme that occupied Hopkins between February and
June 1877 and occasionally afterward. Other sonnets,
particularly *The Starlight Night* and *Spring,* display not
merely a similar mode of feeling, but exactly the same
pattern of thought: a progression from the concrete
beauty of nature described in the octave to its spiritual
analogue or counterpart or significance in the sestet. As
is so often true in Hopkins's poetry, the train of thought
is straightforward, explicit, and simple; only the execution is complex.
   The poem is addressed "To Christ our Lord," and

though after the subtitle Christ is not directly addressed till the tenth line, he is prepared for in the first by epithets given to the falcon. The bird is morning's favorite or darling (*minion* being here used in its earlier, not its later derogatory sense); he is the "kingdom of daylight's" crown prince—the Son, not the King or Father. *Dauphin* is more than an automatic bit of alliteration; it counts for the meaning and for unity. The falcon is not, however, so much a symbol of Christ as a momentary analogue for the duration of the poem—indeed, perhaps not even quite that but simply a foreshadowing image and, in its primary natural sense, the originating factor in the experience of the poem. Though the power and beauty of its flight make it prince of the morning scene, it is not more than a bird, and it is described throughout the octave in the language of the material world, the royal metaphor being in its immediate sense only a metaphor descriptive of the bird's dominance in the scene.

But the sight of its power and beauty awakens the poet, as he says, again explicitly: "My heart [which had been] in hiding / Stirred for a bird,—the achieve of, the mastery of the thing!" Beneath the word *hiding* I hear *hibernating*, but that may be only a chance individual association. At any rate, the poet's heart has been stagnant, in that state common to moods of depression in which one is unable even to wish to be moved—as, a year or two later, referring to Christ, Hopkins told Bridges, "The only person that I am in love with seldom, especially now, *stirs my heart*" (I, 66; my italics). The magnificence of the windhover in flight, however, does stir his heart, and the heart's awakening heralds the turn of the sonnet. The classic and closely parallel representation in English verse of this change of heart is that of the Ancient Mariner, when out of the midst of his wretchedness ("slimy things lived on; and so did I"), he suddenly sees how beautiful are the water snakes. Their beauty stirs his heart to love and admiration, and at once the *particular* creatures—mere snakes—are transformed for the beholder into *universals*, the "happy living things" (failure to recognize this essential step in the progression of the experience is responsible for part of the confusion over *The Windhover*). It is this transformation that then brings the Mariner to spiritual recognition of God: "O happy living things! no tongue / Their beauty might declare: / A spring of love gushed from my heart / And I blessed them unaware. . . . The self-same moment I could pray."

Now in *The Windhover* likewise, under the stimulus of the heart awakened by the singular beauty of a bird in the morning sky, the particular vanishes as a particular, transformed before the awakened vision into the universals "Brute beauty and valour and act, oh, air, pride, plume." This abstract line, which prepares for the "turn" of the sonnet, has itself followed naturally from the elation sparked by the bird's beauty and mastery in flight, for to that overflowing spirit, naturally expansive, a single bright morning today expands into all brightness, all bright mornings. It should not be, but I believe it is, necessary to add that *brute* here is not to be understood as *brutal* but simply as a generic epithet for the animal kingdom in nature. It has been taken to represent such things as the evil part of the sensuous world which the poet must shun, but this introduces something new and irrelevant into the poem and something incompatible with the rest of the line. The word is used merely as we say "man and brute" or "man and beast" ("beast" is the slightly more traditional word for it, but beast can hardly serve as an adjective, which is what the line requires).

It is this whole world, then, of physical beauty and mastery that "here" (at this point of time, now, hereupon) *buckles,* "AND [as the world of matter collapses before the poet's vision and the world of spirit takes its place, the dramatic moment is marked by emphatic type] the fire" of Christ "breaks" through, "a billion times" more lovely and more "dangerous." Only now does the poet address Christ directly: "the fíre that bréaks from thée then . . . O my chevalier." In view of Hopkins's interest in shipwrecks, I suggest that the half-submerged image is of timbers or plates buckling in a fire at sea. Such an image increases the significance while it diminishes the abruptness of the epithet *dangerous,* applied immediately afterward to Christ. The image need not be so specific, however; all that is necessary is that it represent a buckling and a fire of awesome magnitude.

From this point on, the tension that has risen to a climax subsides, and the pitch of the poem drops to a quiet conclusion with the imagery remaining still under the shadow, partly of *buckle* but mainly of *break.* "No wonder" this transformation occurs, Hopkins says —the vision of spiritual beauty, that is, opening out from that of the physical—when the breaking open of the most drab things in life may reveal brightness within. Mere labor of ploughing breaks open the earth, replacing its dull dried surface with a shining furrow; and "blue-bleak" (ash-covered) coals of an apparently dead fire fall apart, breaking open to reveal bright living fire within (the coals of this image are presumably the very large pieces often used in English fireplaces; in this kind of fire the breaking open of the mass is particularly noticeable). Two lines of an early fragment of Hopkins's verse foreshadow this image as well as that of *buckle,* though the latter word itself is not used:

Death's bones fell in with sudden clank
As wrecks of minèd embers will (*Journals,* p. 35).

Some readers take the preceding image to mean that the labor of ploughing polishes the ploughshare,[3] with a moral to be drawn of self-sacrificing labor for God. This reading, as well as the moral drawn from it, ap-

154

pears to me less in keeping with the rest of the poem than the one I have given, and the latter receives further support from Hopkins's observation of nature and use of language elsewhere. During this same summer of 1877, he used the word *plough* to mean *ploughland,* or, more accurately, a ploughed field, in *Pied Beauty,* "Landscape plotted and pieced—fold, fallow, and plough"; and in an earlier notebook he had specifically recorded the visible change in ploughed earth, "the near hill *glistening* with *very bright* newly turned sods" (*Journals,* p. 133; my italics). This reading is also in close keeping with the main analogy of the poem, that of inner beauty revealed through a *buckling* and revelatory *breaking open.*

To return briefly to the octave. Apart from the kingdom-minion-dauphin epithets, all the imagery describes physical movement, action characterized by grace, beauty of form, and easy mastery, all made up of lovely curves. The lines do not express conflict or pain, as some writers maintain. In his elation the spectator both watches and imaginatively shares the flight (*empathy* is an offensive word but perhaps unavoidable). The image of the falcon's "riding" is not the relatively passive one of a rider upon a horse: it is the more direct and thrilling one of "riding the wind" while going his own way, circling, with one wing as pivot, in a smooth curve like that of a horse circling at the end of a fixed rein; movement, finally, smooth and graceful and easy as that of an accomplished skater rounding the turn of a figure eight. Even if the poem as a whole were not clear, it is mysterious to me that some readers have missed the soaring elation of mood, to which most of the language contributes: morning, dauphin of all the kingdom of daylight, dappled dawn, riding, striding high, circling in "ecstasy"; then, with utter freedom, "off" swinging in a new direction. The "hurl and gliding" in flight "rebuff the big wind" not in fight, but in the play and delight of pure mastery. All this is summed up in *achieve* and *mastery, brute beauty,* and the rest; and the "turn" of the sonnet is not to a contrary mood but to a deeper and more thoughtful level of the same one.

In the outline of its thought, then, *The Windhover* is simple, direct, and explicit. Its complexities lie, on the one hand, in the elaboration of the visual imagery interwoven with elaborately echoing patterns of sound, and, on the other, in the play between two counter-pointed sets of opposites. The dominant pair is that of the material and the spiritual, which are expressly brought together by the dauphin-Son parallel and, more literally, by the primary theme of the poet's being stirred by one into more intense awareness of the other. Within the poem, however, these opposites are not in conflict; material beauty is seen wholly as a good, open-ing the heart to the incomparably higher good of Christ.

Of the second pair of opposites one is explicit and major, while the other appears only in shadowy, muted form. The opposition of beauty and terror (or pain), explicitly present in so much of Hopkins's writing, is present here only by implication. The two are not evenly balanced; they are not reconciled either, nor do they need to be. They are brought together in an uneasy harmony through the idea of power in the "mastery" of the bird and the "lovelier, more dangerous" fire of Christ. In *The Windhover* terror or pain is no more than an undertone, the habitually accompanying shadow of all life even at its happiest, reflected here only in one epithet of Christ; in the "gall" and the "gash" of coals against one another, which are only a means to the breaking forth of living beauty from outwardly inani-mate matter (they may possibly also faintly suggest the self-hurt of self-sacrifice that results in spiritual bright-ness, but if so this is very faint indeed, for the inanimate coals are not even remotely personified and any hint of pain is extremely remote if present at all); possibly, but only just possibly, in the known predatory charac-ter as well as the daring mastery of the hawk and the poet's "hiding" heart. Of this last I am especially doubt-ful, however. If the predatory and other painful asso-ciations were actively involved, I think the bird's movements would be described differently: there would be some hint of its diving—a direct, swooping move-ment downward—whereas in the poem all is high and free, soaring and circling, the bird presented as if in pure delight of movement and mastery in the morning air. There are no straight lines in this description; and the "hiding" heart is not pounced upon; it is not even caught up, as it were, by Chaucer's eagle; it rises of itself in delighted admiration, but to behold, not to fly. *The Windhover* thus is not at all a poem of conflict or, as some have even thought, of renunciation and suffer-ing. The faint, shadowy, unresolved suggestion of terror and pain merely gives an edge to the overriding spirit of breathless admiration.

One of the many objections raised by Ivor Winters in his discussion of Hopkins (with particular reference to *The Windhover*) is against "the usual procedure of Hopkins . . . to hurl miscellaneous images at his sub-ject from all sides, rather than to develop one of them fully." It is true that his habit was not usually to con-centrate in each poem upon the systematic exploration of a single image. Few of our older poets, in fact, do this regularly, and Hopkins's images are not on that account miscellaneous or indiscriminately hurled. In *The Windhover* they are woven into a varied pattern but a pattern all the same. Flying, after all, or hovering apparently motionless in air, looks like a defying of gravity, whatever physicists may have to say of it, and it therefore has the appearance of successful risk and daring; animals do have the look, sometimes, of enjoy-ing pure sensation, however otherwise an antiromantic naturalist may explain the appearance. The imagery of *The Windhover* simply puts these and other obvious matters together: minion-dauphin-Son-chevalier-Christ; material beauty and mastery buckling and breaking open to show spiritual beauty beyond—a principle then illustrated by two everyday experiences.

All the images of circling vividly describe the actual movement of the bird and in addition convey the elation produced by the sight. The movement of the verse conveys this too, particularly from the third line on. The first two lines suggest excitement in their reduplicated sounds, but metrically and melodically they are somewhat indeterminate, and in these respects the verse does not get into its really expressive stride till the third line, where one begins to feel the remarkable combination of smoothness and flexibility of tempo that characterizes the rest of the poem. What Hopkins said of a later piece, that "it is most carefully timed in *tempo rubato*" (I, 246), is equally true here. It is in the musical sense a true *rubato*, not casual liberty to slow down or accelerate at will but dynamic flexibility or elasticity of timing in which a *rallentando* itself seems to engender the energy of the subsequent acceleration: time robbed here is paid back there and balance is restored.[4] Mastery of *rubato* in this sense gives life to poetic rhythm wherever it occurs, and in *The Windhover* (after the first two lines) it is peculiarly expressive, reflecting in turn the subtle alterations of movement and feeling.

These complexities are enough. Richness of symbolic meaning cannot be had merely by reading into the poem a mechanical, dictionary-flavored ambiguity in *buckle*. For the interpretation of *The Windhover* at least, an inveterate commitment to irony and paradox is apt to defeat itself by producing only disjointed structure and discordant associations that destroy, by neutralizing, the resonance of the poem. Quite a good deal of the resonance of *The Windhover* derives from simplicity of theme, clarity of structure, and smoothness of movement. This is true even though the final effect is of an extremely complex poem.

It had not originally been my intention to enter into much polemical discussion of other interpretations of the poem; it seemed wiser merely to set forth as directly as possible a reading of it as a coherent whole in which all the parts find a place. Other readings are unconvincing to me because they seem to make of the poem a series of disjointed statements or images or "image clusters," which, taken together, are aesthetically and intellectually unintelligible and are held together by no unity or clarity of either thought or mood: they turn the poem into a conglomerate instead of an organism, or else they secure a factitious unity by ignoring half the poem. One central disputed point, however, teases me into a further comment.

In an extended essay, running to some thirty pages, "What Does *The Windhover* Mean?" Raymond V. Schoder offers the most elaborate, and one of the most widely adopted, readings that I have seen of lines 9 and 10. According to this, the substantives beginning with *brute beauty* are explained as vocatives and *buckle* as an imperative. Such a reading affects and raises difficulties with respect directly to all that follows and indirectly to all that precedes; it is therefore crucial. Father Schoder cites the dictionary sense of *buckle* as "to prepare self for a contest or undertaking; hence to apply self with vigor to a task; to come to close quarters, grapple, engage," and after quoting from Shakespeare "In single combat thou shalt buckle with me," he interprets Hopkins's words to mean something like: O beauty, valor . . . plume, come and buckle ("engage, grapple") "here" (in my heart). To this there are several objections. There is the difficulty of the word *buckle*'s (in this sense) requiring either an object or a completing prepositional phrase, for which *here* seems inadequate; and there is the much greater difficulty and awkwardness in the shift from the second person plural imperative to the third person followed by another second person—this time a singular, *thee*, whose reference must be different from the persons previously addressed—with, in addition, the two

159

thus incompatible parts of the sentence joined by a big, normally coordinating AND. It is as if one Gerard should say, "John and Jane and Jessie, button your coats, AND the fire is burning yóu [Gérard]," the last addressed to himself as "you," that is, or to his heart, not to John, Jane, and Jessie. This is a muddle that we should not expect Hopkins to be guilty of, and it is made no better if one retains this reading of the first clause but interprets *thee* as either the bird or Christ instead of himself.

Father Schoder's main argument for this confused construction is that the abstract nouns must be vocative and not nominative because the last of them, *plume,* is followed by a comma, and "one hardly puts a comma *at the end* of a series of nominatives, separating the final member from the common indicative verb" (p. 296). This principle is indeed generally applicable now that the basis of punctuation has become more frequently grammatical than rhetorical and marks of punctuation also, by custom, sparser; but it was by no means true in Hopkins's day, when punctuation marks were sprinkled more plentifully and were still most often governed by rhetorical considerations. Even today the presence of *here* could easily justify a preceding comma, and in the nineteenth century, after such a series of nominatives as "brute beauty and . . . plume," the comma, representing a slight pause, would have been perfectly normal, as Hopkins's own practice elsewhere demonstrates. I have observed several other passages in his poetry in which a comma separates subject from verb, and there may be more if one looked for them. In the early *Escorial,* with much less reason than in *The Windhover* (with no reason at all, as a matter of fact), *frame* is separated from its verb in the third stanza:

Then fail'd the tongue; the poor collapsing frame,
Hung like a wreck that flames not billows beat—

In the *Deutschland* there is the line, "But Gertrude, lily, and Luther, are two of a town" (stanza 20); and another

instance, "these thy daughters / And five-livèd and leavèd
favour and pride, / Are sisterly sealed . . ." (stanza 23).
All of these might be frowned upon under today's schoolroom standards; that in *The Windhover* is easily defensible
even now. The interpretation of the poem must therefore be
arrived at on other grounds than that of punctuation.[5] A
reading of the ninth line as a series of direct objects of an
imperative *buckle* has also been suggested, but this produces a sentence quite as incoherent as do vocatives. These
are not Hopkins's kind of syntactic freedom; and, even
supposing them conceivable on that ground, they do not in
the end give us an organically coherent poem.

Schoder and a number of other writers also argue that
the sestet must be addressed to the poet's own heart and
not to Christ, mainly on the ground that the expression "ah
my dear" (line 13) could not appropriately refer to Christ.
This view mistakes Hopkins's temperament and the occasionally surprising informality in his relations with Deity; it
was probably a matter of principle with him that he should
speak so in his sermons as well as occasionally elsewhere in
the poems; in a passage to Bridges quoted earlier, he spoke
of being "in love with" Christ. But for the particular phrase
in *The Windhover*, he also had the precedent of "ah my
deare" used similarly in George Herbert's *Love* (III).

II

The two later sonnets often grouped with *The Windhover* present fewer problems of interpretation. Though
in style and imagery they are more startling and are so
much denser in texture that they might have appeared
more difficult, they have in fact been subject to widely
divergent readings only on minor points; their sense, as
a whole, is plain. The three together, I suppose it would
be agreed, are the greatest of Hopkins's baroque sonnets. Bewilderingly rich in sensuous detail and in curli-
cues of thought wound into a simple primary statement,
they have the character evidenced in some of the great-

est baroque painting, that of uniting ebullience of execution with dignity and, in the second poem of the three, even severity of theme. Because of this, they are probably—the two later ones especially—the fullest expression of those incompletely reconciled aspects of Hopkins's temperament, the sensuous and the ascetic.

Spelt from Sibyl's Leaves is a poem remarkable on several counts but most of all, perhaps, for its fusion of emotional intensity and vast religio-cosmic statement within the narrow limits of a sonnet, though, to be sure, that form had to be somewhat enlarged for the purpose. When it was written, Hopkins believed that even on paper it was "the longest sonnet ever made"; and if it is read as he directed, it becomes even longer. "Remember what applies to all my verse," he said: "its performance is not reading with the eye but loud, leisurely, poetical (not rhetorical) recitation, with long rests, long dwells on the rhyme and other marked syllables, and so on." "This sonnet," he added, "essays effects almost musical" and "shd. be almost sung: it is most carefully timed in *tempo rubato*" (I, 245, 246).

Earnest, earthless, equal, attuneable, ˡ vaulty, volumi-
    nous. . . stupendous
Evening strains to be tíme's vást, ˡ womb-of-all, home-
    of-all, hearse-of-all night.
Her fond yellow hornlight wound to the west, ˡ her wild
    hollow hoarlight hung to the height
Waste; her earliest stars, earlstars, ˡ stárs principal, over-
    bend us,
Fíre-feáturing heaven. For earth ˡ her being has un-
    bound; her dapple is at an end, as-
tray or aswarm, all throughther, in throngs; ˡ self ín self
    steepèd and páshed—quíte
Disremembering, dísmémbering ˡ áll now. Heart, you
    round me right
With: Oúr évening is over us; oúr night ˡ whélms,
    whélms, ánd will end us.

Only the beakleaved boughs dragonish ⎸ damask the
    tool-smooth bleak light; black,
Ever so black on it. Oúr tale, O oúr oracle! ⎸ Lét life,
    wáned, ah lét life wind
Off hér once skéined stained véined varíety ⎸ upon, áll
    on twó spools; párt, pen, páck
Now her áll in twó flocks, twó folds—black, white; ⎸
    right, wrong; reckon but, reck but, mind
But thése two; wáre of a wórld where bút these ⎸ twó
    tell, each off the óther; of a rack
Where, selfwrung, selfstrung, sheathe- and shelterless, ⎸
    thóughts agaínst thoughts ín groans grínd.[6]

Hopkins's directions to Bridges raise a question. If
the poem is to be "almost sung," with "long dwells" on
rhymes even when the line is run over, we shall have a
kind of reading associated in modern times only with
the outer suburbs of poetry where Vachel Lindsay and
his brothers have resided, a reading not natural to the
syllabic-accentual rhythms of English poetry. It thus involves a break with tradition as great as that of sprung
rhythm itself, and indeed it almost forces us to conceive
this verse as a new art form somewhat resembling that
which Yeats endeavored to create when he would have
had verses spoken to the psalter, or like Edith Sitwell's
Façade spoken to Walton's music; but Hopkins's work
was without the aid rendered the later poems by the
musical accompaniment, which to the ear at once marks
their mode as a distinct one, by that cue at once preparing the mind to accept a new convention. Whether or
not his directions, written to Bridges less than three
years before his death though he was now applying
them back to all his verse, represented his conception,
from the beginning, of the proper reading of it cannot
now be determined with certainty. Probably they did
not, in spite of the instructions for *rallentando* that he
had sprinkled among earlier poems. The *Eurydice*, he
had written in 1878, must not be read "slovenly" with

the eyes but with the ears, "as if the paper were declaiming it at you. For instance the line 'she had come from a cruise training seamen' read without stress and declaim is mere Lloyd's Shipping Intelligence; properly read it is quite a different thing. Stress is the life of it" (I, 51–52). Hopkins had never shrunk from "declaim" or the oracular when it was warranted, and from the period of the *Deutschland* on he was evidently influenced more than most contemporary poets by the prevailing style of musical performance described in chapter 4. Undoubtedly, however, the influence of the art of music increased after about 1880, when he had become thoroughly engrossed in music, was composing airs, and had invented, as he said, "a new [musical] style, something standing to ordinary music as sprung rhythm to common rhythm: it employs quarter tones" (I, 103).

For *Spelt from Sibyl's Leaves*, however, the direction "almost sung" is scarcely needed, for the lines cannot easily be read in any other way. The first three almost sing themselves, and they do so without too much mannerism, for their timing is unmistakable, the sonorous spoken beats falling with almost metronomic regularity as the opening series of parallel epithets perforce establishes a kind of chant (the *rubato* mainly comes later). The beats are established so clearly that even the pause replacing one of them before the close of the first line—the equivalent of a whole measure's rest in music, "vaulty, voluminous, . . . [the marks of suspension indicate a rest] stupendous,"—falls into place without oddity and with remarkable expressiveness, for what it does, in effect, is to propel the final word, reinforced by the cumulative weight of all the preceding epithets in the line which have seemed to pile up during the pause, into the movement of the following line. The only drawback is one for which Hopkins was not responsible, namely, that *stupendous*, the word upon which the movement hinges, is not the word it once was, our increasingly shrill use of superlatives having since his day weakened it sadly, so that for it to count as it should, one has to make a deliberate effort to clear it of trivial associations, a misfortune similar to though not quite so bad as that which befell Keats's phrase (in the *Ode on Melancholy*) "and let her rave" in consequence of the later coarsening not of "rave" only, but of the whole phrase "let her rave."

In the first three and a fraction lines of *Spelt from Sibyl's Leaves* are conveyed both the visual and the emotional impact of the beautiful but also abysmal coming of night. About the visual images of the third line, however, there has been some dispute:

Her fond yellow hornlight wound to the west, | her wild
    hollow hoarlight hung to the height
Waste . . .

Leavis tells us that "of course" the "yellow hornlight" describes the setting moon and "hoarlight" the "cold, hard starlight," a reading that has been followed by many. It is not quite "of course," however. As neither moon nor stars *waste* with the advance of evening, even if the moon is represented as setting, Leavis must, and does, ignore that word as if it did not exist, in spite of its prominence and in spite of the fact that doing so decapitates the sentence; this will not do. Moreover, another meaning, one that includes *waste*, is both more exactly observed from nature and more in keeping with the sense and mood of the poem. As evening advances, both the warm yellow afterglow of sunset in the west and, overhead, the less friendly and less human, more cosmic-looking "wild hollow" pale light in the dome of the upper sky "waste" (i.e., fade) before the oncoming dark. Then, as this light drains away, the stars do explicitly appear, but, far from wasting, they are bright, "fire-featuring heaven." [7]

In this sonnet the material world and its spiritual analogue are not so formally separated in octave and sestet as they were in *The Windhover*. From the start, evening is more than the single, or even the generic, evening of nature; it is immediately "time's" night toward which she "strains," and the heaven that is "fire-featured" by the stars is spiritual heaven as well as sky. *Feature* is a significant word, carrying, as it usually does in Hopkins, the implication of individual identity: the pattern of stars maps the identifiable face or form of the heavens, in contrast with the annihilating change going on below. As evening advances on the natural level, earth, her "dapple" gone, becomes undifferentiated darkness except where individual leaves are still outlined sharply and ominously against the faint remaining light in the sky. Like the phrases "fire-featuring heaven" and "wild hollow hoarlight," the line "only the beak-leaved boughs dragonish damask the tool-smooth bleak light; black . . ." is scarcely to be matched in its union of visual precision and imaginative suggestiveness, here bringing into focus the threat which is the theme of the poem. Rarely, too, does a sound pattern—"beak-leaved" and "bleak light" and "black" played off against "drag[onish] damask" and the onomatopoetic "tool-smooth"—so dramatically reinforce what is said.

There is a peculiar split, however, between the ostensible statement of the poem and its emotional impact, and more strange is the fact that this does not seem to injure but if anything reinforces its power. The poem asserts that ultimately man has but two choices, right and wrong; and, this being so, of course the literal statement offers hope of a right choice. But in the tone and the direction of the poem there is no hope. It is not merely that the importance of choosing right is emphasized by vivid warning of the consequence of a wrong choice; it is that the possibility of the right and hence of a fortunate outcome is scarcely contemplated and is nowhere present in the imagery except momentarily in the stars, which vanish from the poem as soon as they appear, and that except for the lovely phrase "fire-featuring heaven," which describes them and does carry more beauty than threat, all the most powerful language and imagery of the poem convey the "black," not the "white," alternative. The mood of the first half-dozen lines is a complex one. There is some elation in it as well as solemnity; there is also a foresense of doom, but as if of doom accepted, so that one seems a part of that march of doom itself and not only its victim. The elevation is therefore not that of hope but of prophetic recognition and foreknowledge. As the poem advances, however, all elation fades away with the fading light as foreknowledge passes imaginatively into experienced doom. The conclusion then comes as an unmatched expression of pure reflexive, self-torturing pain, "a rack / Where, selfwrung, selfstrung, sheathe- and shelterless, thoughts against thoughts in groans grind," a line so powerful and felt to be so all-encompassing that no influence from the stars early in the poem survives. The power is felt in spite of and not, I think, because of the distorted stresses indicated by Hopkins, though these do, in the last four or five lines, contribute to the measured rhythm that beats into the mind the sense of doom.

It is not the concluding line alone that produces the appalling effect. Throughout the poem the handling of the prevailing and unifying image of evening is in keeping with this tone. Though some of the opening epithets are neutral or even beneficent—notably "attune-able," "home-of-all," and, at least nominally, "womb-of-all" (though in fact this latter suggests not so much the fruitful as the all-enveloping womb)—the whole progression of the poem is toward night, and from the beginning it is the final night, "time's" night that "will end us," no mere portion of the diurnal cycle and no prelude either to eternal day. This theme begins to be apparent early, when "hearse-of-all" appears last and most prominent among the opening epithets. "Wild hollow hoarlight," too, is poetically so superior as nearly to obliterate the preceding, more friendly "fond yellow hornlight"; but both, in any event, "waste." The draining away of color into pure form is a natural imaginative analogue of the change from transient to permanent.

The statement of the poem, then, is about choice but its spirit is not of choice but of doom. I do not quite know why this contradiction should not injure the poem, but to me it does not seem a flaw, possibly because it corresponds to a recognizable human experience in which the intellect may conceive an alternative that is without reality to the imagination and emotions. In the poem, it is as if this contradiction itself were felt as the real implicit theme.

The flaws, or at any rate what strike me as flaws, in *Spelt from Sibyl's Leaves* are elsewhere and real, though they only momentarily weaken the effect of the whole. Two or three lines or half lines I think must be among the worst Hopkins ever wrote. In love of wordplay, he is not outdone by the Elizabethans; and in the artifice of sound patterns, Euphues is Simple Simon beside him. The motives, however, were mainly different. With the Elizabethans one has the feeling that modern English was still so fresh that its resources had not yet been fully explored. The rhymes and puns had not all been made in their modern forms—or at any rate not too often—and the sounds of the language had not all been matched up. Consequently, even in their most labored wordplay, something of the air of discovery survives; its general freshness is still felt though the particular *jeu* has grown stale. In Hopkins, however, play of sound and word is usually the result of an overriding passion for unity or, as Charles Williams called it, reversing the terms, "the unity of his passion," in which "the intense apprehension of the subject provides two or more necessary words almost at the same time." Referring especially to such alliteration as, in the *Deutschland*, "Thou hast bound bones . . . fastened me flesh," Williams explained, "It is as if the imagination, seeking for expression, had found both verb and substantive at one rush, had begun almost to say them at once, and had separated them only because the intellect had reduced the original unity into divided but related sounds."[8] This way of describing one of the obvious features of Hopkins's style may appear fanciful, but it does draw attention to what most readers feel most of the time, the organic rather than mechanical character of the interplay of sound and sense.

But there are lapses, most notably when Hopkins's love of ingenuity—probably pride in ingenuity, too—tries to justify itself by a kind of schoolmen's logic and produces only a strained and frigid result. In *Spelt from Sibyl's Leaves*, frigidity sets in with, though not as a consequence of, the *rubato* that follows the opening lines, at which point Hopkins departs on one of the philological cruises that he loved: "her earliest stars, earlstars, stars principal." "Stars principal" has the look of being present as a gloss on the preceding, as if the poet felt obliged to explain that "earl" is not an irresponsible sound echo but has logic behind it. All that this third appositive does, however, is to chill further the already chilled passage, for, led astray as he sometimes could be by the sound track, Hopkins refused to see how deeply irrelevant this verbal excursion really is, so irrelevant to the main line of the poem that the availability of a logical, or philological, justification for "earl" is seen to be pure chance, and its being brought forward at all merely emphasizes the irrelevance.[9] A few lines later another lapse of the same kind occurs, only it is worse, in "Disremembering, dismembering." It is worse because of the undignified as well as irrelevant associations of the colloquial and somewhat childish first word, the seeming inaccuracy in meaning of the second—*dismember* does not suggest the *fading out* of distinctions between objects as evening deepens but the *scattering* of fragments, which leaves them visually distinct—and the prominence given to both by the fact that each—even, unnaturally, the second—carries two metrical stresses: "Dísremémbering, dísmémbering." Most of this part of the poem, except for the fifth line, which is a fine one, suffers from these lapses and also from a good deal of rhythmic distortion. All comes right again, however, in the simplicity of "Oúr évening is over us," and the tone of the poem does not thereafter sink. I do not much like the words "Heart, you round me right / With," [10] yet their rhythm and dynamics—their musical dynamics, that is—have power to round the corner of the line and bring all to bear upon what follows with "oúr évening," in a way somewhat like that in which, at the beginning, "stupendous" and the pause preceding it bring the weight of the first line to bear upon the same word, *evening*. Evening, of course, is the main thematic image of the poem; and though the word itself occurs only twice, each time the highly original technical resources brought to bear on its context heighten the magnitude and portentousness of the image.

For anyone acquainted with the published portions of Hopkins's devotional writings it is scarcely possible to doubt that the "rack" of suffering in the last line is, literally and theologically, Hell.[11] The sense of the illimitable throughout the poem, however, and the overwhelming sense of fate in the final expression of pain transcend any narrow theological threat, and we are left at the end of the poem with a vast, an all-encompassing universe of approaching darkness and abstract pain. Faulty or not, this poem is one of Hopkins's greatest achievements. I am not sure that the sonnet form has ever produced such massive effect in so small a space.

III

Though he himself did not explicitly connect them, the late sonnet *That Nature is a Heraclitean Fire and of the comfort of the Resurrection* is a natural companion to *Spelt from Sibyl's Leaves*. Hopkins liked to work with associated and contrasted pairs. Even the early *Heaven-Haven* was to have had its counterpart; the longing for safety and repose in the haven "out of the swing of the sea" was to have been answered by its opposite, the wish for action and danger: "I must hunt down the prize . . ." in "those wastes where the ice-blocks tilt and fret, / Not so far from the pole." Among the finished poems, the "Leaden" and "Golden" Echoes are carefully matched; *The Candle Indoors* has its express "companion" in *The Lantern out of Doors;* and, not quite so symmetrically ordered but still clearly related in more than a bird's name, are *The Sea and the Skylark* and *The Caged Skylark. Heraclitean Fire,* like *Sibyl's Leaves,* is marked by a partial return to the thematic structure of *The Windhover* and others of the earlier poems, a structure in which a concrete natural scene, descriptively elaborated, leads on to the statement of a spiritual analogue or conclusion. Like *Sibyl's Leaves* also, *Heraclitean Fire* has a cosmic theme, but its mood and statement, by contrast, almost throughout are marked by triumph and elation.

Cloud-puffball, torn tufts, tossed pillows ǀ flaunt forth,
    then chevy on an air-
built thoroughfare: heaven-roysterers, in gay-gangs ǀ
    they throng; they glitter in marches.
Down roughcast, down dazzling whitewash, ǀ wherever
    an elm arches,
Shivelights and shadowtackle in long ǀ lashes lace,
    lance, and pair.
Delightfully the bright wind boisterous ǀ ropes, wrestles, beats earth bare
Of yestertempest's creases; ǀ in pool and rutpeel parches
Squandering ooze to squeezed ǀ dough, crust, dust;
    stances, starches

Squadroned masks and manmarks ∣ treadmire toil there
Footfretted in it. Million-fuelèd, ∣ nature's bonfire burns
   on.
But quench her bonniest, dearest ∣ to her, her clearest-
   selvèd spark
Man, how fast his firedint, ∣ his mark on mind, is gone!
Both are in an unfathomable, all is in an enormous dark
Drowned. O pity and indig ∣ nation! Manshape, that
   shone
Sheer off, disseveral, a star, ∣ death blots black out;
   nor mark
                Is any of him at all so stark
But vastness blurs and time ∣ beats level. Enough! the
   Resurrection,
A heart's-clarion! Away grief's gasping, ∣ joyless days,
   dejection.
            Across my foundering deck shone
A beacon, an eternal beam. ∣ Flesh fade, and mortal
   trash
Fall to the residuary worm; ∣ world's wildfire, leave but
   ash:
             In a flash, at a trumpet crash,
I am all at once what Christ is, ∣ since he was what I
   am, and
This Jack, joke, poor potsherd, ∣ patch, matchwood,
   immortal diamond,
          Is immortal diamond.

   The poem is much longer even than *Sibyl's Leaves*.
Hopkins called it a sonnet with two codas; Bridges
said there are three, a difference of definition only, the
truth of the matter being that the poem has little of
the character of a sonnet at all, though the first eight
lines do employ conventional Petrarchan rhyme. It has
a "turn" of thought too at the close of the ninth line,
but then it has another, sharper turn in the middle of
the sixteenth. Its main thematic form is, therefore, a
three-part one, yet it can also be looked upon as two-

part, an ambiguity created by the fact of the central lines' facing both ways. The first part of the poem, written in language remarkably full of movement, conveys a windy delight in change, the arrival of a bright windy day after a storm. This clearing is described in terms of Heraclitean flux, terms adapted to include all four of the traditional Greek elements of matter, though certainly not in any spirit of Heraclitean gloom: wind (*air*), now dominant after tempest (*water*), dried *earth*, through one revolution of the perpetual change, with the primary element of *fire* underlying all: "Million-fuelèd, nature's bonfire burns on," as the cycle concludes. Subsequent lines introduce a new theme, man, and in that respect look forward to the conclusion, which concerns man, not nature; but they also face back to the first section of the poem in dealing with man simply as part of nature and therefore impermanent. They also stand out alone, however, for they constitute the dark part of the poem, given over to mourning individual mortality: individual man, the "clearest-selvèd spark" of nature, does not recur in the Heraclitean cycle; on the contrary, as a unique being he perishes, and his work and his memory soon perish too.

The final section of the poem opens with an abrupt reversal of this mood, perhaps too abrupt a reversal, for the bare exclamation "Enough! the Resurrection, / A heart's-clarion!" cannot instantaneously translate the reader from the "unfathomable dark" of eternal death to joyful resurrection. (It is possible that this passage might have been altered if the poem had undergone final revision; it survives only in a single version that Hopkins had marked "provisional only.") There is, to be sure, a beautiful approach to the final statement, but it comes afterward, leaving the abruptly exclamatory Resurrection clarion standing stark, without, in spite of the word "clarion," any reverberation at all. Once the concluding lines are under way, however, they transcend all their oddity, their statement being approached through lines of timeless, unmannered (unless perhaps Shakespearean-mannered) language and imagery:

> Across my foundering deck shone
> A beacon, an eternal beam. Flesh fade, and mortal trash
> Fall to the residuary worm; world's wildfire, leave but
>   ash.

This is the grand style, very grand; and the inspired epithet "residuary" transforms it into that exceedingly rare thing (not, if I remember correctly, known to Arnold), the grand style ironic. Sometimes the line between the grand and the grandiose, like that between the simple and the simpleminded, is a hairline, but I think there is no room for doubt here.

A good deal was said earlier about Hopkins's use of coordinate and parallel grammatical elements. The matter under discussion there was the obscurity so often inherent in coordinate constructions. In *Sibyl's Leaves* and *Heraclitean Fire* the use of coordinate elements, predominantly appositional, though not, or only once or twice, a source of obscurity,[12] is pronounced to the point of mannerism; it is in fact a prevailing mark of the style in these two and such other of the baroque pieces as *Harry Ploughman* and the "Echoes." Apart from the question of obscurity, one would expect such sequences of phrase or epithet to result in diffuseness, and in the longest of these poems, the "Echoes," they do; but not in *Sibyl's Leaves* or in *Heraclitean Fire*, where the effect is of density rather than diffusion. Moreover, though strings of appositives as a rule are apt to bring movement and even statement to a standstill, in these two most successful of the late baroque poems they do not do so. Closely patterned sound—alliteration and many varieties of assonance—helps propel one phrase into the next, but this aid alone would not be enough—at least it does not keep the Leaden or Golden Echo from sagging. *Sibyl's Leaves* and *Heraclitean Fire* are borne forward additionally by a driving movement of meaning, of statement, which finds expression in extremely strong, vivid verbs and verbal elements: *strains,* for example, and *waste, overbend, whelms, end (us), selfwrung, selfstrung, grind,* in *Sibyl's Leaves.* In *Heraclitean Fire,* moreover, a good many of the coordinate elements are themselves verbs, and strong ones, so that action is piled upon action: *flaunt* and *chevy; throng* and *glitter; lace, lance,* and *pair; ropes, wrestles, beats; parches, stanches, starches.* All within the first seven lines, these words themselves stir up a great windy commotion. The character of the verbs here is of course thematic also, and it changes with the changing statement, for at the end, where the concrete representation of Heraclitean flux gives way to a final affirmation of permanence, verbs of movement vanish, leaving nothing but *am* and *is, was,* and *am,* and *is*—*becoming* at last giving way to *being.*

In these two poems more than elsewhere, Hopkins has turned a potential source of weakness into strength. At its best everywhere, however, his baroque style, loaded though it is with a quantity of descriptive epithet and appositional elements great enough to sink most verse, does not sink but moves on with unfailing energy, in constantly circling progression, to some— whatever it may be—conclusive statement that serves as its goal. Among the other late baroque poems there are many fine passages and many imaginative, quintessentially exact epithets such as those through which everyday toil is transcended at the end of *Felix Randal* ("Didst fettle for the great grey drayhorse his bright and battering sandal") and parts of *Tom's Garland* and *Harry Ploughman;* there are many beautiful things in the *Echo* poems; there is a fresh conjuring up of summer in the *Epithalamion,* which, however, remains a fragment, broken off as Hopkins encountered the difficulties of his real subject. But neither these nor the other completed poems reach the heights of the *Sibyl* and *Heraclitean* sonnets or the earlier *Windhover*, which together stand as the peak of Hopkins's achievement in his more extreme baroque style.

8

"The Times Are Nightfall": Poems in the Plain Style

THOUGH MUCH of the mature writing of Hopkins occupies something of a middle ground in style, differences are usually apparent, and in their more extreme manifestations his two styles lie at nearly opposite poles. Most commonly, too, they are associated with contrasting states of mind. The language of elation, cheer, high confidence is nearly always baroque, and the plain style is usually a vehicle for despair or dejection; but as we have seen with his more native baroque work, the distinction is not absolute. That style could on occasion be made fit for any mood, high or low; and on the other hand, though we associate the plain style particularly with the "terrible sonnets," the first of the plain poems is at least nominally an expression of confidence. *Andromeda,* written in August 1879, represents a deliberate departure from the style of the *Deutschland* or *The Windhover* or *Duns Scotus's Oxford,* three poems that together illustrate the varied resources of the baroque style of his first mature years, toward, to employ his own words again, "a more Miltonic plainness and severity." And though, as he also said, it did not turn out very severe or very plain, it is marked by easily identified changes.

Now Time's Andromeda on this rock rude,
With not her either beauty's equal or

Her injury's, looks off by both horns of shore,
Her flower, her piece of being, doomed dragon food.

Time past she has been attempted and pursued
By many blows and banes; but now hears roar
A wilder beast from West than all were, more
Rife in her wrongs, more lawless, and more lewd.

Her Perseus linger and leave her tó her extremes?—
Pillowy air he treads a time and hangs
His thoughts on her, forsaken that she seems,

All while her patience, morselled into pangs,
Mounts; then to alight disarming, no one dreams,
With Gorgon's gear and barebill / thongs and fangs.

Most immediately evident in this new style is a sharp
reduction in the number of descriptive epithets and
complete disappearance of the *ad hoc* compound ones
that had become one of the hallmarks of Hopkins's
verse. "White-fiery" and "whirlwind swivellèd," "wind-
beat whitebeam" and "mealed-with-yellow sallows," the
"rash-fresh re-winded new-skeined score," "rolling level
underneath him steady air"—combinations such as
these are entirely absent, and the few epithets that
remain seem to underplay rather than to risk overplay-
ing their function. A second major change partly consequent upon the first is a reduction almost to the vanishing point of the parallel, and especially appositional,
constructions; only one of these remains, "her flower,
her piece of being." A third conspicuous difference—
actually these are all so interdependent that they may
better be looked upon as aspects of a single change—
is the disappearance of variety (Ivor Winters would
say of miscellaneousness) in the imagery. It follows
naturally from these changes, which are all in the direction of retrenchment of language and image, that *Andromeda* and the subsequent poems written in the new
style have all the concentration and none of the expan-

siveness of Hopkins's other writing. They are nearly all sonnets, and none strains the limits of the form; they require, as a rule, no six- or eight-foot lines, and no codas. Finally, the new style is marked in most instances by a return to old, relatively conventional rhythm, an iambic pentameter handled with only a shade more freedom than may be found in other nineteenth-century sonnets. The effect of all these changes is not as negative as this enumeration representing them as a series of abstinences might imply. For one thing, in *Andromeda* the plainness of style is considerably disguised by an elaborate employment of classical myth. It is the only poem of Hopkins's founded on myth and almost the only one in which the structure is determined by elaboration of a single extended symbol or symbolic story. This use of myth, actually here approaching allegory, mitigates the effect of plainness, for though momentary metaphors are almost entirely excluded, the single mythical one runs throughout the whole.

Though Hopkins's referential use of the Andromeda legend is straightforward, the thematic equivalents of the story are not quite beyond dispute; and as some or all of these equivalents were to become part of the substance of the "terrible sonnets" in which the style is carried further in the direction of severity, it seems best to be explicit at once about them. The poem has been commonly described as a sonnet on the Catholic Church represented under the figure of "Time's" Andromeda. Gardner so reads it (as do two of the writers in *Immortal Diamond*), and on ready biblical grounds he supposes the "rock rude" to be St. Peter. The "wilder beast" of the seventh line he believes to be such evils as "rationalism, Darwinism, the new paganism of Swinburne and Whitman, possibly Nietzsche"; and Perseus is Christ. Perseus may well be Christ, but I find it difficult to imagine Hopkins going out of his way, deliberately and altogether irrelevantly, to characterize St.

Peter as a "rude" rock. Alan Heuser has a slightly different and more likely explanation of the poem as "a public sonnet on the political situation of the Church," more specifically, of the "Roman Church Militant in England." The "rock rude" is then England itself, which surely it is. Perseus, he thinks, is St. Michael or St. George, and the wild beast "industrial mob rule." [1]

There is a third possibility, differing from Heuser's rather in emphasis than in substance. It is that Andromeda may be the spirit of England itself or ideal England—Britannia, in short. Certainly "a wilder beast from West than all were" seems too specific to stand for a catchall series ranging from rationalism and evolution to Swinburne and Whitman; and though Heuser's "industrial mob-rule" is specific enough and not out of keeping with Hopkins's thought, its place of origin would be thought of commonly as rather the north of England than "west"; and as the legendary Ethiopian princess Andromeda must have looked *east* from her shore, Hopkins presumably had something specific in mind by turning her dread outlook to "West." The dragon may have had industrialism or even Whitman in his wake, but his head and fangs I think were the Irish troubles, which were a source of deep concern to Hopkins even before he was sent to Dublin in 1884; and it must, I think, be Ireland to which Andromeda "looks off" awaiting the wild beast. Though the situation of the Catholic Church would have been involved also, the proper heroine of the sonnet still may be England-Andromeda-Britannia, Hopkins being an ardent, only moderately enlightened imperialist and, as he said, "a very great patriot" (I, 131). The two "horns of shore" from which she looks off are geographically specific, either Land's End and the western reaches of Scotland or else the narrower horned points of Holyhead and St. David's Head—either, that is, the outer or the inner western horned outline of the home island —both pairs of horned points looking west to Ireland,

and beyond to America, of whose support of violent Irish nationalism Hopkins wrote indignantly at a later date: "Are the [Irish] tenant-farmers satisfied? They are less so than ever before; their spokesmen in and out of parliament more violent, their champions in Ireland and America more bent on outrage, as dynamite and laying London in ruins, than when the Irish were without power and without redress." [2] These words were written almost eight years after the composition of *Andromeda*, but Hopkins's concern with the Irish question dated back to his undergraduate years, when in the Balliol Debating Society he had brought forward a "motion in defence of the Fenians" (*Journals*, p. 133). The Irish land agitation that had broken out in 1878 became acute in 1879; in August, the month in which *Andromeda* was composed, Davitt founded the Land League, and following events elicited from Hopkins that same November the comment ". . . and the Government is arresting Irish agitators, that will do far more harm in prison than on the stump." [3] To the end of his life, though with great reluctance, he favored Home Rule for Ireland, partly from a sense of justice but also in the belief that some change was inevitable, and in the half-despairing hope that the granting of Home Rule might forestall greater violence or even an Irish war of independence. The conflicts that eventually became tragic for him were already under way and he was already deeply concerned with them.

Whoever the Andromeda of the poem may be, how-ever, whether she represents England or the Catholic Church in England, her uncertain identity is less important than it would appear to be. Though it is not one of Empson's enriching ambiguities, it impairs the effectiveness of the sonnet little, since both meanings can be subsumed under the more general and perfectly clear sense that something of the greatest public value in today's world waits to be saved, and the mythological metaphor of Andromeda herself does not demand anything more specific. However, it is material to the effect of the poem that the wild beast seen from the horns of shore be recognized as Ireland, because this gives precision, point, and vividness to a group of images that under any other reading are arbitrary and blurred into ineffectiveness.[4]

Apart from its symbolic metaphor, *Andromeda* is plain if not severe. Not only are descriptive adjectives reduced to half or a third of the usual number, but their character is even more restrained than their number, for they are nearly all abstract and unsenuous; even "rude" in the first line, when placed beside "rock," suggests rather more of substance than appearance. The "pillowy air" upon which Perseus arrives in the sestet is the conspicuous exception, and *pillowy* is probably also the least happy word in the poem, being more reminiscent than one likes of Leigh Hunt or the early Keats, soft where softness is at best irrelevant. But *lawless, lewd, wilder, rife,* and *doomed* are characterizing epithets essential to the statement, not in any usual sense descriptive; all of them are violent, yet none are showy and none visual or otherwise concrete.

With the language thus deprived of nearly all of Hopkins's habitual means of poetic heightening, one may wonder what remains. Much does, though the means are scarcely noticeable in themselves. The remark of a recent writer in another connection that in poetry the word *now*, denoting as it does merely time, is only a mechanical narrative word, not an "affective" one,[5] the other day brought home forcibly what I take to be a quite opposite truth, that inconspicuous words having to do with time are often highly charged with feeling in poetry (and not in poetry alone: one thinks of such an evocative title as, in its English form, "Last Year at Marienbad," in which the ostensibly specific but actually indefinite expression of time is as suggestive as the romantic place-name). When Drayton's best sonnet turns, its pivot is *now:* "Now, at the last gasp of

Love's latest breath"; and flowers are not the sole charm of Tennyson's "Now sleeps the crimson petal, now the white." When these common words signifying time are not factually necessary, they are apt to be strongly "affective" words. In certain situations the tense of the verb itself sufficiently establishes the time, and if one says "now" in addition (or a generic, not literal, "yesterday" or "tomorrow"), one has said something else and something more, something that is almost wholly in the dimension of feeling. These words of time are in fact such sensitive expressions that even when they serve a narrative or informative function, by a mere slight change from their normal position they may become dramatically charged. One thinks of Hamlet's "Now might I do it pat" or Yeats's rationally meaningless but poetically powerful "Now as at all times I can see in the mind's eye" (the full effect of which, however, requires the remaining lines).

Initiating the new style, Hopkins began to create his effects from such small but still explosive charges as this. *Andromeda* opens with this portentous *now* and immediately gives notice of symbolic use of the myth in the more portentous *Time's Andromeda*. This epithet is followed by a harsh image made harsher by inversion in "rock rude," and the entire opening is held in syntactic suspense heightened by stark and stripped word order in the phrase that holds off the verb, "With not her either beauty's equal or / Her injury's." All this is very fine and is made finer by tension established between images of the fragile and the hard—*beauty* and *flower* set in opposition to *rock rude, dragon,* and even to the *horns of shore,* which says something merely geographical while verbally suggesting something quite different. There is little here that is not to be found at times in Hopkins's more florid writing: the inversions, the grammatical suspense, the contrasting imagery are not new. They have new prominence, however, because they are not overshadowed by rich imagery or by the sound pattern and because they do not seem to spring from the pattern as they do in such pieces as *The Leaden Echo;* rather, they spring directly from the thing said and the feeling about what is said. The pruning away of nearly all descriptive epithets and appositives exposes to view a structure the elements of which are put together so starkly that even a slight inversion of word order acquires significance.

It is only in the octave of *Andromeda* that Hopkins's new style appears at its best; the conclusion is not quite up to this level. Though not elaborate in the baroque way, the sestet is mannered, and its oddities have an air of contrivance. The interrogation with which it opens ("Her Perseus linger and leave her to her extremes?"), the intrusive "pillowy air," and the later disjointed or loose syntax of "then to alight" all draw attention without being particularly expressive; and the anticipated happy outcome, huddled as it is into a line and a half, does not ring with full prophetic conviction. In spite of the somewhat disappointing close, however, *Andromeda* is a fine sonnet, composed in an almost traditional and almost severe English poetic style harking back to Milton, and to Wordsworth when Milton was running in his head. Though its mythological imagery has pictorial elements that modify the severity of style and its theme is at least nominally a happy one— Christ will rescue Andromeda, whoever she is—still this sonnet in style and at least to some extent in theme foreshadows the later sonnets written in Ireland.

Andromeda had no immediate sequel. Soon after it was written, temporary moves followed by a heavy load of work and an even heavier heart among the appalling conditions of the poor in Liverpool, and then by the final year of his Jesuit tertianship, prevented his writing much for some three years. During this time, too, another interest claimed most of whatever time and creative energy Hopkins could muster, the composition of music. In poetry the first successful production of this lean period was *Felix Randal*,[6] which is written in elaborate sprung rhythm and has a brilliant and highly sensuous descriptive close but which elsewhere is relatively plain and restrained in diction. *Brothers,* begun possibly before *Andromeda* but not finished till a year later, is simple in style but far from severe. As Hopkins was aware, though he hoped he had got around the weakness by a change from the original stanza, it is too much in the simple-Wordsworth manner (I, 86, 106), really a post-Wordsworthian sentimentalized simplicity that does not do justice to the perceptively observed subject and that is further marred by an unfortunate personal tone. One sees through these and the far superior *Spring and Fall,* which followed in September 1880, not quite a continuation of the plain style of *Andromeda* but a continued and deliberate exploration of various kinds of simplicity and directness. Like *Felix Randal, Spring and Fall* is restrained in the quantity of its descriptive detail. With a subject, Margaret weeping over the ending of summer, that offers every opportunity for the elaborate baroque treatment of nature such as we had in *The Starlight Night* or *Spring* and other sonnets of earlier years, this poem sets the scene at the end of the second line in exactly two words—"Márgarét, áre you griéving / Over Goldengrove unleaving?"— and of these two, *Goldengrove* is only half descriptive, the other half being place-name.[7] Its image is transformed and intensified a few lines later in more imaginative form: when she is older, Margaret is told, she will no longer weep over the falling leaves nor even "spare a sigh / Though worlds of wanwood leafmeal lie," though the forests themselves should fall, to lie as grim and dead as the fallen leaves ("Though forests low and leaf meal lie" is an earlier, canceled version in MS B). Except for the two compound epithets in this line, the poem is plain, spare, and intensely concentrated, though the plainness is momentarily disguised by the distortion of extreme inversions following the opening couplet.

The rhythm of this poem Hopkins described as sprung, but it is rather different from any that he employed elsewhere. Most of it would pass muster among the sixteenth- and seventeenth-century verses of seven and eight syllables that lean to the trochaic but equivocate. It has the occasional initial or final monosyllabic foot that one finds there, but—for once effectively used —the "St. Dorothea" (or Shakespeare's "Whý should thís désert bé") rhythm also appears in several lines ("Sórrow's spríngs áre the same," and cf. lines 1 and 14). This effect may be what he had been striving for in some of his earlier, unsuccessful experiments. It is at any rate here a finely wrought lyric measure; its effect is more springy than sprung, yet it is grave enough for its theme.

Nearly all the important later poems of Hopkins were written after his removal to Dublin, and the plain style reappears there, where we are most familiar with it, in the "terrible sonnets" ("terrible" is an embarrassingly overcharged name under which to classify a group of sonnets, but with the precedent behind it of Bridges and Dixon and many subsequent writers, it has grown into a half-official title to which one may as well succumb). Ivor Winters launched his celebrated attack on the poetry of Hopkins through a discussion of one that he regarded as typical of these late sonnets, the one beginning, "No worst, there is none." The poem deals, he says, primarily with a particular and personal experience, but it offers "so little generalization that we can feel no certainty regarding the nature of the experience beyond the fact that it has generated a desperate emotion." It fails, therefore, because the reader is shown no "particular motive" or cause for the desperation; and the omission, Winters says, impels him to ask the poet, " 'What do you know of these matters? Why are you so secretive? And above all, why are you so self-righteous in your secretiveness?' " [8]

186

One may question the assumption upon which such a criticism rests, but on this occasion it is not necessary to do so, for Hopkins was not being secretive; he was in fact, in view of his circumstances, remarkably explicit in one sonnet of the group though not in this one. These "terrible" sonnets, though they do not record in chronological order a succession of episodes or states of mind, nevertheless make up a sequence or cluster of poems springing about a central situation, in reading which, unless one is prepared on a priori aesthetic grounds to rule out all connected series of poems qua series (at what loss when it comes to Shakespeare's sonnets), one does not ask that what is relevant to all must be repeated in all: the reader's mind need not be wiped blank between poems in order to come at the next freshly. The main "cause" behind the terrible sonnets is set forth quite as explicitly as need be in the "Stranger" sonnet; but as it is shown even more fully in Hopkins's prose, brief passages from that source may serve as an additional commentary on the sequence.

During Hopkins's final years in Ireland, the earlier sources of his unhappiness, those dating back to *The Wreck of the Deutschland* and earlier, were intensified and compounded by others. No doubt his temperament subjected him to suffering that was in some degree neurotic; but the sources of pain that underlay the *Deutschland* had been by no means all neurotic, and the years in Ireland provided more than enough external and rational grounds for suffering. His loneliness in alienation from family and friends and the lack of success in his profession pressed upon him as heavily as ever, and the partial smothering of his creative powers through ill health and overwork, as well as through absence of appreciation and encouragement by an order which at the time could make no use of his best talents —these circumstances had changed, if at all, only for the worse. No one now doubts the truth of a statement made at the beginning of the private note in which during the last year of his life he summed up his position, "I do not waver in my allegiance, I never have since my conversion to the Church." This loyalty, in fact, is what fixed unalterably and sharpened one of the horns of his dilemma in Ireland. The other horn was his passionate love of England, "wife to my creating thought," no less passionate for being critical, protective, and anxious. His work in Ireland, mainly the examining of large numbers of students in classics in University College, seemed to him of little use, for the institution was accomplishing scarcely anything of what Newman had hoped originally. But for him the gravest problem was something else: "Meantime the Catholic Church in Ireland and the Irish Province in it and our College in that [he has just noted that his salary contributes to the Jesuits' work in the College] are greatly given over to a partly unlawful cause, promoted by partly unlawful means, and against my will my pains, laborious and distasteful, like prisoners made to serve the enemies' gunners, go to help on this cause." In his dilemma, the more fully he did what he knew to be his duty, the more he contributed to the aid of England's enemies in Ireland, a situation to him nearly intolerable. Involved in this also, and an added grief to him, was the recognition of what he could not help seeing as shocking moral imperfections in both the objects of his loyalty, his Church (or more exactly, its clergy) and his country, a recognition forced upon him now, on one hand by eyewitness experience of the Church's activities in Ireland, and on the other by the to him detestable character and policies of Gladstone and his followers, and additionally by horrifying reports of cowardice and panic among the English troops at Majuba, this last a national disgrace that he could scarcely bear to think of. The times were "nightfall" indeed, to him. Unable to fall back on self-righteousness, however, he blamed himself too; and his painful meditation on "serving the enemies' gunners" closed in utter desolation. "All my undertakings miscarry: I am like a straining eunuch. I wish then for death. . . ." [9] Though this was written in 1889, the situation was essentially the same through all the Dublin years. In 1885, the year in which the most despairing sonnets were probably composed, he told his mother: "The grief of mind I go through over politics, over what I read and hear and see in Ireland about Ireland and about England, is such that I can neither express it nor bear to speak of it" (III, 170). Two of the sonnets of that year express a wish for death, and in the next year what begins, in a letter, as praise of Coventry Patmore's poetry—"Your poems are a good deed done for the Catholic Church and another for England, for the British Empire"—quickly turns into mourning for the state of England (III, 366–368). Even to Bridges he broke out with some violence against the activities of the clergy in Ireland, though in former years he would have done anything rather than feed fuel to Bridges' dislike of his Church: "One archbishop backs robbery, the other rebellion; the people in good faith believe and will follow them. You will see, it is the beginning of the end" (*Letters*, I, 252). Bridges himself would scarcely have used stronger language.

Meantime his own poems, unpublished and all but unread, could not function as "good deeds" done for either the Church or the Empire, and even his religious devotion was in certain respects unproductive, for his views were evidently distrusted by his superiors. The official Jesuit history of University College in Dublin notes that his "somewhat obstinate love of Scotist doctrine" had "got him into difficulties" with his superiors; [10] and when Bridges asked him to write so harmless a thing as "a short paper on English scanning," his response was: "I should like to do this if you still want it, but all that we Jesuits publish (even anonymously) must be seen by censors and *this is a barrier which I do not know how anything of mine on a large scale would ever pass,*" adding, however, that a short paper on scansion would "no doubt" get through (*Letters*, I, 200; my italics). Even with the qualification of his "no doubt" clause, and allowing for possible exaggeration, this response provides substance for his repeated accounts of himself as "time's eunuch," betraying as it does something of the habitual frustrations under which he lived, frustrations partly of his own making but partly not.[11]

The "Stranger" sonnet, written probably in 1885, is a condensed summary of the foregoing circumstances, which together made up much of the cost of his life's dedication. In language it is the most direct of all his poems, and in theme it is the explicit center of the "terrible" sequence.

> To seem the stranger lies my lot, my life
> Among strangers. Father and mother dear,
> Brothers and sisters are in Christ not near
> And he my peace / my parting, sword and strife.
>
> England, whose honour O all my heart woos, wife
> To my creating thought, would neither hear
> Me, were I pleading, plead nor do I: I wear-
> y of idle a being but by where wars are rife.
>
> I am in Ireland now; now I am at a third
> Remove. Not but in all removes I can
> Kind love both give and get. Only what word
>
> Wisest my heart breeds dark heaven's baffling ban
> Bars or hell's spell thwarts. This to hoard unheard,
> Heard unheeded, leaves me a lonely began.

Severity of style and condensation here reach their extreme limit. There is scarcely an adjective, scarcely an image, scarcely any metaphor; and there is not one vividly descriptive or sensuous word. The diction, moreover, is not perceptibly raised above the commonplace: no dignity is bestowed by high Latinized abstractions or absolutes, or by that great occasional poetic resource of abstraction, the time-and-space sublime. Yet the power of the poem is not simply owing to the biographical sincerity of its direct and honest statement of despair, with which the reader must sympathize. It is a created poem, and its language is poetically heightened and intensified, though by almost imperceptible means.

The first quatrain is brought to its end by an alliterative paradox summing up, from one point of view, the subject of the poem, "And he my peace my parting, sword and strife." This is succeeded by the only other figure, a quiet metaphor focused in a single word, *wife,* which gains force from its rhyme and its position at the end of a run-on line that causes it to be followed by a faint real or imagined pause not afforded by the syntax alone, "England, . . . wife / To my creating thought." The only strikingly Hopkins-like touch in the style of the poem, apart from its grammatical condensations, is the final word in which a common verb, *began,* is wrenched into a substantive. If this forcing of language is too mannered for some tastes, it nevertheless has virtue, devoid as it is of sensuous or metaphorical coloring, in preserving the severity of style and still bringing the poem to a close with the force and condensation commonly secured only by metaphor.

For the rest, the plain language receives its poetic heightening from elaborately patterned sounds, including repeated words, and from a varied speed of movement within a strict frame of rhythmic time. The alliteration, however, is severely controlled; there is no chasing of the letter, no indulgence in free association guided by the letter, such as one feels in the Echo poems; here pattern and meaning are fully interdependent. Though the sound pattern is less obvious than in the baroque poems because the words themselves are inconspicuous, it is no less important an element in the poetic texture. Finally—and this is characteristic of

Hopkins's later style—the poem is full of small, sometimes scarcely noticeable inversions of normal word order and reversals of preceding word order. In prose, the opening sentence might be "My lot lies . . . , my life lies . . . ," but in the poem the second element reverses the order of the first. In the third line, "are in Christ not near" is a very slight departure from normal order. The second quatrain opens with a normal, though complex, order of words, but this opening is followed by an inversion which has the effect of tortured syntax because the words are nearly the same as before: "England . . . would neither hear me, were I pleading, plead nor do I," which is again reversed in "I weary" and "idle a being." This intricate interweaving of the direct and the reversed, which continues throughout the sonnet, is a main source of its poetic and also its emotional tension.

In the earlier discussion of Hopkins's obscurity, something was said of his extreme and striking inversions, which in addition to obscurity often produce a feeling of violent dislocation. The effect of these was not always happy (the opening of *Peace*, for one instance, to me is funny rather than impressive, its syntax dodging about elusively in literal—and I fear deliberate, though not deliberately funny—imitation of the flitting "wooddove Peace" who herself kept eluding the poet). Hopkins appears to have discovered inversion as a conscious resource quite suddenly in 1879, not long before he wrote to Bridges on the subject. Earlier he had varied his word order mainly in conventional ways, as by placing in initial position an adverbial phrase or clause. With the sonnet to Henry Purcell, however, he began to employ an unnatural order of words in conjunction with, and often not separable from, unusual ellipses, interrupted syntax, and various other daring constructions; "with the reversal / Of the outward sentence [that] low lays him, listed to a heresy, here" is an instance in that sonnet, and its prominence in *Andromeda* has already been noted. Hopkins's style is not characterized by that long-range suspense created by delay and displacement, of which Yeats was such a great master; his displacements are apt to be short-range but more intricately patterned than those of Yeats, and the tension they produce has a different character; they create tightness rather than a wide arc of suspense.

The psychological basis of this and certain other sources of poetic tension arising from the texture of the poet's language is the same as that commonly associated with skillfully handled meter: it is the constant, minute interplay upon the mind of expectation or prediction by turns aroused, disappointed, satisfied in expected or unexpected or half-expected ways, so that an ever-varying microscopic suspense becomes part of the verbal texture. The effects of alliteration also and of other kinds of sound pattern rest in part upon this basis; it is one reason their success varies so greatly from one passage and one poet to another: prediction must not be too readily and blandly fulfilled, as it often is in the alliteration of Swinburne, yet it must be answered, whether loudly or faintly, directly or obliquely, if expectation with its accompanying tension is to remain alive.

Inversions, then, including particularly reversals but also other intricate displacements in the order of words, are a characterizing feature of the writing of Hopkins's last decade. It appears typically in the first two quatrains of *Ribblesdale:*

Earth, sweet Earth, sweet landscape, with leavès throng
And louchèd low grass, heaven that dost appeal
To, with no tongue to plead, no heart to feel;
That canst but only be, but dost that long—

Thou canst but be, but that thou well dost; strong
Thy plea with him who dealt, nay does now deal,
Thy lovely dale down thus and thus bids reel
Thy river, and o'er gives all to rack or wrong.

In the baroque poems the inversions are not always conspicuous, being obscured by so much else; and in fact where the imagery is most luxuriant and the language most elaborate, particularly where long series of appositional and other parallel elements abound, the inversions are apt to be fewer. *Spelt from Sibyl's Leaves,* for instance, has but two, both slight though the second brings the poem to its appalling close on the word *grind.*

It is in the plain sonnets that inversion is most essential, for there it combines with alliteration, assonance, and patterned, often symmetrical, repetition of words—as in the already noticed double chiasmus "Me, were I pleading, plead nor do I: I weary of idle a being"—to produce the poetic heightening, as well as the extreme tension, that transforms their otherwise plain and pictureless language. Obviously, where ornament is absent every feature counts, and in the terrible sonnets the tragic theme is matched by this kind of severe distinctiveness. That the "theme" sonnet of the series can be at once so literally informative, so bare of any other means of heightening than these, and still so poetic is its particular distinction.

Though often spare, no other late sonnets are quite so bare as this central one; in none is the diction so factual and prosaic, and no other is quite without imagery or concrete metaphor. In the other terrible sonnets, however, the images that do occur are not, as in the baroque poems, descriptively elaborated; they are more often compressed and most sparing of adjectives: "creep, / Wretch, under a comfort [that] serves in a whirlwind," or "leave comfort root-room," or "The times are nightfall" (this last the opening of a sonnet that is not the least distinguished of the sequence, though little known because it appears among the unfinished poems and fragments). In other respects, except, that is, for their use of some restrained imagery and metaphor, the remaining sonnets in the series are written in the same plain style as the "Stranger" sonnet. Metrically, only the one called "Patience" is out of the ordinary, and that only in two or three somewhat oddly counterpointed lines. All are marked by these inversions and interruptions of word order that produce tension and pattern in the language, often without being individually conspicuous. Here and there, however, they stand out, and in one sonnet the word order seems again, as with the "wooddove Peace," designed to be onomatopoetic. The poet describes self-torture by means of deliberately tortured syntax and reflexive reduplication of the key words.

My own heart let me more have pity on; let
Me live to my sad self hereafter kind,
Charitable; not live this tormented mind
With this tormented mind tormenting yet.

I cast for comfort I can no more get
By groping round my comfortless, than blind
Eyes in their dark can day or thirst can find
Thirst's all-in-all in all a world of wet.

Soul, self; come, poor Jackself, I do advise
You, jaded, let be; call off thoughts awhile
Elsewhere; leave comfort root-room; let joy size

At God knows when to God knows what; whose smile
's not wrung, see you; unforeseen times rather—as skies
Betweenpie mountains—lights a lovely mile.

For his most violent distortions of language I think Hopkins always took particular care to have a rule or precedent ready. Thus, in the opening quatrain of this poem the syntax, though it is often thought loose, is strict; the order, however, is unnatural, and the tension of the passage derives from both the strictness and the displacement. Let me live, the passage says, hereafter kind, charitable, to my sad self; not live yet ("yet" in the sense of "still," "continually") tormenting [no. 3] this tormented [no. 1] mind with ("by means of") this tormented [no. 2] mind: the words that would normally have followed the second "live" have been placed last; "tormenting yet" is adjectival and parallel in construction with the preceding "kind"; the rest falls into place of itself. This is mannered surely enough but not objectionably so, for though the theme is most serious, there is a certain amount of play in the tone, and the poem itself is a call away from self-torture to something at least distantly resembling play; the tortured syntax then at once expresses and faintly mocks the self-torment. While these distortions, recurring throughout the sonnet, keep up its emotional as well as verbal tension, the element of play rises to the surface in the extravagant colloquialism of the sestet, not only in the self-depreciatory "Jackself" and the canine-flavored "call off," but in the punning of "God knows," which I think is to be taken primarily in the colloquial sense ("I will go sometime but God knows when"). The poet's concluding advice to his Jackself then is: Let joy grow ("size") at whatever time it will ("at God knows when") and in response to whatever occasion comes along (or else, let it grow to whatever proportions it will), joy, whose smile is not wrung (cannot be compelled), but rather, at unforeseen times (if one will only relax instead of hunting desperately with the "blind eyes" of an earlier line) will spring up of itself and light "a lovely mile" as skies do by making a pied pattern between mountains (it is joy's smile, not God's, that is in question, I think, partly but not only because of the semicolon preceding *whose*).

This is a sonnet in which contrasting sets of feelings or attitudes are to be represented: one attitude sensible, half relaxed, capable of ease and flexibility and gentle play, the attitude already imaginatively achieved in the sonnet even while it is still ostensibly only trying to dissolve its opposite, self-torment. Harmony and balance

196

between these two states of mind are attained partly by the combination of extremely colloquial diction with an order of words that is equally extreme in its artificiality, and partly by the distribution of imagery. Self-torment finds it objective correlative in a paradoxical formulation of unparadoxical fact, blindness in daylight and thirst in the midst of water when one is adrift on the salt sea; the relaxed mood is objectified mainly in the brief, gay image "skies betweenpie mountains." As in all these late, plain sonnets, the images are presented with the utmost economy; nothing visual or otherwise sensuous is elaborated.

Another sonnet in which two states of mind are represented, a poem not quite so successful in achieving its balance, is the one already mentioned upon which Winters founded so much of his attack upon Hopkins. "No worst, there is none" is in some respects the least satisfactory of the "terrible" series, but its weakness is not perhaps quite what Winters points to. Though there is a central vagueness as he says, it does not result from any absence of circumstantial statement but from an indecisiveness about what constitutes the central emotion and theme. The poem says two things, and the two are inherently related, much more naturally so than the two moods of "My own heart." Yet the reader is left with the feeling that they have canceled each other out, or he is left standing cold between the two:

No worst, there is none. Pitched past pitch of grief,
More pangs will, schooled at forepangs, wilder wring.
Comforter, where, where is your comforting?
Mary, mother of us, where is your relief?
My cries heave, herds-long; huddle in a main, a chief-
woe, world-sorrow; on an age-old anvil wince and sing—
Then lull, then leave off. Fury had shrieked 'No lingering! Let me be fell: force I must be brief.'
O the mind, mind has mountains; cliffs of fall
Frightful, sheer, no-man-fathomed. Hold them cheap

May who ne'er hung there. Nor does long our small
Durance deal with that steep or deep. Here! creep,
Wretch, under a comfort serves in a whirlwind: all
Life death does end and each day dies with sleep.

The opening concentrates upon the subjective experience of desolation, of despair piled upon despair; this
is the first theme. The second is a statement made about
it, that because man cannot bear such pain long, therefore relief of a sort, if only numbness, sleep, or death,
always comes. The essential connection between the
pain and the relief is obvious of itself and is expressed
several times. Fury's shriek includes the brevity as well
as the violence of her assault, the "cries" at the end of
the anvil image "lull' and "leave off," and a direct statement follows, with force derived from a remarkable
linguistic texture in the words "Nor does long our small /
Durance deal with that steep or deep. Here! creep. . . ."
On the intellectual level these contrary states of mind
are logically put together; what unites them is just what
Hopkins has said, that man's power to suffer agony is
short. Yet this does not produce an emotional or a poetic
resolution in the actual poem, though the reason for its
not doing so is somewhat elusive. We do not know
quite where we are, whether we stand with the agony or
with the relief, or whether we should move from one to
the other, though we do not quite do this either. In "My
own heart" resolution came about through an irony that
to some extent colored the whole, but Hopkins was not
often ironical and is not so in this sonnet of despair. No
tone, therefore, is available to draw the poem together,
and no state of mind or mood is created from within
which the contrary elements are held in focus; nor is
the feeling created of progression from one state to the
other. This lack of resolution is a flaw at a very deep
level. On other levels, particularly in the expressiveness
of its imagery, the sonnet ranks with the best. In the
sestet, where Hopkins allows himself freedom to ex-

patiate a degree or so beyond the bounds of plainness through a sustained metaphor, the images of which, still bare of descriptive elaboration—mountain, "cliffs of fall," man who has "hung there," and "comfort [that] serves in a whirlwind," all these in "the mind, mind"— have remarkable power in themselves, a power increased, too, from another tragic association that inevitably arises with these images. The cliffs of Dover in *Lear*, where "hangs" the samphire gatherer, are cliffs of fall too, and they are truly cliffs of "the mind" though named Dover. This sonnet is so moving in its detail that it may often be read without any disturbed sense of underlying weakness. Yet the relief and the despair do, within the frame of the poem, somehow wrongly neutralize each other.

Andromeda preceded the terrible sonnets by nearly six years, during which the plain style remained little exercised; [12] yet as the first avowed venture into this style it belongs with the group, just as do the two final poems written a few months before Hopkins's death, "Thou art indeed just, Lord" and *To R. B.* They are all bound together, though it may be by chance, in theme as well as in style, for they all deal with one or more aspects of what was summed up in the "Stranger" sonnet: the critical conflict of England, Ireland, and the Church as reflected in his own pain of torn loyalties and helplessness, and the related frustration of his creative powers by forces both internal and external.

Written before Hopkins himself became imprisoned in the Irish situation, *Andromeda* has more cheer and more detachment; and it must, one supposes, have been chance alone that led him to try the new style first upon a theme that would afterward become central to the more self-involved sonnets. Yet it does almost seem as if at some point an obscure sense of form had been at work to effect the homogeneity of the plain sonnets, even in bringing them to a close with one that is developed, like the opening one, by progressive elaboration of a single metaphor drawn from ancient traditional, but not this time mythological, material. Though the theme of the final sonnet is personal—the poet's loss of inspiration through absence of "that fine delight that fathers thought"—its tone, as if it were bringing all these matters to a close, is more detached than that of the preceding "terrible" ones. For the process of poetic creation, Hopkins finds his metaphor, his in fact symbolic story, in the human sexual and reproductive cycle, which he follows in explicit detail from the initial "delight" through phallic imagery:

> the strong
> Spur, live and lancing like the blowpipe flame,
> Breathes once and, quenchèd faster than it came,
> Leaves yet the mind a mother of immortal song.

Personal as the substance is, it becomes objectified through this meditative exploration of the symbol, and the result is a poem whose tone is rueful but marked with repose and resignation. It is at once the most personal and most impersonal of them all, *Andromeda* excepted.

This sonnet to Bridges thus brings to conclusion the plain poems which owed so much to him. They bear no resemblance at all to Bridges' own poetry. In the creation, however, of this antithetical poetic self of Hopkins (to borrow and distort Yeats's term), sympathetic identification with Bridges' taste played a part; and it is appropriate, if presumably accidental, that Hopkins's final poem should have been addressed to the critic without whose influence and encouragement these poems of his second self would probably not have come into being.

Notes

CHAPTER 1: BEGINNINGS

[1] In *Once a Week*, Feb. 14, 1863. This version is reprinted in *Letters*, III, 437–438. By 1871, the date of the revised version now printed in *Poems*, the archaisms ("what time," etc.) had been pruned away and the descriptive language much improved.

[2] The sources of the story are Numbers 13–14, Exodus 12–17, Deuteronomy 1.

[3] There is one exception. The sonnet "See how Spring opens with disabling cold," except for its first line, is as clearly Miltonic as the others are Shakespearean.

[4] This sonnet and the lines from *A Soliloquy* are quoted from *The Poems of Gerard Manley Hopkins*, published by Oxford University Press. Copyright The Society of Jesus 1967.

[5] John Sparrow shows the extent to which this kind of gruesome imagery pervaded early nonconformist hymnology (Martha Winburn England and John Sparrow, *Hymns Unbidden* [New York, 1960]), but that tradition would not account for its appeal to either Christina Rossetti or Hopkins.

CHAPTER 2: THE DRAGON IN THE GATE

[1] Bridges' notes in *Poems* (2d ed., 1930; omitted from 3d ed.). Extended studies of the poem have been published by W. H. Gardner, *Gerard Manley Hopkins: A Study* . . . (2 vols.; New Haven, 1948–1949), I, 38–70; Robert R. Boyle, S.J., "The Thought Structure of *The Wreck of the Deutschland*," in *Immortal Diamond*, ed. Norman Weyand (New York, 1949), pp. 333–350; John E. Keating, *The Wreck of the Deutschland: An Essay and Commentary*, Research Series VI (Kent, Ohio: Kent State University, 1963); Todd K. Bender, *Gerard Manley Hopkins: The Classical Background* . . . (Baltimore, 1966), pp. 71–96; and John Pick, *Gerard Manley Hopkins, Priest and Poet* (2d ed.; New York, 1966), pp. 40–51. That of Philip M. Martin,

Mastery and Mercy (London, 1957), is a devotional rather than a literary study.

This chapter was published in slightly different form in *PMLA,* LXXXI (1966), 110–122, and that version was reprinted separately by the Modern Language Association in 1967.

[2] This theme of conversion must provide the essential parallel upon which the poem is founded and not, as some writers have suggested, one between the poet's experience and that of a nun drowned in the disaster, for the latter resemblance is too slightly sketched and embraces too little of the poem to be more than incidental; taken as a structural theme, it leaves out most of the poem. For an instance of that view, however, see Boyle, "Thought Structure," esp. pp. 335, 339.

[3] Editorial in *The Times,* Dec. 13, 1875. This and some extracts from the news accounts in *The Times* are reprinted in *Immortal Diamond,* pp. 354–374. See also *Letters,* III, 439–443.

[4] *Journals,* pp. 71, 190. This must have meant not only giving up pleasure walks in wood or field but also walking with downcast eyes at other times. In 1874 Hopkins noted, "All this ["a lovely day," etc.] I would have looked at again in returning but during dinner I talked too freely and unkindly and had to do penance going home" (*ibid.,* p. 249).

[5] I read the line without a stress on *me*—"Thóu mástering-me / Gód" (differing in this from Gardner, *Poems,* p. 221)—taking *mastering me* as a single proclitic epithet of God, the equivalent of *masterful* or *overmastering,* made personal for the sake of the theme of Part I. For fuller consideration of the metrical character of this and other passages, see chapter 3.

[6] *Devotional Writings,* pp. 175, 195. Because of its metrical significance, this passage is dealt with more fully in the next chapter.

[7] F. R. Leavis (*New Bearings in English Poetry* [London, 1950], pp. 179–180), mistakenly I think, sees the two images in this much-discussed stanza as symbolizing two successive and contrasting experiences. Keating (*The Wreck,* pp. 60–61) also reads it differently, finding "ironic humor" in the image of the steady water. Still another interpretation is offered in Gardner's notes and a fuller version of my own in *MLN,* LXV (1950), 306–311.

[8] One might not hazard this reading if the poet were any other than Hopkins, but of course no other poet would have written the line, whatever the meaning. *Instressed* and *stressed* in this passage are usually taken to be grammatically parallel, but to read them so seems to me to produce a meaningless tautology as well as a feeble and pointless anticlimax uncharacteristic of Hopkins. John Pick feels that a virtue may be made of what I can see only as a defect: "The impact," he says, "is heightened by the reversal of the expected word order" (*Gerard Manley Hopkins,* p. 44n). Cf. the discussion of this in Gardner (*Gerard Manley Hopkins,* I, 56–57), and the extended discussion by Boyle ("Thought Structure," pp. 343–348), which I find equally unsatisfactory. The natural reading seems to me the one I have given, and it is in keeping with Hopkins's practice of taking accepted idioms or constructions and stretching them slightly beyond their ordinary use. The employment of a participle as the equivalent

202

of an elliptical clause is common, though it more often precedes than follows the main statement (e.g., "Planted early enough, the seed will sprout in May," but also, "This will grow indoors, given plenty of sun"). Hopkins used it a number of times elsewhere: clouds "shew brighter *shaken* in Penmaen Pool" (in the poem written immediately after the *Deutschland*), more eccentrically in "Aftercomers cannot guess the beauty *been*" (*Binsey Poplars*) and "nor he for his bones *risen*" (*The Caged Skylark*). For some account of Hopkins's use of the word *instress* itself, see chapter 5.

[9] *Devotional Writings*, pp. 197, 202. The attraction of this doctrine for Hopkins is again shown in his Latin verses, the "May Lines." See this and the comment by Father Turner quoted in Gardner's notes to the poem.

[10] *The Times*, Dec. 11, 13, 1875 (reprinted, with minor variants, in *Immortal Diamond*, pp. 368, 374).

[11] I owe the suggestion of the liturgical association to Rev. Robert Boyle, S.J. Professor Hugh Kenner too thinks this would naturally have been present to Hopkins's mind and additionally suggests that the association strengthens the supernatural implications of the passage. As Hopkins was both classicist and priest, the word must, I should think, carry both its general linguistic and this particular liturgical force. In his article "Evolution, Myth, and Poetic Vision" (*Comparative Literature Studies*, III [1966], 16), Walter J. Ong, S.J., describes the nun's cry as "one of recognition and acceptance" but does not suggest a supernatural presence.

[12] It may be worthwhile to draw attention to the solution of one small mystery that has puzzled numerous readers. At the end of stanza 29, the nun is described in contradictory images: she is "to the blast / Tarpeian-fast, but a blown beacon of light." The rock from which Roman traitors were hurled seems irrelevant. But in *Paradise Regained*, which Hopkins studied with great care, its associations are different. Rome is described and then the Capitol, "on the Tarpeian rock, her Cittadel / Impregnable." This has been pointed out by Arthur W. Pitts, Jr., in the *Explicator*, XXIV, no. 1 (Sept. 1965), and it is undoubtedly the association intended: the nun is fixed and firm like the impregnable rock, yet her cry rides through the air like the blown flame of a beacon torch.

[13] *Devotional Writings*, pp. 200, 308 (my italics); the word is used in the same sense also on page 146. The meaning is not particularly rare, and its analogy with the "fetching" of butter in a churn is obvious. For its use by Scott and others, see *OED*, *English Dialect Dictionary*, and Yeats's introduction to *Irish Fairy and Folk Tales*.

[14] I have given the reading in some detail because the passage is an important link in the thought and has been read quite differently by Gardner in his notes to the poem. He takes *mark* to be a noun, *fetched* a verb, so as to read (as I understand him) "The uttermost mark [that] our giant fetched." This seems to me to have little or no meaning in its context; the sense of *mark* is vague, and *fetched* more than a little slangy, as well as wrenched into a wrong tense: present, perfect, or future would be conceivable, but not the simple past.

There is a verbal parallel to the reading I have suggested in the sentence opening the sestet of *The Soldier,* written a few months later, "Mark Christ our King," as well as the thematic parallel in the "last or first . . . men go" of stanza 8. Cf. also the several uses of *mark,* together with other ideas and images reminiscent of the *Wreck,* in a sermon of 1879 (*Devotional Writings,* pp. 28–29).

15 MS B gives the stresses only in the second line, which is the more important one for the sense here. Those in the first are the natural ones but are confirmed by Gardner (*Gerard Manley Hopkins,* I, 284) from manuscript authority, which I suppose to be MS A.

16 *Letters,* II, 71–72, and cf. 85–86. He described the poem "Pied Beauty" as a curtal sonnet, that is, a poem shorter than a standard sonnet but preserving the same interior proportions. There is some discussion of these matters in Alan Heuser, *The Shaping Vision of Gerard Manley Hopkins* (London, 1958), pp. 82–84.

17 *Letters,* I, 47; and cf. his justification of another poem on the same ground: "Though the analogy in the Candle sonnet may seem forced, yet it is an 'autobiographical' fact that I was influenced and acted on the way there said" (I, 85).

18 See George T. Wright's interesting discussion in *The Poet in the Poem* (Berkeley and Los Angeles, 1960), pp. 92 ff.

CHAPTER 3: EVOLUTION OF THE NEW RHYTHM

1 Influential published accounts have been those of Harold Whitehall, "Sprung Rhythm," in *Gerard Manley Hopkins: By the Kenyon Critics* (Norfolk, Conn., 1945); W. H. Gardner, *Gerard Manley Hopkins: A Study* . . . (2 vols.; New Haven, 1948–1949), I, chaps. 2 and 3 *passim,* and II, chaps. 2, 3; Walter J. Ong, S.J., "Hopkins' Sprung Rhythm and the Life of English Poetry," in *Immortal Diamond,* ed. Norman Weyand (New York, 1949), chap. 4; Paull F. Baum, "Sprung Rhythm," *PMLA,* LXXIV (1959), 418–425.

Much of the present discussion was published in a somewhat different form in "Sprung Rhythm: A Chapter in the Evolution of Nineteenth-Century Verse," *PMLA,* LXXX (1965), 237–253.

2 Letter of October 1878, nearly three years after the *Deutschland* was begun (*Letters,* II, 14).

3 George P. Marsh, *Lectures on the English Language* (New York, 1859), pp. 525, 540, 579.

4 Robert Bridges, "Wordsworth and Kipling" and "Letter . . . on English Prosody," in *Collected Essays and Papers,* II (London, 1933), 30–31, 71; Edward Thompson, *Robert Bridges* (London, 1944), p. 79.

5 For the influence particularly of Wesley on Blake, see Mrs. England's account in Martha Winburn England and John Sparrow, *Hymns Unbidden* (New York, 1960).

6 *Journals,* pp. 267–290. For evidence of the date, see the preface, pp. xxvi–xxvii.

7 On grounds of taste and "sincerity," Bridges and C. C. Abbott

doubted Hopkins's authorship of this poem in spite of strong evidence that it is his. Their opinion, with which on critical matters of this kind I should ordinarily find myself in agreement, was influenced by the fact that the Jesuit father who discovered the poem printed it (posthumously) as a production of Hopkins's last years, which it certainly could not have been. Gardner's evidence for placing it in 1871–1873 is beyond dispute, as is its strong resemblance to the other poem of this period, *Rosa Mystica,* of which his authorship is proved by the existence of an autograph manuscript with his own revisions. The earlier date removes the only solid basis for doubting the authenticity of *Ad Mariam,* and Hopkins's authorship seems now unquestionable, though one may well wish he had written neither of these poems. See *Letters,* I, xvii; Gardner, *Gerard Manley Hopkins,* II, 91–94; and the notes to the poems. One other poem exists in an autograph copy dated August 1871, but it yields nothing for our purpose: it is the revised version of *Winter with the Gulf Stream,* in conventionally handled *terza rima.* The date of this autograph may not represent the date of the revision.

[8] *Letters,* III, 228–229; I, 44–45. For both talents and scandal, Swinburne of course was the talk of Balliol. He had left the university not long before Hopkins entered but had maintained friendship with his former tutor Jowett, who was also Hopkins's tutor. No literary and classical undergraduate could have escaped the excitement of his reputation. Hopkins recorded that he saw Swinburne on the day he (Hopkins) took his degree in 1868. His interest did not flag. Shortly before his death he wrote to Bridges about Swinburne's latest volume, "There is some heavydom, in long waterlogged lines (he has no real understanding of rhythm, and though he sometimes hits brilliantly at other times he misses badly)." Usually Hopkins expresses a mixture of admiration and reprehension: Swinburne's "genius is astonishing, but . . ."; "for music of words and the mastery . . . of a consistent and distinctive poetic diction . . . it is extraordinary. But . . ."; "a delirium-tremendous imagination" (*Letters,* I, 304, 79, 202; II, 99, 156–157).

Apart from comments in the letters, there are enough verbal and stylistic reminiscences, chiefly of *Atalanta,* the first *Poems and Ballads,* and *Songs before Sunrise* (1871), in Hopkins's poetry to show how closely he read these works. For brief illustration, cf. Swinburne's "towery tresses" of Crete and "The firewhite faith of Poland without spot" (from *Ode on the Insurrection in Candia* and *The Eve of Revolution*) with Hopkins's *Duns Scotus's Oxford,* "Towery city," and "Who fired France for Mary without spot," and with "whitefiery" in the *Deutschland* (stanza 13). The mannered string of possessives that conclude this poem may have been suggested by a similar construction used for the expression of a similarly grand thought in Swinburne's line "The world's heart's thanksgivings" in *Blessed among Women.* This poem, which appeared in *Songs before Sunrise,* suggests Hopkins throughout in style, imagery, rhythm, and stanza form. See Swinburne, *Complete Works* (Bonchurch ed.; 20 vols.; London, 1925–1927), II, 126 and elsewhere.

[9] In his study of Hopkins ("The Poetry of Gerard Manley Hop-

kins," in *The Function of Criticism* [Denver, 1957]), to be referred to again later, Ivor Winters takes as sprung any spondaic substitution, but surely the effects are very different.

[10] As discussion of fundamental prosodic theory would take me too far afield, conventional terminology seems the only possible one here. Inaccurate and ambiguous though it is in certain respects, it is too closely associated with what poets thought they were doing and what readers thought they were hearing to be supplanted at present in this kind of study. I shall therefore not stop to justify the use of particular terms and concepts that may be debatable.

[11] Swinburne, *Works,* VII, 333. Apart from the rhythm, cf. the image of unmaking man here and later ("To make me and unmake me," p. 348) with a similar image in the first stanza of the *Deutschland.*

[12] There are other possible ways of reading the line ("máde măn," for example), but they would be even farther from the blank verse norm.

[13] Hopkins appears to have accepted the widespread notion—inherited, I think, somewhat inaccurately from Horace—that the second foot of an iambic line is irreversible (*Letters,* II, 78 and elsewhere). Neither he nor other metrists seem to have noticed what fine effect that particular inversion can sometimes produce.

[14] Logaoedic, that is, in the sense merely of mixed kinds, without consideration now of the question of equal or unequal timing.

[15] See, for example, *A Christmas Carol,* in *Works,* I, 346–347.

[16] During his summer holiday in 1873, Hopkins read with interest the volume of Arnold containing *Rugby Chapel* and *Heine's Grave,* the meter of which, described by Enid Hamer as "the saddest and sombrest of all anapaests" and by others as cadenced or free verse, is, however classified, logaoedic. These may have reinforced the influence of Swinburne. See *Letters,* III, 58.

[17] Elsewhere Hopkins explicitly rejected the usual emendation regularizing the line, "Why should this a desert be" (*Letters,* I, 45).

[18] Swinburne's 1866 volume contains a longish poem, *St. Dorothy,* on the same subject. It is odd that both men independently should have selected this minor saint, yet the poem of Hopkins's seems to have been composed in 1864. Gardner's tentative date, 1866, would resolve the mystery, but House and Storey's account of the manuscript seems to rule out any but the earlier date; and there is no evidence and probably not much likelihood that either poet knew the other's unpublished work. So we have tentatively to suppose the two poems to be independent, or only indirectly connected through some common source. There is no resemblance between the poems apart from their subject (Gardner, notes to the poem; *Journals,* pp. xvii–xviii; Swinburne, *Works,* II, 1–15). Mabel P. Worthington, who kindly checked exhibition records for me in London, noted that a watercolor by Burne-Jones, "The Martyrdom of St. Dorothea," was exhibited at the Royal Water Colour Society in 1867, but this was after both poems had been written.

[19] "Syncopation," though in some respects a more accurate term, has too many wrong connotations and implications.

As we should expect, Hopkins also had much to say about alliteration. Gardner notes (*Gerard Manley Hopkins,* II, 138–140) that some of the discussion derives from the lectures of Marsh. But Hopkins had long been familiar with the alliterative devices and the assonance and consonance employed by Swinburne, not only the familiar twins ("mother of months," etc.), but also elaborate interlaced patterns. "A flower-bud of the flower bed" might have been written by Hopkins under the influence of his later Welsh studies, but it is in *Atalanta* (p. 301).

[20] "Sprung Rhythm," in *Kenyon Critics,* p. 41, and cf. pp. 35–36. Cf. *Letters,* II, 22, "an easily felt principle of *equal strengths*" (Hopkins's italics); I, 81–82, "Since the syllables in sprung rhythm are not counted, time or equality in strength is of more importance than in common counted rhythm, and your [Bridges'] times or strengths do not seem to me equal enough."

[21] Yet timing was of undoubted importance. In 1880, R. W. Dixon wrote to Hopkins: "I asked Bridges whether the foundation of it [Hopkins's new prosody] did not lie in fixed quantity, and he said that it did, but that much more was involved in it" (*Letters,* II, 35). Hopkins's reply to this letter is discussed later in the present chapter.

Since this chapter was written, an important note has been printed in full for the first time (*Poems,* 4th ed., pp. 255–256). In Bridges' hand but clearly, as the editors say, Hopkins's own note, it appears in MS A as a preface to Bridges' transcript of *The Wreck of the Deutschland.* It seems to be an early acount of the "new rhythm" (which here is given no name), and its impersonal and at the same time slightly self-conscious opening—"Be pleased, reader, since the rhythm in which the following poem is written is new, strongly to mark the beats . . ."—suggests to me that this may have been an introduction sent to *The Month* when (or after) Hopkins submitted the poem (Professor N. H. MacKenzie, who knows the manuscripts intimately, tells me he thinks this may be so). Its tone seems directed toward a general (and perhaps not entirely sophisticated) public rather than to friends or fellow poets or other men of letters. At any rate, according to this preface, *The Wreck* is to be read with emphasis on the rhythm and rhyme, and the reader is warned against reading it as if it were prose; but his reading must bring out "the meaning and feeling of the words." Either Hopkins had not yet developed in technical terms his theory or definition of sprung rhythm, or else he was deliberately avoiding the terms in this note. He makes, however, one rather complicated statement. "If the beating syllable is of its nature strong, the stress laid on it must be stronger the greater the number of [unstressed] syllables belonging to it, the voice treading and dwelling: but if on the contrary it is by nature light, then the greater the number of syllables belonging to it the less is the stress to be laid on it, the voice passing flyingly over all the syllables of the foot and in some manner distributing among them all the stress of the one beat." This passage is puzzling, for it appears directly to controvert Hopkins's other important statements about equality of "length" or "strength." It seems, in fact, to emphasize *difference,* in such situations, between the lengths or strengths of different feet. Solution of the contradiction is not facilitated by the fact that there has been disagreement about the identity of two lines that he brings forward (but does not quote) to illustrate his point, the sixth and seventh lines of either stanza 31 or stanza 30. To take up the long argument here is impractical, and in any event the answer to this problem would not really solve the main difficulty in Hopkins's account. If the note is earlier than his other known discussions of sprung rhythm, the discrepancy may mean not only that his new rhythm was originally *heard* rather than invented by theory, as we know it was, but also that his theory and his analysis had lagged behind his accomplishment. What he says here about the handling of a light stress as the number of unstressed syllables increases is consistent with his other statements, but that concerning the strong syllabic stress is not easily reconciled with the metrical principles that he set forth elsewhere. It could be fitted into his theory as the description of an expressive modification of the rhythm but not as part of its fixed basis.

22 See Bridges' discussion of accentual verse in *Milton's Prosody* (Oxford, 1921), pp. 89–93.

23 *Letters*, II, 41. Outrides, which I do not think do what Hopkins claims for them here, are discussed in the next chapter. The *Deutschland* contains none.

24 Stresses on *almost, unmade,* and *thee* are from MS B; the others represent my reading.

25 In Part I only. In Part II, the first line has three stresses. The remaining lines are the same throughout the poem: l. 2, three stresses; l. 3, four stresses; l. 4, three; ll. 5 and 6, five; l. 7, four; l. 8, six.

26 In Hopkins's poetry, the stresses cannot always be determined by either the alliteration or the rhyme; he frequently employs alliteration in obviously unstressed syllables and occasionally uses an unstressed syllable for his end rhyme. *The Wreck of the Deutschland* is known to have been influenced by Welsh verse, and there is one Welsh form (well known and known to Hopkins) that *requires* the rhyming of an accented with an unaccented syllable. If Hopkins needed a precedent, he had one at hand.

27 *Devotional Writings*, pp. 175, 195. The image of God's "finger" is of course familiar in iconography, but it is often understood only in a generalized sense, with little awareness of the specific meaning essential to this passage.

28 ". . . pást áll / Grásp Gód, thróned behínd." The stresses are marked in MS B.

29 See the facsimile of the manuscript of *Harry Ploughman* (*Letters*, I, facing p. 262), where *curls, hurls,* and *furls* are marked with a circumflex over the vowel, which means that the vowel is to be dwelt on in such a way as makes "one syllable nearly two," though the first two of these rhymes occur in run-on lines, "cûrls / Wag" and "hûrls / Them."

30 The newly printed note from MS A (described in note 21, above) also deals with this subject. Hopkins writes there of "letting the scansion run on from one line into the next, without break to the end of the stanza: since the dividing of the lines is more to fix

the places of the necessary rhymes than for any pause in the measure." Alone, this statement would seem intended almost to obliterate the line; but on the other hand, at the beginning of the note, he explains the fixed number of beats in each line of the stanza and enjoins the reader to avoid "disguising the rhythm and rhyme." These two statements together represent perhaps a less sophisticated version of what he said elsewhere on the subject. The problem seems to me to be mainly that of formulating advice for the reading of poetry (not of Hopkins's alone) in which the larger rhythmic and melodic strains are important but too commonly neglected. It is a well-known problem in musical performance also: presence or absence of this awareness of the larger elements of form often distinguishes a great from a merely competent musician. Earlier criticism (literary or musical) had had little to say about this; and in the absence of any existing critical vocabulary, Hopkins was perhaps having to grope for his expression.

[31] See note 8, above; still better, see the poems; and cf. the similar stanza employed in *To Victor Hugo*, published in *Poems and Ballads* (*Works*, I, 274–280).

Chapter 4: Later Rhythms

[1] So he defined it in his "Author's Preface." Sometimes, however, he seems to have regarded a single reversed foot, if it is in a sensitive position in the line, or two nonconsecutive feet, as sufficient to produce a counterpointed rhythm. This appears from his illustration from *Paradise Regained* in *Letters*, II, 15, and from his notes to certain poems.

[2] Bridges, *Poetical Works* (2d ed.; London, 1936), p. 265.

[3] That the marks in the final text are Hopkins's is established by the history of MS B, in which, according to Bridges' preface to the notes, the emendations and corrections were made by Hopkins—together with Bridges' note to this poem stating that the accents printed are from those "corrections in B." I have added, also from B, the arc connecting *rescue* and *and,* which in Hopkins's notation indicates that two syllables are to be slurred into one (see facsimile of MS in *Letters*, I, facing p. 262), even though the slur here bridges a comma. Hopkins was aware that he had made these lines regular, for he described the meter of the whole poem as "Standard [i.e. iambic pentameter] rhythm, with one sprung leading and one line counterpointed." The ninth is the line with "sprung leading," the fifth the counterpointed line; this fourteenth one, therefore, he evidently recognized as regular. The marks from the earlier version in MS A and Gardner's effort to explain and justify the B reading on oratorical grounds may be found in *Gerard Manley Hopkins: A Study . . .* (2 vols.; New Haven, 1948–1949), I, 93–94.

[4] The underslung loop is Hopkins's symbol for outrides; I have added stress marks to the preceding line to establish the rhythm without having to quote more of the sonnet.

⁵ The markings are those of MS B: the superscribed arc slurs two syllables almost into one: ⌣ is here the same as ⌢ elsewhere, a foot with stress reversed. Gardner prints a number of other stresses which he says are from MS B, but these I do not find.

⁶ G. F. Lahey, S.J., *Gerard Manley Hopkins* (London, 1930), pp. 103–104; Gardner, *Gerard Manley Hopkins,* I, 98–100. Lahey appears to have been writing without precise knowledge of the markings in the manuscripts.

⁷ No poems known to be earlier than *The Windhover* have outrides, and they are not mentioned in letters till some three months later. The first line, which contains none, can be read as two (or one and a half) paeonic feet if one disregards the fact that the poem as a whole is written in five-stress lines; or the five-stress and paeonic rhythm may be compromised in the first line though not throughout the poem: "I cáught this mŏrning mórning's mĭnion, kíng-"—not a very satisfactory reading, however.

⁸ Metrical marks are from MS B.

⁹ The song has been given a musical setting, though not as a maidens' chorus, by Robert Parris in "The Leaden Echo and the Golden Echo, for Baritone and Orchestra" (1960), performed, with considerable success, I understand, at George Washington University in 1963.

¹⁰ *Letters,* I, 120. This statement, however, was not made till 1881, when Patmore's *Essay* had stirred Hopkins's interest.

¹¹ These observations have been somewhat reinforced by the newest edition of Hopkins's *Poems.* In previous editions and in letters, some of his musical directions for reading the poems have been published. *Spelt from Sibyl's Leaves* was described as "most carefully timed in *tempo rubato*" (*Letters,* I, 246); in *Hurrahing in Harvest* three words, and in *The Starlight Night* half a line, were marked "*rall.*" or "*rallentando*" (notes to *Poems,* 3d ed., pp. 226, 229). The new fourth edition prints from subsequently discovered autograph manuscripts a number of such marks in the sonnets of 1877, most of them *rallentando,* and these would particularly exemplify the prevailing musical style of which I have spoken. The manuscripts also contain indications for *sforzando* and *staccato.* All these, in addition to numerous other passages in the letters, give evidence of the degree to which Hopkins's poetry was influenced by the other art of music and also by what is today regarded as a debased style of musical performance.

I am under obligation to Professor Dolores M. Hsu, a musicologist at the University of California, Santa Barbara, who has confirmed the accuracy of my impressions of nineteenth-century musical performance, which, with only a rusty and limited knowledge of musical history, I should not have ventured to present on my own authority alone.

CHAPTER 5: ROOTS OF OBSCURITY

¹ There is a single exception, cited here earlier in chapter 2. He was not "over-desirous" that the literal meaning of quite everything in

the *Deutschland* be unmistakable (*Letters*, I, 50). This reserve, I think, concerns his suggestion of a miraculous event, which he would not have felt free to make as an open assertion. It was a particular exception for a particular reason.

2 For another similar instance of tortuous syntax, see the discussion of "My own heart" in chapter 8.

3 See, however, Sister M. Adorita Hart in *MLN*, LXX (1955), 345–347, for a third, ingenious reading, very tentatively advanced. The possibility presented there seems to me too remote to be entertained unless other evidence were at hand.

4 This guess of mine will not hold if the "early draft" of the poem dated October 2, 1879 (now first cited in *Poems*, 4th ed., p. xlvii), represents the very earliest work on the poem, for Hopkins's letter is dated August 14, and though it may have been written over a period of time it must have been finished before October.

5 The reader wishing to trace more fully Hopkins's uses of the terms *inscape* and *instress* will find them conveniently indexed in the *Letters* and the *Journals*. In the *Devotional Writings* they are also indexed, but incompletely; the following additions, some of them important, have been noted: pp. 123, 136–139, 145, 202, 285. Extended discussions will be found in the books by Gardner, Heuser, Peters, Pick, and others; and in Marjorie D. Coogan, "Inscape and Instress: Further Analogies with Scotus," *PMLA*, LXV (1950), 66–74. For *instress*, however, I can find no single definition that fits its use in every context. I have sometimes wondered whether, as may easily happen with a word not fixed to standard use by any dictionary, *instress* may not have been found a convenient term, at different times, for two or three slightly different purposes.

6 The quaking aspen and certain other white poplars have a leaf stalk exceptionally long, slim, and flattened, with the leaf blade set at right angles to the flat plane of the stalk, so that in a faint breeze that fails to stir other leaves, or in a stronger current of air that in other trees causes the mass of leaf and branch to move mainly as a unit and in a single direction, on the poplar each leaf and small spray will be literally "set on a flare," moving not in one direction only but in all. This is a conspicuous and not at all a recondite feature of the poplar, which in a less urban age than ours must have been common knowledge and which even now is familiar to most people who have more than a literary acquaintance with trees. Cf. "gliding and winding of white-poplar sprays in the wind" (*Journals*, p. 143) and, of course, the "airy cages" of *Binsey Poplars*.

7 An early version of the poem (printed in facsimile, *Letters*, III, facing p. 145) at first glance seems to support this latter reading, but on reflection may instead be taken to support the other. It therefore provides no real solution.

8 The second is the reading of Gardner, Pick, and Heuser. Cf. also the view of N. H. MacKenzie (*Poems*, 4th ed., pp. xliv ff., and *The Month*, n.s., XXX [1965], 348) that the sonnets of 1877 "form a sequence related with unusual immediacy to the flow of the changing seasons." If he is right, the literal reading will scarcely stand because foliage on February 24, the date of the poem, would be less advanced than the imagery suggests.

[9] Gardner in his note to the poem and Raymond V. Schoder, S.J., in his "Interpretive Glossary of Difficult Words in the *Poems*" (in *Immortal Diamond*, ed. Norman Weyand [New York, 1949], p. 202) takes *delves* as the plural of an obsolete word, *delf*, meaning pit or mine. This seems much less likely than that Hopkins should have used a known and current verb as a substantive, as he did on a later occasion ("a lonely began"). His insistence upon the "current language heightened" usually though not quite invariably precluded his use of a truly *obsolete* word. An earlier version of the line, just recently printed in notes to the fourth edition of *Poems*, "diamond wells," reinforces the parallel grammatical reading.

CHAPTER 6: BRIDGES AND THE TWO STYLES

[1] Jean-Georges Ritz, *Robert Bridges and Gerard Hopkins . . . A Literary Friendship* (London, 1960).

[2] The critical response to the first edition of the poems is surveyed in the first chapter of Todd K. Bender's *Gerard Manley Hopkins: The Classical Background . . .* (Baltimore, 1966).

[3] Letter from Bridges to Hopkins's mother, August 4, 1890, quoted in Ritz, *Bridges and Hopkins,* pp. 152–154. This was not the sole cause for delay, but the others, which are evidently not attributable to Bridges, have not fully come to light; they had to do with the affairs of the prospective publisher Daniels.

[4] Essays of F. R. Leavis are "Gerard Manley Hopkins," in *New Bearings in English Poetry* (London, 1950; first published in 1932), and "Gerard Manley Hopkins" and "The Letters of Gerard Manley Hopkins," in *The Common Pursuit* (London, 1952). Quotations are from the latter, pp. 63–66.

[5] Sir Herbert Read, *Collected Essays in Literary Criticism* (2d ed.; London, 1951), p. 352.

It would not have seemed necessary to treat this subject as extensively as I have done if the views of Leavis and Read had become outmoded; but though more moderate views are expressed from time to time, even now—or at least as late as 1966—responsible writers continue to attack Bridges bitterly on the same grounds as before.

[6] *Letters,* I, 31–32. The autograph dates of the poems are printed in the notes to *Poems.*

[7] Bridges' destruction of his letters to Hopkins, which had been returned to him after the latter's death, has been regarded with black suspicion or ascribed to "conceit" or to an unpleasantly cautious desire to protect his own reputation (see Leavis in *The Common Pursuit, passim,* and Read, *Collected Essays,* p. 352). Edward Thompson, however (*Robert Bridges* [London, 1944], p. 119), notes that Bridges destroyed many of his letters to other friends also; and discussing the matter in his Preface to Hopkins's *Letters* (I, v–vi), C. C. Abbott reminds us of Bridges' wish that no biography of himself should be published. (Cf. also Ritz, *Bridges and Hopkins,* pp. xi–xvi.) Evidence is lacking for even a well-informed guess at his motive in

destroying his own letters to various correspondents, though it is not an unusual thing for a man to do.

8 Now no. 31, "In All Things Beautiful," *Poetical Works* (London, 1936), p. 202.

9 Now no. 23 in *Poetical Works*, p. 198.

10 *Letters*, I, 56–57, 67–75, and similarly at intervals throughout subsequent letters.

11 *Letters*, I, 52, 54, 65, 77, 79, 121, 153, 218; II, 100, 110; and cf. in III, 351, Patmore's letter asking to see his poems: "Mr. Bridges and Mr. Gosse have excited much desire in me to see some of your Poems in MS." They proved not much to Patmore's taste, however. Cf. also Bridges' statement to Patmore, quoted (from an earlier article by Derek Patmore) by D. Anthony Bischoff, S.J., in his valuable article "The Manuscripts of Gerard Manley Hopkins," *Thought*, XXVI (Winter, 1951), 551–580.

12 The manuscript was dated August 12, 1879.

13 I am pleased to see that in the fourth edition of *Poems*, published after the above was written, one of the editors, Professor N. H. Mac-Kenzie, expresses briefly a similar view (pp. xlix–l).

CHAPTER 7: THREE BAROQUE SONNETS

1 The following are among the most influential or the fullest studies of the poem: I. A. Richards, "Gerard Hopkins," *Dial*, LXXXI (1926), 195–203; Herbert Marshall McLuhan, "The Analogical Mirrors," *Kenyon Review*, VI (1944), 322–332 (reprinted in *The Kenyon Critics*, 1945); Raymond V. Schoder, S.J., "What Does *The Windhover* Mean?" in *Immortal Diamond*, ed. Norman Weyand (New York, 1949), pp. 275–306; Archibald A. Hill, "An Analysis of *The Windhover*: An Experiment in Structural Method," *PMLA*, LXX (1955), 968–978; Robert Boyle, S.J., *Metaphor in Hopkins* (Raleigh, N.C., 1961), chap. iv. A more recent and well-argued discussion (with much of which, nevertheless, I cannot find myself in agreement) is that of G. Giovannini, "A Literal Gloss of Hopkins' 'The Windhover,'" in *Linguistic and Literary Studies in Honor of Helmut A. Hatzfeld*, ed. A. S. Crisafulli (Washington, 1964), pp. 204–212. The study by F. X. Shea, S.J., "Another Look at 'The Windhover,'" *Victorian Poetry*, II (1964), 219–239, presents one of the best interpretations I have seen (though it too differs from my own), along with other valuable discussion of Thomist and Scotist elements in Hopkins's thought. My own discussion here is founded on my earlier brief note, "Hopkins' *The Windhover*," *Explicator*, XVIII, no. 4 (Jan. 1960).

2 Todd K. Bender, *Gerard Manley Hopkins: The Classical Background . . .* (Baltimore, 1966), pp. 74 ff.

3 The best argument that I have seen for this interpretation is that of William D. Templeman, "Ruskin's Ploughshare and Hopkins' 'The Windhover,'" *English Studies*, XLIII (1962), 103–106. Persuasive though it is, on the whole it seems to me outweighed by the considerations I have outlined.

⁴ I find that I am using an outmoded conception of *rubato*, but I let it stand because it is clearly what Hopkins had in mind. According to the latest edition of Grove's *Dictionary*, the term is no longer interpreted as requiring that the "stolen" time be paid back but only that the preceding tempo be resumed.

⁵ It is almost but not quite certain that the comma should appear after *plume* in the final text of *The Windhover*. It is present in two earlier autographs in MS A but absent in Bridges' copy in B, which was corrected by Hopkins. Though B, the latest and best text, is that generally followed in all editions of the poems, it contains an occasional error in Bridges' transcription that was not caught when Hopkins made his corrections, and this is probably one of them. The comma from A was printed in the early editions, was removed in conformity with the B text when the third edition was revised in 1956, and has just now again been restored in the fourth edition. The *presence* of the comma, as explained above, tells nothing about the syntax; its *absence*, if not a slip, would of course rule out a vocative altogether; furthermore, if the vocative were intended, Bridges' error in copying (assuming that it *was* an error) would seriously have injured the sense and would consequently have been somewhat less likely to escape the notice of both himself and Hopkins.

⁶ Stresses are printed as in the fourth edition of *Poems* except that I have recorded an additional one from MS B on *óver* (line 8) because the line has been read differently (without reference to MSS) in one of the best essays on sprung rhythm.

⁷ Cf. F. R. Leavis, *New Bearings in English Poetry* (London, 1950), pp. 183 ff. Cf. John Pick, *Gerard Manley Hopkins, Priest and Poet* (2d ed.; New York, 1966), pp. 141–143; and W. H. Gardner, *Gerard Manley Hopkins: A Study* . . . (2 vols.; New Haven, 1948–1949), II, 313–314, who also agrees mainly with Leavis though earlier (I, 166–167) he had expressed a different view. Cf. *Journals:* "Sunset . . . , sky round confused pale green and blue with faint *horned* rays" (p. 146) and, in an account of northern lights, "beams of light and dark very like the crown of *horny* rays the sun makes behind a cloud" (p. 200; my italics). Among his early philological notes, one of the longest is on the word *horn*, which he connects with, among many other words, *corona* and a Latin word for *spiral* that may possibly have suggested the expression here "*wound* to the west." A similar note connects the word *hollow* with *hole* and *hell*, but also with *caelum* (sky) (pp. 4, 12). Cf. the comments (in *Essays in Criticism*, XIV [1964], 327–331) of Andor Gomme, who criticizes Leavis and interprets the passage much as I have done.

⁸ Hopkins's *Poems* (2d ed.; 1930), p. xi.

⁹ William J. Rooney points out in somewhat different terms the failure of the play on *stars* in " 'Spelt from Sibyl's Leaves'—A Study in Contrasting Methods of Evaluation," *Journal of Aesthetics and Art Criticism*, XIII (June 1955), 510n.

¹⁰ The verb *round* has been variously glossed as "whisper," "round upon him," "counsel," and so on, but I do not think any specific gloss matters or is quite adequate here. What the word functionally does is turn the sonnet, turn the whole preceding description upon

the subsequent statement; we can gloss *round,* for this purpose, as we please.

¹¹ Cf. especially the meditations on hell and death in *Devotional Writings,* pp. 241–247.

¹² One grammatical ambiguity has been observed in the sixth line of *Heraclitean Fire,* where the subject of the verb *parches* is in doubt, and the manuscript reading as between "rut peel" and "rutpeel" is uncertain. The whole passage reads best if *wind* (l. 5) is taken to be subject of the second group of verbs—*parches, stanches, starches*—as well as the first.

CHAPTER 8: "THE TIMES ARE NIGHTFALL"

¹ W. H. Gardner, *Gerard Manley Hopkins: A Study* . . . (2 vols.; New Haven, 1948–1949), I, 185–186, and notes to *Poems; Immortal Diamond,* ed. Norman Weyand (New York, 1949), pp. 338, 206; Alan Heuser, *The Shaping Vision of Gerard Manley Hopkins* (London, 1958), pp. 77, 114. With reference to Darwinism, incidentally, it is a mistake to suppose that Hopkins rejected the whole theory of evolution. His recorded objections have to do with aesthetic details rather than essential theory. In 1874 he argued that Darwinism does not necessarily imply man's descent from the ape but only that both spring from a common ancestor, and "these common ancestors, if lower animals, *need not have been repulsive animals*" (*Letters,* I, 128; my italics). He recommended the modified Darwinian views of St. George Mivart, who "is an Evolutionist" yet is able to be "very orthodox"—or so Hopkins thought; eventually Mivart was excommunicated for certain later writings. In a letter of 1883 to Bridges discussing music, Hopkins expressed dislike of Vernon Lee's notion (as restated by himself) "that we enjoy music because our apish ancestors serenaded their Juliet-apes of the period in rudimentary recitatives and our emotions are the survival—that sexual business . . ." (*Letters,* I, 172). As far as I know, Hopkins never expressed disbelief in the general theory of evolution.

² *Letters,* III, 287; cf. also (p. 169) his notice of the "stars and stripes" being flown at an Irish political meeting in 1885.

³ *Letters,* III, 243. August 1879 was important also in the history of the Catholic university to which Hopkins was later appointed. *Andromeda* was written on August 12 and sent to Bridges two days later. Heated parliamentary debate upon an act establishing the Royal University in Dublin, to succeed what was left of Newman's foundation, was just then drawing to a conclusion, and the act was passed on the fifteenth. Abbott's notes (*Letters,* I, 316–317) give a brief summary of the university's history and the controversies over its management before it was turned over to the Jesuits. The subject was of active interest to Jesuits at the time, and of course it was one of the entanglements in the whole Irish question.

⁴ The beast should be the Irish troubles even if *Andromeda* is believed to be the Church, because Hopkins would be apt to see those

conflicts, especially in view of the involvement of many of the Irish Catholic clergy, as alienating English sympathies and hence bringing the progress of conversions to a halt.

⁵ William J. Rooney, " 'Spelt from Sibyl's Leaves'—A Study in Contrasting Methods of Evaluation," *Journal of Aesthetics and Art Criticism*, XIII (June 1955), 509.

⁶ *Morning, Midday, and Evening Sacrifice*, written sometime during the same month as *Andromeda*, is a devotional piece in which Hopkins's striving for a popular style led to what amounts to a metrical parody of *The Charge of the Light Brigade*. Though he omits the eighth line of Tennyson's stanza, the parody is so insistent that "Rode the six hundred" intrudes quite loudly into the reader's mind to complete Hopkins's seven (Tennyson's stanzas vary in length, but memory sets the pattern by the first). The poem is insignificant except as showing again the strength of his desire for an audience.

⁷ Golden Grove, in Wales, which Hopkins may perhaps have visited, was the birthplace of the poet Vaughan, whose work he admired. In 1879 he had written to Dixon about Vaughan's poetry and life as given in the edition and memoir of H. F. Lyte (1847), where the place-name is prominent (*Letters*, II, 23–24). He was probably also familiar with the name from its importance in the life and work of Jeremy Taylor, whose *XXVIII Sermons Preached at Golden Grove* and devotional book *The Golden Grove* he very likely knew. His notebooks refer to other work of Taylor, whose suspected leaning toward Catholicism would have attracted his interest. In *Spring and Fall*, the place-name origin remains in the capitalization of the word, but its chief function is of course its condensed suggestion of autumn.

⁸ Ivor Winters, "The Poetry of Gerard Manley Hopkins," in *The Function of Criticism* (Denver, 1957), pp. 107–108.

⁹ *Devotional Writings*, pp. 261–262. Cf. Father Devlin's analysis of Hopkins's situation at this time (pp. 218–219); also the letter to his mother and "Additional Notes" (*Letters*, III, 184–185, 446–447); the letters to Bridges (*passim*, from p. 189 on); and an extract from Bridges' letter to Hopkins's mother after his death, referring to the "mental trouble" suffered by Hopkins from being faced with what Bridges called "the disloyal plotting" of the Jesuits in Ireland (*Journals*, pp. xii–xiii).

¹⁰ *A Page of Irish History* . . . , 1930, as quoted in *Letters*, I, 319–320, note V.

¹¹ *Devotional Writings*, p. 262; cf. letter to Bridges (p. 222), "It kills me to be time's eunuch and never to beget" and the late sonnet, "Thou art indeed just, Lord," from which the phrase has become familiar. Father Devlin notes (from unpublished letters to Father Keating) that "there were Jesuits themselves among Hopkins's contemporaries who felt that he was being wasted and misused," though Devlin does not think blame is to be laid "at any particular door." It is known, too, that English converts (for quite natural human reasons) did not have an easy time in the Church. This had been one explicit reason for the elder Hopkins's distress when his son first became a convert (*Letters*, III, 435). It is also well to recognize,

on the other hand, that Hopkins himself was not in intellectual matters the most adaptable of men.

12 *The Candle Indoors* and *The Handsome Heart,* though in earlier editions printed after *Andromeda,* were written earlier in the same summer (see *Letters,* I, 84 ff.). In the second of these, which is less elaborate than most of the baroque pieces, Hopkins may have been feeling his way toward the new style.

Index